CultureShock!

A Survival Guide to Customs and Etiquette

Tokyo

Yuko Morimoto-Yoshida

Marshall Cavendish
Editions

This edition published in 2008 by:
Marshall Cavendish Corporation
99 White Plains Road
Tarrytown, NY 10591-9001
www.marshallcavendish.us

Other Marshall Cavendish Offices:
Marshall Cavendish International (Asia) Private Limited. 1 New Industrial Road, Singapore 536196 ■ Marshall Cavendish Ltd. 5th Floor, 32–38 Saffron Hill, London EC1N 8FH, UK ■ Marshall Cavendish International (Thailand) Co Ltd. 253 Asoke, 12th Flr, Sukhumvit 21 Road, Klongtoey Nua, Wattana, Bangkok 10110, Thailand ■ Marshall Cavendish (Malaysia) Sdn Bhd, Times Subang, Lot 46, Subang Hi-Tech Industrial Park, Batu Tiga, 40000 Shah Alam, Selangor Darul Ehsan, Malaysia

Marshall Cavendish is a trademark of Times Publishing Limited

ISBN 10: 0-7614-5502-7
ISBN 13: 978-0-7614-5502-8

Please contact the publisher for the Library of Congress catalog number

Printed in China by Everbest Printing Co Ltd

Photo Credits:
All black and white photos from the author except page xii (Corel Stock Photo Library), page 13 (Japan Tourism Bureau).
Colour photos from Getty Images pages a, i, j–k; Photolibrary pages b–c, d–e, f–g, h, l–m, n–o, p ■ Cover photo: Corbis

All illustrations by TRIGG

ABOUT THE SERIES

Culture shock is a state of disorientation that can come over anyone who has been thrust into unknown surroundings, away from one's comfort zone. *CultureShock!* is a series of trusted and reputed guides which has, for decades, been helping expatriates and long-term visitors to cushion the impact of culture shock whenever they move to a new country.

Written by people who have lived in the country and experienced culture shock themselves, the authors share all the information necessary for anyone to cope with these feelings of disorientation more effectively. The guides are written in a style that is easy to read and covers a range of topics that will arm readers with enough advice, hints and tips to make their lives as normal as possible again.

Each book is structured in the same manner. It begins with the first impressions that visitors will have of that city or country. To understand a culture, one must first understand the people—where they came from, who they are, the values and traditions they live by, as well as their customs and etiquette. This is covered in the first half of the book.

Then on with the practical aspects—how to settle in with the greatest of ease. Authors walk readers through how to find accommodation, get the utilities and telecommunications up and running, enrol the children in school and keep in the pink of health. But that's not all. Once the essentials are out of the way, venture out and try the food, enjoy more of the culture and travel to other areas. Then be immersed in the language of the country before discovering more about the business side of things.

To round off, snippets of basic information are offered before readers are 'tested' on customs and etiquette of the country. Useful words and phrases, a comprehensive resource guide and list of books for further research are also included for easy reference.

CONTENTS

FOREWORD

Tokyo is a place of continuous renewal. Its landscape has been altered several times during the course of its history by fire, war, or natural disaster—but the people of Tokyo ('Tokyoites') have turned each occasion into an opportunity for rebirth, and the metropolis has bounced back bigger and better than before. Even during the two centuries when Japan was technically closed off to foreigners and travel within the country was somewhat restricted, people of the capital eagerly adopted new trends in thought, technology and fashion to which they were exposed. Today, Tokyoites are still attentive to changing trends and eager to latch onto them. To fall behind would be unbearable. However, they are apt to grow weary of new trends quickly and constantly seek new targets for their attention.

What are the origins of this ability to recover from adversity and this appetite and passion for things new? Perhaps they come from deep within ancient Japanese traditions. Shinto, the country's indigenous belief system, offers the idea that destruction and rebuilding are rites of purification, like a cleansing of the soul. Buddhism, a religion introduced to Japan from China, offers the idea that life is transitory, so people should not get too attached to the things of everyday life. To this day, Tokyoites appreciate traditional but fleeting seasonal events, and participate in a variety of rituals and celebrations with ancient roots—all with the latest technical gadgets tucked away in their pockets.

This contradicting, unique character of the society can be better experienced by people who live in Tokyo than by those who simply visit the city. Residents can easily see what is the leading trend. People dress according to the latest fashion style; 'in' restaurants and entertainment spots come and go; the latest electronic gadgets rapidly sell off the shelves; popular actors and actresses appear in every magazine and television show. When one trend changes, everyone shifts to the new one. At the same time, enjoyment of seasonal events gives rhythm to people's lives and participation in traditional rituals and celebrations connects them with the past. In time, newcomers learn to appreciate both the subtle and not-so-subtle contrasts of this ambivalent culture; this appreciation is a sure sign that Tokyo has become home.

AUTHOR'S NOTES

As you read through this book, please note the following:

- Throughout the book, Japanese words are written in *romaji* (Japanese words transcribed into the English alphabet; also known as 'romanisation').
- The prices mentioned in this book are estimates and are generally stated in Japanese yen.
- Many of the resources listed in this book include website addresses, all of which have English language pages. If you go to these websites and encounter a Japanese language home page, though, please be patient—look for a little icon that says 'English' and click on it.

Every effort has been made to ascertain that the information in this book is accurate; my apologies if you find that places and websites mentioned have changed or disappeared. This is just a fact of life in this ever-changing metropolis that is at the same time very international and Japanese.

ACKNOWLEDGEMENTS

This book could not have been completed without the help and support of many people. Especially, I owe a great deal to the following people and would like to express my sincere appreciation to them.

First and foremost, I would like to thank Lynn Witham, who was courageous enough to suggest me as an author for this book, and who supported me in every step of the creation process from drafting to editing to completion. We discussed ideas openly, and she provided continuous moral support. This would never have come to pass without her.

I received much support from Kay Jones who edited several drafts and offered valuable feedback on many topics. Together with Anthony Pan, she enhanced the focus and readability of the sections on history and religion. Tony also gave generously of his time for reviewing and editing the final drafts. Their knowledge and insights about Japanese culture were just impressive.

Other fellow interculturalists based in the San Francisco area and who have extensive experience with Japan offered ideas and insights about the unique features of Tokyo. Masahiro Shintani, a Tokyoite himself, was always gracious in answering questions about deep issues, and Chris Brannen shared thoughts and impressions. Dave Dickey and others at Meridian Resources were particularly good sports in offering their observations and intuition.

Kristy Buckingham is owed great thanks for being the first reader of the draft and for diligently editing what now seems like just a rough sketch.

As for the Japanese support crew, I am especially grateful to Masazumi Akita who kept me informed on current events and trends in Tokyo and who introduced me to a wonderful photographer, Akiko Watanabe. Watanabe-san wandered around every corner of Tokyo in search of good photo opportunities, and the results of her efforts are included in this book. Shu Ikkatai offered some photographs as well, which were much appreciated.

In addition, I wish to express gratitude to the expatriates in Tokyo who shared with me their experiences of living in the city. Their comments and stories added depth to the content of the book. Thanks are due to friends and friends of friends who referred me to these expatriates.

Hosts of other people were gracious in suggesting ideas, giving information and encouraging me in many ways. Finally, I would like to thank my family for their continuous support and encouragement during this entire adventure.

Yuko Morimoto-Yoshida

MAP OF JAPAN

MAP OF TOKYO

Japanese businessmen crossing the Shibuya Intersection.

FIRST IMPRESSIONS

CHAPTER 1

'The first charm of Japan is intangible
and volatile as a perfume.'
—Lafcadio Hearn,
(a journalist of the 19th century
who became a Japanese citizen)

YOUR FIRST IMPRESSIONS OF TOKYO will depend on your prior knowledge, interests and expectations as well as on your experiences during the first few days in the city. To help you visualise what to expect, described below are some common first impressions that represent unique aspects of Tokyo and that will provide good snapshots of life there. You may find it interesting to write down your own first impressions and later review them to see whether or not your subsequent experiences have changed your perspectives.

Most foreigners going to the Tokyo area pass through Narita New Tokyo International Airport. Although the airport bears the name of Japan's capital, it is actually located in Narita City, 60 km (about 37 miles) away. The ride into the centre of Tokyo normally takes 1.5 to 2 hours, giving foreigners the impression that the city is quite a distance from the airport.

As public transportation is convenient and reliable, most newcomers (and Japanese) take a bus or a train from the airport to downtown Tokyo. Travellers taking the bus will be politely welcomed at the bus ticketing counter by clerks who provide information and sell tickets, and at the pavement by attendants who load suitcases and remove their hats and bow as the bus departs. This experience gives foreigners the impression that Japanese people are very polite in their interactions with customers. Foreigners may also notice that buses generally depart exactly on schedule.

After arriving in downtown Tokyo, many travellers take a taxi, a subway or a train to get to their final destination. This is when the real adventure for newcomers begins. Subway and train stations are often crowded with people crossing paths and heading in every direction. The situation is extreme during the famous Tokyo rush hour and can be overwhelming for newcomers who are not used to being in crowds. It is difficult to believe how Japanese people, who impress foreigners with their politeness, push others to squeeze themselves into the train and bump into others on the concourse without seeming to care and without apologising. Understandably, this contrast in behaviour can be confusing for foreigners.

Music in the Toilet?

Japanese people are very attentive to detail and seem to enjoy using complex, high-tech devices in many aspects of their lives. Sometimes it is difficult for the uninitiated to figure out what the equipment is meant for. One good example is the high-tech toilet. These days, toilets in many of Tokyo's homes and public buildings are equipped with numerous controls—one to heat the seat, one to rinse your body parts, one to adjust the strength of the water flow, one to flush, one to dry your body parts, and even one to turn on music! It is interesting to note that the music is not provided for your entertainment; it is provided so that you will not cause unpleasantness for others while you are doing what you have to do in the toilet!

Speaking of confusion, figuring out complex train maps and train station layouts are daunting tasks for newcomers, and determining which train to take may seem utterly impossible. The good news is that Japanese people are helpful and there are signs and instructions in English and other foreign languages around, so if you look carefully and ask for help when necessary, you will eventually find your way.

Train stations are sometimes very noisy due to the sheer volume of people and the frequent announcements by the automated tape and the stationmaster. The announcements are to inform travellers that specific trains are approaching, have arrived, and are leaving. These announcements are also made in the train, often in English as well as in

Japanese. This is yet another form of customer care, albeit one that creates noise.

In contrast, Japanese passengers are usually quiet. Many people use their time on the train to take a nap or to check or send emails on their cellphones. It is very interesting to watch how people skilfully type on the cellphone keys using only their thumb!

When newcomers finally arrive at their hotel, they may decide to explore the neighbourhood, as in busy areas the streets are full of people, even late at night. What first attracts attention is the Tokyo skyline, dotted with concrete skyscrapers, some of which are decorated with impressive neon signs and gigantic video screens showing news or advertisements. What becomes evident upon further exploration is that, interspersed among these symbols of modernity and industrial advancement, are many old shrines and temples reminiscent of a quieter era.

Newcomers who arrive during winter or early spring notice that many Japanese people wear white masks over their nose and mouth. This is to guard against spreading germs and inhaling flu viruses. People who suffer from pollen allergies also use masks.

Visitors who arrive in Tokyo on a rainy day will notice that many people carry giant umbrellas. Tokyoites rely mainly on public transportation and sometimes have to walk long distances between different forms of transportation, so they take precautions to stay dry. Conveniently, many stores provide plastic bags in which customers can store their umbrellas while they are shopping. Some stores even have machines through which you slide your umbrella and it will automatically be covered by a plastic bag!

One of the best times to arrive in Tokyo is during the spring cherry blossom season when pale pink flowers can be seen everywhere. There is nothing that compares with the beautiful sights and fragrant aromas of this season. It is quite heartwarming to find a single cherry tree in bloom among several tall buildings; it seems like an oasis in the desert. To welcome spring and cherish the flowers that bloom for only one week during the season, Japanese people often go

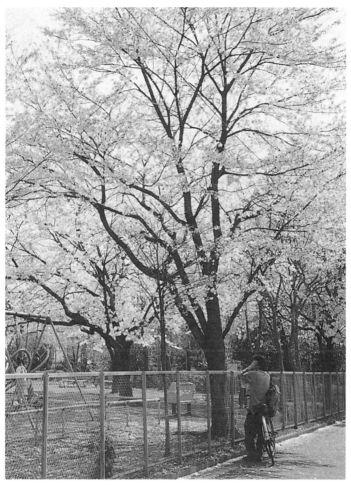

Cherry blossoms in a Tokyo park herald the arrival of spring.

to parks to have parties under the cherry trees. Foreigners are often surprised to see that although Japanese people are usually quiet and reserved, they can be rather loud and wild during these parties.

On the surface, Tokyo is a modern, gigantic metropolis. At first, you may be overwhelmed by the city's complexity, but eventually you will get to know your way around and find remnants of the old city among the new. On the surface, the city's residents may seem to be in a perpetual rush.In time you may observe that, on a deeper level, their lives follow a natural rhythm punctuated by seasonal events. Finally, while Tokyoites are generally very polite, reserved and attentive to detail, you may be surprised to see that at times, they can be somewhat aggressive in a crowd and vocal during parties. Such contrasts in the city and in its residents would probably best summarise common first impressions of Tokyo. As you stay longer in Tokyo, you may find some explanations for such contrasts and you may identify other contrasts that will make your stay even more interesting.

OVERVIEW OF JAPANESE LAND AND HISTORY

CHAPTER 2

'Unlike Americans but like other peoples of East Asia,
the Japanese have a strong consciousness of history.
They see themselves in historical perspective. They
will delve a thousand years and more into their past i
n analysing their contemporary traits.'
—Edwin O Reischauer
(previous US ambassador to Japan)

KNOWLEDGE OF THE CITY'S BACKGROUND helps newcomers to increase their understanding of the place, people and the society today. This chapter offers information about the geography, history, religions and belief systems that have influenced the Japanese people.

GEOGRAPHY

Japan is made up of four main islands: Honshu, Shikoku, Kyushu and Hokkaido. Tokyo is located near the centre of Honshu, the largest island. Administratively, Japan is divided into 47 prefectures, each with its own government; these prefectures are further categorised into 11 regions without governments. Tokyo is one of the 47 prefectures, and the capital of the country.

Situated in the Kanto Plain, the Tokyo Prefecture, together with surrounding prefectures, is categorised as part of the Kanto region. The land area of Tokyo is about 2,000 sq km (approximately 769 sq miles), and is rather flat with no high mountains.

Tokyo metropolis is administratively divided into three main parts: 1) the 23 wards (*ku*) in the eastern part; 2) the Tama area, consisting of 26 cities (*shi*), three towns (*machi*), and one village (*mura*), in the western part; and 3) two islands (*shima*), Izu and Ogasawara (consisting of two towns and seven villages), located south of the mainland. In this book, the name 'Tokyo' mainly refers to the 23 wards, as these are the centres of government, commerce, and foreign affairs. 'Greater Tokyo' refers to these wards, the Tama area and the surrounding prefectures.

Neighbourhoods in Tokyo

There is no one focal point in Tokyo; there are several areas that serve unique functions and offer distinctive atmospheres. Six of these areas are described below.

Asakusa/Ueno (Taito-ku)

Located in Taito-ku in the eastern part of Tokyo, Asakusa is considered to be 'downtown Tokyo' and is the place to experience the atmosphere of **'Old Tokyo'**. The **Sensoji**, a Buddhist temple believed to have been built in the 7th century, is a famous landmark. Leading up to the temple are rows of small shops selling traditional Japanese crafts, and in the streets nearby, rows of traditional wooden houses stand side by side. Many families residing in this neighbourhood have lived here for several generations and cherish its ambience.

Just west of Asakusa, Ueno and its surrounding areas form a bustling commercial centre with many wholesale shops dealing in food, clothing and electronics. Major attractions include the food and flea market at **Ameya Yokocho (Ameyoko)** and the **Akihabara** electronic district where more than 600 shops sell electronic appliances at discount prices. The large **Ueno Station** used to be the junction of major train routes and served as the entrance to Tokyo for people travelling from other regions of the country. Although Ueno Station lost its former status after the introduction of bullet trains that use Tokyo Station as their hub, it continues to be one of the major transportation hubs of Tokyo. The focal point of this area is **Ueno Park**, located just across from the station. In spring, the park is crowded with people enjoying the cherry blossoms. Adjacent to the park are museums and a zoo.

Marunouchi (Chiyoda-ku)

The Marunouchi area in Chiyoda-ku serves as the core of economic and political activities in Japan. The focal point in Marunouchi is **Tokyo Station**, the hub that connects all of the country's major railroad lines, including the bullet trains. As many prominent Japanese companies and banks have their headquarters located here, in the day the atmosphere buzzes with the energy of people proud to be at the centre of Japan's business scene. At night, the streets are quiet and the buildings dark, save for the lights still burning in the windows of the many who are working late.

The National Diet Building in Kasumigaseki.

The **National Diet** building, which houses the national government of Japan, is situated in the Kasumigaseki area adjacent to the business district.

The oldest and most important landmark in the Marunouchi area is the **Imperial Palace**. At one time it was the headquarters of the Tokugawa Shogunate, which ruled Japan for more than 250 years (1603–1868). After the Shogunate lost power and was dissolved, the emperor gained control and relocated here from his residence in Kyoto. Since then, the royal family has resided in the palace. The current emperor and empress, symbolic figures of the country, still reside there. The palace is surrounded by the original moat, built for protection from possible revolts. Today, the pavement around the moat is popular with joggers, the lush trees and gardens provide a relaxing green backdrop and quiet contrast to the hustle and bustle beyond.

Ginza (Chuo-ku)/Hibiya (Chiyoda-ku)

Adjacent to the financial and business district of Marunouchi is the Ginza and Hibiya area. Ginza is the most expensive and high-class shopping area in Japan and its main street, **Chuo Dori**, is to Tokyo what Fifth Avenue and the Champs-Elysées are to Manhattan and Paris respectively. The old department stores and private shops located here have long histories and established reputations for quality and service.

These private shops specialise in items such as crafts, jewellery, *kimono* and made-to-order suits; and they have been catering to well-heeled customers for several generations. Foreigners entering these shops for the first time may be intimidated by the stores' appearance. However, perseverance will be well-rewarded by a fascinating cultural experience. The displays of elegant, formal *kimono* and accessories for men, women and children are exquisite and the prices breathtaking.

In recent years, several world-famous brands such as Tiffany, Louis Vuitton and Hérmes have opened branches here, adding an international flavour to the streets.

In addition to upmarket shopping, Ginza offers fine dining and posh nightclubs. Most people who wine and dine here do so only on corporate expense accounts, as the costs can be exorbitant.

Several theatres are located in the Hibiya area adjacent to Ginza. Here, people can enjoy musicals, concerts and plays. Many patrons of the arts like to stop at the prestigious **Imperial Hotel** for pre- or after-theatre snacks or meals.

Shibuya (Shibuya-ku)/Shinjuku (Shinjuku-ku)

Shibuya and Shinjuku are popular with people who prefer more casual and less expensive shopping, dining, and entertainment options than those offered in and around Ginza. Both areas host busy railway and subway junctions on public transportation routes, connecting the inner and outer areas of the Tokyo region.

Shibuya is where the younger crowds gather. Teenagers hang out in the game centres, movie theatres and fast food shops, while college students congregate in the inexpensive pubs. Both frequent the department stores, many of which target young customers. The most popular meeting point in Shibuya is by the bronze statue of a dog named '**Hachiko**', located in the square in front of the station. However, the square can get so crowded, especially at rush hour, that it is almost impossible to locate anyone.

Shinjuku offers a bit more variety, with the eastern and western parts projecting entirely different images. The eastern part is as congested as Shibuya but draws a much older crowd. A few major department stores as well as discount electronic shops are located here. Shinjuku is the location of the famous **Kabuki-cho**, an area lined with small bars, strip clubs and porno shops. As there are usually many drunken people roaming the street, Japanese and foreign women who walk alone here are likely to be harassed. Rumour has it that the *yakuza* (the Japanese equivalent of the Mafia) is involved in many of the nocturnal activities.

Compared to the somewhat darker eastern part of Shinjuku, the western side, with its concentration of high-rise buildings, has a more modern and polished image. Prominent landmarks include the **Tokyo Metropolitan Government Office** towers, which dominates the skyline, the **Shinjuku**

An average afternoon crowd crosses the road at Shibuya Intersection.

Park Tower Building (where the popular Hotel Park Hyatt Tokyo is located) and the **Shinjuku Sumitomo Building**, which offers spectacular views of Tokyo.

Aoyama/Akasaka/Roppongi (Minato-ku)

The Aoyama, Akasaka and Roppongi neighbourhoods in Minato-ku offer trendy, fashionable neighbourhoods with a cosmopolitan flavour.

These neighbourhoods host a large expatriate community, resulting in the establishment of international schools, apartments with Western-style fixtures and amenities, and grocery stores that sell international goods. More foreigners than Japanese people congregate in some of the clubs and restaurants in these areas.

Aoyama has lovely tree-lined streets where pedestrians enjoy strolling, browsing in elegant boutiques or relaxing and people-watching from inside the many cafés with street views. Akasaka is known for its many embassies and luxury hotels. Roppongi is one of the most popular entertainment areas in Tokyo for people in their twenties.

The Waterfront

Created from landfill in the 1990s, the Waterfront is a newly developed area that is still expanding. The Shiodome and Odaiba sections host several office buildings, upscale hotels, shopping areas and parks that were built to satisfy the varied needs of residents and visitors.

The Suburbs

Compared to the 23 land-scarce wards of Tokyo, the suburbs in the western part of the metropolis have more space and offer more affordable housing. Many young couples with small children live here and make the daily one- to two-hour commute to their offices in central Tokyo. People living in the wards enjoy visiting the suburbs on weekends to experience a quick 'nature getaway'. Here they can hike, fish, enjoy the fresh air and find respite from city life.

TOKYO IN JAPANESE HISTORY

Japan, or Nippon, has a long and colourful history. Most historians divide this history into periods based on a variety of names relevant to the times, such as those of ruling families, political or military leaders, significant symbols and events, or locations of activity. This section offers a glimpse of the history of Tokyo within the context of the country's development and traces its rise to its current status as the country's centre of government and commerce.

Early History (Prior to 1185)

The earliest written accounts of Japan are found in Chinese chronicles that had references to inhabitants of Japan visiting China as early as AD 57. But archaeologists have found pottery and other evidence confirming that human activity took place in Japan during the Jomon Period (11,000–300 BC), and recent findings suggest the possibility of even earlier activity.

The next segment of early Japanese history is known as the Yayoi Period (300 BC–AD 300), named after an area near Tokyo University where a second distinctive type of pottery was reportedly found. Around this time, metalworking and rice cultivation were introduced to Japan, probably through contact with people on the Korean peninsula and the Asian continent.

During the Kofun Period (AD 300–593), so named because of the existence of many large tombs (*kofun*) built for leaders, most human activity in Japan seems to have been centred in the Yamato Plain. It was on this plain, located in the mid-western part of Honshu Island (in the general area of today's Nara Prefecture), that a clan of people known as Yamato gained power over other clans in the region and established a court.

The rulers of this clan claimed to be direct descendants of the Sun Goddess (called Amaterasu) and are believed to be ancestors to the imperial family of modern Japan. By the middle of the 6th century, the Chinese writing system and Buddhism had been introduced to the Yamato rulers via China and Korea. These were important developments as, subsequently, scholars began using the Chinese writing system, and Buddhist teachings began influencing the political structure and values of the Yamato court.

In the Asuka Period (AD 593–710), Prince Shotoku, serving as regent of the Empress Suiko, sent several diplomatic missions to China. He also issued the 'Seventeen Article Constitution', a document that emphasised the importance of reverence for Buddhism, ethical behaviour among people and loyalty to imperial rulers. It established a political and religious foundation for early Japan. Also during this period, Japan began to be known by a pair of Chinese characters pronounced *Nihon* or *Nippon* in Japanese (literally 'sun origin', often loosely translated as 'Rising Sun'). Westerners developed the word 'japan' in their attempts to simulate the Chinese pronunciation of these same characters.

At the time of the Nara Period (AD 710–784), a capital called Heijokyo was founded in Nara; and during the Heian Period (AD 794 to AD 1185), Heiankyo in Kyoto was established as the capital. The plans for both cities were modelled after the Chinese capital Chang-an (now called Xi'an), which was then the ruling centre of the Tang Dynasty. This was just one reflection of the extent to which early Japanese society was influenced by China.

Though close contact with China continued during the Heian Period, the Japanese began to develop their own distinct culture, including the development of the arts. The origins of some forms of Japanese literature, art and architecture still enjoyed today can be traced to this period of time in the country's history.

Another focal point at this time was the development of a writing system that, unlike Chinese characters alone, could reflect the language spoken in Japan. Scholars set about modifying and simplifying Chinese characters and eventually created the *hiragana* and *katakana* writing scripts. These new phonetic scripts combined with Chinese characters resulted in a more useful writing system. This facilitated the expression of thoughts and emotions as well as the proliferation of literature and poetry. The famous Japanese classic, *The Tale of Genji*, written by Lady Murasaki Shikibu, is a hallmark achievement of this period.

This was a time of prosperity during which the aristocracy devoted themselves to indulging in cultural pursuits, rather than to governing their territory. Within the aristocracy, rivalries developed and the power of the Heian court diminished. Significant unrest and lawlessness rose, especially in rural areas, amongst the populace. In an attempt to maintain order in their individual territories, local leaders created small groups of armed guards known as *samurai* (warriors). The *samurai* from different areas began to form alliances based on financial and military might, and over time, a *samurai* class (that later became based on heredity) emerged.

The Feudal Period (1185–1602)

Two of the most prominent clans at the time were the Taira and the Minamoto. Their rivalry culminated in a decisive war in 1185, in which the Minamoto clan emerged victorious. Interestingly, a powerful member of the Taira clan who had established a home in the Tokyo region was said to have aided the Minamoto clan members in achieving victory. The residence of this Taira clan member was called Edo, a centuries-old name for Tokyo.

In 1192, the reigning court appointed the head of the Minamoto clan, Minamoto Yoritomo, as the first *shogun* (general) of Japan. Minamoto's shogunate (a military government headed by the *shogun*) was based in Kamakura, just west of Tokyo. His appointment signalled a shift eastward in control and political power, and set the stage for the development of the Kanto region.

The *samurai* were attracted to several geographical features of the Kanto Plain: the natural ridges surrounding the plain offered protection from invaders; the broad, flat lands were perfect for exercising horses; and the confluence of rivers and tributaries provided irrigation as well as a means of transportation. As the might of the Minamoto Shogunate grew, the position of the Kanto Plain, where modern Tokyo is located, shifted from the periphery to the centre of political and cultural activity in Japan.

The emperor and the *shogun* began to share authority in governing the country, although the emperor and aristocracy remained in Kyoto. This dual power structure would continue for several hundred years, during which time the authority of the *shogun*—as well as military and political activity in the Kanto region—would grow steadily, while the emperor's position became largely symbolic. The *samurai* class eventually became the dominant social class in the country, and each shogunate, with few exceptions, was headed by the most powerful *samurai* clan of its period. Some positions of power in the shogunate were given to members of other clans that pledged their allegiance to the ruling *shogun*.

This period of Japanese history is usually called 'feudal', as subordinates were expected to demonstrate loyalty to their military leaders (*samurai* and/or the *shogun*) in exchange for societal privileges or rights to land.

In 1338, the Muromachi Shogunate, ruled by the Ashikaga clan, succeeded the deposed Minamoto (Kamakura) Shogunate. This military regime was based in Kyoto, giving rise to a resurgence of emphasis on aristocracy and culture. Many aspects of traditional Japanese culture, such as *Noh* theatre, flower arrangement and the tea ceremony, had their origins in this period.

Three Famous Heroes

Oda Nobunaga, Toyotomi Hideyoshi and Tokugawa Ieyasu are three famous historical figures who are portrayed frequently in Japanese literature, movies, and drama even today.

They all contributed to the unification of Japan in the late 16th century and are known to have distinct personalities. The difference among them is illustrated well in the following anecdote:

Each of the men received a little cuckoo as a gift and replied as follows:

Nobunaga: "If the cuckoo doesn't sing, I'll kill it."
Hideyoshi: "If the cuckoo doesn't sing, I'll make it sing."
Ieyasu: "If the cuckoo doesn't sing, I'll wait until it does."

Gradually, the Muromachi Shogunate also declined and the country was ravaged by civil strife as regional warlords (*daimyo*) vied with each other and with the Shogunate for power. In 1573, a *daimyo* named Oda Nobunaga brought down the Muromachi Shogunate. He is famous for laying the groundwork for the unification of Japan, although he did not succeed in his quest. His successor, Toyotomi Hideyoshi, completed the process and gained the title of regent to the emperor. Known for his extravagant tastes, Hideyoshi built elaborate and imposing castles. Born a commoner, Hideyoshi's 'rags to riches' success story makes him one of Japan's favourite historical heroes.

After Hideyoshi died in 1598, his successor, Tokugawa Ieyasu, persuaded the emperor to confer on him the title of *shogun*.

The Tokugawa Period (1603–1868)

The Tokugawa Shogunate formally began in 1603 and retained power until 1868. Tokugawa chose his own territory of Edo as the seat of government. From this point on, the city (now called Tokyo) would remain the political and cultural centre of Japan.

According to legend, Edo was founded by the previously mentioned Taira clan member who established his home there. The name 'Edo', literally meaning 'door to the bay', was supposedly derived from the location of his home. Edo took on added significance when Ota Dokan, a powerful resident of the Kanto region, built a fortress there in 1457. It is said that Tokugawa Ieyasu built his castle on the remains of the fortress. This castle—the remnants can still be seen on the grounds of the Imperial Palace of Tokyo—became the seat of the Tokugawa Shogunate.

Historians have offered a number of reasons why Tokugawa Ieyasu chose Edo as his seat of power. It was located in the Kanto Plain, the largest bed of fertile soil in the country. Its strategic location allowed it to serve as both a port city and as a nexus between western and northern Japan, with natural barriers that made it relatively easy to defend. Some historians also believe that Tokugawa wanted his base to be located away from Kyoto, the seat of imperial power and a frequent source of political struggles and intrigue. Edo eventually became so closely identified with the Tokugawa regime that the terms 'Tokugawa' and 'Edo' are used almost interchangeably to characterise this era and its culture.

After the Tokugawa Shogunate was established, it instituted a number of measures to ensure its strength and longevity. These measures not only transformed the entire society, they also had a major impact on Edo, the political capital. Suspecting that free trade with foreign countries might allow the *daimyo* to build wealth, foreign trade was restricted to two ports in Kyushu. Christianity, introduced in 1549 by Jesuit missionaries, was suppressed for fear of undermining loyalty to the *shogun*. Afraid that social mobility might cause political disorder, the Tokugawa regime established a clear hierarchy among the social classes (warriors, peasants, artisans, and merchants, in descending order), which were made hereditary and marriage across class lines was prohibited.

The Tokugawa policy that had the most dramatic impact on life in Edo involved the system of *sankin kotai* (alternating obligatory visits). Under this system, almost all *daimyo* were required to maintain at least one residence in Edo where their wives and children would live permanently, while they themselves were required to divide their time equally between their residences in Edo and their home domains. The system was a huge financial burden on the *daimyo* but, with their families held hostage in Edo, it also reduced the potential for revolts. A by-product of this system was the improvement and expansion of the transportation network between Edo and regional towns, completely transforming Edo.

In order for Edo to function as the country's political centre, the Tokugawa Shogunate built a castle, numerous bridges and waterways. Moreover, once Edo became a place of residence for all *daimyo* and their entourages, the city had to support a huge concentration of *samurai*. A flourishing community of merchants, craftsmen, artisans, and other workers developed.

The *daimyo* and their followers lived in the castle's vicinity, generally to the west and south. This hilly part of the city was commonly known as Yamanote (literally, 'hand of the mountain'; commonly translated as 'High City'). The *daimyo* residences reflected its owners' power and status, and some were truly elaborate estates. Commoners, including merchants, craftsmen, artisans and workers, lived east of the castle in the flat area known as Shitamachi (literally, 'bottom town'; usually translated as 'Low City'). Their activities centred round Nihombashi and Asakusa. In the early years of the Tokugawa Period, rows of small wooden houses were built to accommodate the burgeoning population. Residences of both commoners and *daimyo* were periodically destroyed in the fires that swept the city. In the destructive Great Fire of Meireki (1657), even part of Edo Castle was severely damaged.

The Tokugawa Period lasted over 250 years and was generally peaceful. By the 18th century, it had also become quite prosperous. As a result, many *samurai* did not have occasion to engage in battle, even though they cherished their reputations as warriors. Although merchants held the lowest rank in society, in time many became rich and an earthy, hedonistic culture catering to the tastes of commoners developed in Shitamachi. Kabuki theatre became a popular form of entertainment, as did the elegant pleasure quarters where courtesans plied their trade. The demimonde pleasures of urban commoners, as well as landscape scenes (such as views of Mount Fuji), were captured in a new art form—prints created from woodblocks, called *ukiyo-e* ('pictures of the floating world').

The relative stability of the Tokugawa Period was dramatically interrupted in 1853 when Commodore Matthew Perry of the United States sailed into Japan with four huge warships, demanding that the country open its doors to foreign trade. Having been isolated from much of the outside world for over 200 years, the Tokugawa Shogunate felt threatened by the display of advanced weaponry and acquiesced to Perry's demands. This submission to foreigners fuelled the social discontent that was simmering due to a declining economy and a weakened social hierarchy. Among the *samurai,* anti-Tokugawa forces rallied around the symbol of the emperor. After a series of battles between supporters of the emperor and those of the Tokugawa regime, the Shogunate collapsed in 1868 and Japan was jolted out of isolation.

The Meiji Period (1868–1912)

The beginning of the Meiji Period saw the restoration of the emperor's authority. The imperial capital was officially relocated from Kyoto to Edo and renamed 'Tokyo', or 'Eastern Capital'. The imperial family moved into Tokugawa Castle, which became known as *kokyo*, meaning 'imperial residence' (better known today as the Imperial Palace). Policies of the new government were formulated and implemented by a handful of relatively young supporters of the emperor.

In the early years of the Meiji Period, the government felt an urgency to modernise, and especially to learn from the West. Japanese scholars and others were sent abroad to learn science, technology and foreign languages, and the government hired foreigners to assist in the development of banking, education, transportation and other infrastructure systems.

By 1872, technological progress was clearly visible. A British-built railway connected Tokyo with Yokohama; buildings in Ginza sported gas-lit lamps and fire-resistant red brick construction; pedestrian and boat traffic were supplemented by horse-drawn carriage and buses, and later the electric trolley.

Social changes during the Meiji Period were no less momentous. The former social hierarchy was banned and *daimyo* were forced to surrender their land. A national military was formed and the *samurai* class was summarily abolished. Marriage between people of different classes was permitted and commoners were allowed to change jobs. Freedom of religion was proclaimed and compulsory education instituted.

The Meiji leadership wanted to turn the country's capital into a cosmopolitan city worthy of international respect. Tokyo became the cultural centre of Japan—the place that set the standards in, among other things, fashion and food. Japanese people began wearing Western clothes instead of *kimono*. Dairy products and meat were introduced into the Japanese diet, and *sukiyaki* (sliced beef cooked with vegetables) became a favourite dish.

Admiration of Western culture was exemplified with the building of the Rokumeikan (Deer Cry Pavilion) in Hibiya. Here, high-ranking government officials and others from the Japanese social elite entertained Westerners with ballroom dancing, music recitals and elaborate dinners. Designed by a British architect, the Rokumeikan was where Japanese people, dressed in tuxedos and ballroom gowns, could show the world how advanced and civilised they had become.

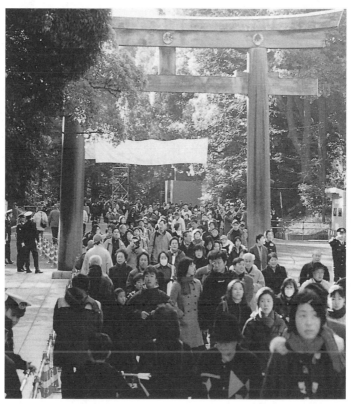

The Meiji Shrine, built in honour of the Meiji Emperor, crowded with people on New Year's Day.

Artists portrayed the changes. Woodblock prints, which during the Tokugawa Period had depicted the world of the Edo commoner, now displayed symbols of modernity: trains; red brick buildings; men and women in Western dress; and the Meiji Emperor and Empress attending ceremonial events in Western garb.

After a couple of decades, this emulation for all things Western was more than the conservatives could bear. A return to traditional values was promoted and, although this movement eventually lost steam, practices such as ballroom dancing all but disappeared.

Japan's modernisation movement originated from its ambition to gain the respect of Western powers and membership in the elite world community. As Japan's economy and military grew stronger, the self-confidence of the Japanese people grew, as did their desire to emulate Western powers by building an empire.

This was enhanced when victory over China in 1895 resulted in the acquisition of Taiwan. In 1905, the Japanese took special pride in defeating Russia, a European power, over issues concerning Manchuria and Korea. By 1910, Japan had annexed Korea. When the Meiji Emperor died in 1912, the curtain was drawn over a remarkable period in Japanese history. Japan had transformed itself from a feudal country cut off from the outside world to an industrialised nation and a burgeoning world power.

The Taisho Years and the Great Earthquake (1912–1925)

The Emperor Meiji was succeeded by his son, the Emperor Taisho. In poor health for most of his reign, Taisho had little say in governing the country. His son (who would later become Emperor Hirohito) began serving as regent in 1921.

When World War I broke out in 1914, Japan sided with the Allied Powers of Britain, France and Russia. Japan continued its policy of territorial expansion after the war by seizing and occupying German territories in China. During the conflict, Japan received massive orders for military goods from its European allies, turning a trade deficit into a trade surplus. The country experienced an unprecedented economic boom, and Tokyo was one of the primary beneficiaries. This was most evident in the growth of the Marunouchi area, where the headquarters of many Japanese conglomerates were located.

The economic boom accelerated a process that began during the Meiji Period—the development of an urban working-class culture distinct from that of the Edo commoners and that of the high culture of the wealthy in Yamanote. Since the Meiji Period, Tokyo's population had grown substantially and large numbers of women entered the workforce, especially in light industry and services. Universal education ensured most Japanese were literate. By the late Meiji and

Taisho eras, Tokyoites were enjoying newspapers, magazines, photographs, records and movies—all products of the new industrial age. In sports, baseball had begun to surpass *sumo* (a form of Japanese wrestling) in general popularity.

Tragedy struck on 1 September 1923, when Tokyo was jolted by a huge earthquake. The Great Kanto Earthquake destroyed much of Tokyo as well as Yokohama. Estimates vary, but most researchers concur that well over 100,000 people died and more than 50,000 injured. It was a traumatic event in Tokyo's history and reconstruction took years. Avenues were widened and many buildings replaced with Western-style structures. A celebration was held in 1930 to mark the completion of the reconstruction,though the actual work continued for several more years.

The Rise of Militarism and World War II (1926–1945)

When Emperor Hirohito ascended to the throne in 1926, Japan was facing a time of challenge. Efforts at reconstruction and recovery from the earthquake had drained the economy. A few years later, the worldwide depression that started in New York in 1929 wreaked further havoc on Japan. While the government grappled with the economic situation, the military gained power.

By 1931, the Japanese military had occupied the whole of Manchuria and in 1937, Japan invaded China proper. Subsequently, during the early 1940s, Japan provoked Western nations by attempting to gain control over Southeast Asia. To stop the expansion of Japanese control in Asia, the United States, Britain and other world powers imposed an embargo on exports to Japan. In December 1941, panic over dwindling oil supplies led Japan to attack the United States at Pearl Harbor in Hawaii—Japan had officially entered World War II.

From 1942–1945, the United States carried out air raids on the city of Tokyo. These had a devastating effect; estimates of the number of casualties run as high as a quarter of a million people. The most intense bombing occurred in March 1945 when an estimated 80,000–100,000 people lost their lives. By the end of the war, much of the city lay in ruins. In August 1945, in an attempt to defeat Japan and end the war, the United States dropped atomic bombs on Hiroshima and on Nagasaki. It is estimated that over 200,000 people died; countless numbers were injured and large areas of both cities were destroyed.

The Post-War Years: Recovery and Reconstruction (1945–1970s)

At the conclusion of World War II, Japan was devastated and Tokyo was in ruins. Air raids had destroyed much of the city and more than a million people were left homeless; disease among residents was rampant. There was an acute shortage of food and other necessities. Conditions were miserable for everyone in Tokyo.

September 1945 saw the occupation of Japan by the Allied powers, but in many ways it was an American occupation under the command of General Douglas MacArthur. He projected self-confidence, and, under his command, the occupation was more benevolent than many had expected. Given the demoralised state of the Japanese people and the loss of confidence in their militarist leaders, MacArthur was able to command respect. Some people referred to him as 'the last *shogun*'.

While there were incidents of tension between the Americans and the local populace, on the whole there was relatively good cooperation between the two sides. In part, this was due to the fact that the Americans appeared to be making a concerted effort to help rebuild the Japanese economy. The American presence was most evident in Tokyo where MacArthur and the American forces were based—many buildings in the Marunouchi area and others were requisitioned for use by the occupying forces.

From his headquarters in Tokyo, MacArthur oversaw the process of remoulding Japan into a democratic society, stripping the emperor of divine status and disassembling commercial conglomerates. Occupation forces drafted a new constitution, which came into effect in 1947, which would be the foundation for Japan's post-war society. To prevent further attempts at territorial expansion fuelled by militarism, Japan relinquished its right to maintain military forces or to engage in war. Equal rights for men and women were granted. The formation of a two-house legislature called the Diet (*Kokkai*) was mandated, and every citizen aged 20 or older was given the right to vote.

The occupation was formally concluded with the ratification of a peace treaty between the United States and Japan in 1952. Japan was now on the way to rebuilding its economy and society.

The event that signalled Japan's full recovery and return to the limelight in the world stage was the 1964 Tokyo Olympics. Japan engaged in an earnest endeavour to showcase itself to the world, building a cluster of remarkable sporting venues for the games. A network of highways improved the flow of traffic in the city. The year also marked the debut of the high-speed bullet train, or *shinkansen*, linking Tokyo and Osaka. By all measures, the Olympic games was a resounding success; a milestone in the history of Japan as well as that of Tokyo.

Industrialisation and urbanisation continued apace as the 1960s and 1970s marked an age of steady economic growth for Japan. The country became a major producer of world-class goods for both the domestic and international markets. As Japan prospered, the standard of living improved. Many households could afford electrical appliances such as television sets and washing machines, and private ownership of automobiles increased.

Modern Japan (1980s–Present Day)

In the 1980s, continued growth and low-interest rates enticed Japanese companies and individuals to invest in real estate and the stock market. As a result, both markets skyrocketed and Japan experienced a 'bubble' in its economy. Large companies used their profits from investments to purchase properties in other countries. Individual investors spent their gains on luxury goods, overseas travel as well as expensive restaurants and entertainment. The booming economy attracted foreign investors and many foreign companies established subsidiaries or regional headquarters in Tokyo. The metropolis soon became known as a centre of international business.

In the early 1990s, the 'bubble' burst and Japan paid a very high price for having partied hard. The stock and real estate markets tumbled and the economy fell into a serious recession. Many companies could not sustain their competitiveness in the world market, as they had insufficient funds to continue developing new products and services. Some even went bankrupt because they could no longer repay their debts to the financial institutions from which they had borrowed. Left with a heavy burden of bad debt, many financial institutions eventually followed suit.

Job security became a significant concern for Japanese workers, as many companies that had previously practised lifetime employment were forced to implement restructuring plans that included employee layoffs. These layoffs, combined with hiring freezes in struggling companies, resulted in a significant increase in the unemployment rate. All of this led to a drop in consumer spending which further drained the economy. Tokyo was also hit hard by the recession. In the last decade of the century, real estate values declined substantially, corporate revenues dropped and consumer spending slowed.

After the turn of the century, Japanese economy slowly recovered from the severe economic downturn it experienced in the 1990s. However, the impact of the economic downturn on peoples' lifestyles and working styles has been significant and the nation's future direction is still difficult to predict. Yet, it is clear that Tokyo is well-positioned to remain as the centre of the country's economic, political and cultural centre.

RELIGION AND BELIEFS

Japanese people have a relatively pragmatic attitude towards religion and spiritual life. Although most people do not consider themselves devout followers of any particular faith or belief system, elements of Confucianism, Buddhism and Shinto have become integrated into the cultural fabric of their lives and permeate their world outlook if only at a subconscious level.

Confucianism

Although it is not considered a religion, Confucianism has had great influence on the Japanese people. The teachings of Confucius were brought to Japan in the 3rd century, promoting social order and the observance of hierarchy. In particular, the *samurai* found the emphasis on hierarchical relationships appealing, as they could use it to foster loyalty from subordinates. Likewise, the Tokugawa Shogunate strongly promoted Confucianism to create social order and strengthen loyalty to the regime. Throughout Japanese history, Confucianism has also been used to reinforce an indigenous tendency towards subordinating or even sacrificing oneself for the good of the group. This tendency is still a strong component of Japanese morality.

Buddhism

Buddhism, which originated in India, was introduced to Japan in the 6th century via China and Korea. By the turn of the 7th century, it had been promoted heavily by the ruling elite and made into the state religion; numerous temples were built.

The central belief of Buddhism is that everything in this world is transient, and that life produces suffering due to attachment to material things; one can achieve nirvana only by freeing oneself from the self and its desires. Concepts rooted in Buddhist thinking can be found in various aspects of Japanese culture, including the arts, architecture, and even gardening. One of the reasons Japanese people love cherry blossoms may be that they cherish things that last for a short period of time, savouring every moment.

Shinto

Shinto is the indigenous religion of Japan. It spread among the people long before Confucianism and Buddhism were introduced. It is animistic and based on the belief that *kami* (sacred spirits) reside in natural elements such as mountains, rivers and forests. These *kami* must be honoured if humans want to comfortably share their environment with them. Shinto priests perform purification rituals in the presence of the *kami* to promote harmony between human beings and nature, and when people visit Shinto shrines, they typically cleanse their hands and mouths with water. An associated purification ritual is the annual cleaning of homes in preparation for the new year.

According to the Japanese creation myth, the first emperor was a descendant of the Sun Goddess, Amaterasu. This myth has been used by Japanese leaders to their advantage throughout the nation's history. In the late Tokugawa Period, it was used to enhance the status of the emperor and to emphasise the unique character and superiority of Japan, the country and its people.

At the end of the Tokugawa Period, regional leaders used the myth to rally people around the emperor in order to overthrow the Tokugawa Shogunate. Subsequently Meiji leaders infused politics and education with Shinto precepts. In the 1930s and 1940s, during Japan's war efforts in Asia and the Pacific, these same beliefs were articulated to stir up nationalism and militarism. After World War II, the Allied occupation forces strongly encouraged the adoption of democracy and other Western ideals. Henceforth, the emperor was no longer considered divine and Shinto was separated from politics.

Today, Japanese people go to Shinto shrines to mark milestones and turning points in their lives, and to celebrate seasonal events. After the birth of their children and when they have reached the ages of three, five and seven, parents visit shrines to pray for a happy life for their offspring. Before school entrance examinations, students and their parents often go to shrines to pray for good luck. And people of all ages go to Shinto shrines on New Year's Day to pray for health and happiness throughout the year.

During some Shinto festivals, people carry around *mikoshi* (portable shrines) in the belief that this will exorcise evil spirits in the neighbourhood. Participation in Shinto ceremonies and rituals is open to all, regardless of religious beliefs or affiliation.

While Buddhism teaches that people can achieve enlightenment in the next world, Shinto guides life in this world. Buddhism offers a more positive perspective on life after death than Shinto does. That may be one reason why there is a saying that Japanese people are 'born Shinto and die Buddhist'; they go to Shinto shrines when babies are born, and have Buddhist funerals whether or not they have been to a temple when they were alive.

Christianity

Christianity accounts for only about 1 per cent of the Japanese population today, yet various customs and practices of Christianity have become popular, more as social customs than as religious practices. Christian wedding ceremonies, with brides wearing white wedding gowns, are considered more fashionable than traditional Shinto weddings with couples dressed in *kimono*. Many Tokyoites, especially young people, enjoy the festive atmosphere of Christmas, holding parties to celebrate the occasion.

In modern Japan, people have the tendency to adopt whichever practices of Confucianism, Buddhism, Shinto and Christianity they think are most suitable to any given situation or time of year. Adherence to any doctrinal truths or ideals assumes relatively low priority in the lives of most Japanese people, who tend to be more concerned about leading a good moral life in harmony with nature and other human beings.

TOKYOITES

CHAPTER 3

'The Japanese in general did not develop a clear-cut concept
of the human individual qua individual as an objective unit
like an inanimate thing, but the individual is always found
existing in a network of human relationships.'
—Hajime Nakamura
(scholar of Asian studies)

Tokyo is a crowded metropolis with a population of just over 12 million, which is about 10 per cent of the total population of Japan. This chapter offers insights about the people of Tokyo ('Tokyoites') by highlighting stereotypes and reality, traditions, and their cultural values.

STEREOTYPES AND REALITY

As in other big cities in the world, Tokyo residents are not necessarily people who were born and raised in the metropolitan area. Many moved here from other parts of Japan when they were young, when they entered college, or when they joined a company. Yet, people in other parts of Japan attach certain labels or traits to Tokyoites, most common of which are: 'snob', 'elite', 'cold', 'fast-paced' and 'busy'. These labels may be somewhat accurate. Tokyoites must function in this crowded metropolis, interacting daily with people from diverse regions and backgrounds. Consequently, they tend to ignore what others are doing and approach strangers with a reserve that may be interpreted as coldness or snobbishness.

The inhabitants of Tokyo and those of Osaka (the second largest city in Japan, located in the western part of the country) have a kind of rivalry. People from Osaka tend to think that Tokyoites are rather obnoxious, while Tokyoites regard the people of Osaka as being rather vulgar, given that the latter tend to be more direct and talk more openly about money than do the people of Tokyo. These contrasting perceptions might be caused by the historically different functions these cities served. Since the Tokugawa Period (1603–1868), Tokyo, which was then called Edo, has been the centre of politics in which bureaucrats play a major role.

Osaka, in contrast, has long been known for its commercial endeavours in which merchants play the primary role in society.

Within Tokyo, people who live in the downtown area claim themselves to be *edokko* (natives of Edo) and display traits distinct from those of the previously mentioned stereotypical Tokyoites—they are generally more open, sentimental, short-tempered and caring. *Eddoko* is a title conferred only on those who are at least third-generation born in Tokyo and residents of the downtown area. The term was created during the Tokugawa Period when *samurai* (warriors) held all the power in society. Civilians (such as merchants, artisans, and craftsmen) flourished as a separate and somewhat extravagant culture, distinct from the disciplined *samurai* culture. The civilians proudly called themselves *eddoko* and tried to enjoy life, resisting the heavy regulations imposed by the authorities. But as Tokyo was transformed into a

Japanese Names

- Japanese people usually call each other by their family (last) names. Given (first) names are used only among close friends, couples or family members.
- They usually add '-*san*' after the family name. For example, a person whose family name is Suzuki will be addressed as Suzuki-*san*. The suffix '-*san*' is never added to one's own name and is sometimes omitted when older people call younger people (e.g. teacher, boss).
- The suffix '-*sama*' can be used instead of '-*san*' to indicate more formality. For instance, an important

cosmopolitan society and the mobility of its residents increased, the number of *edokko* declined.

Among foreigners, common first impressions of Tokyoites are that they are polite, organised and hard-working. These impressions may change over time as they get to know them better.

Men and Women in Tokyo

The lifestyles of families in Tokyo have been greatly affected by the recession that started in the early 1990s, by women's role in the society and by the ever-increasing costs of education.

Many middle-class males in Tokyo work for relatively large companies and are called *sarari*-man (salary man) because they spend their lives working for a salaried wage. Lifetime employment, promotion based on seniority and long working hours described the life of these employees until recently. With the economic downturn, lifetime employment is no longer guaranteed in many companies, and a greater number of people now change jobs mid-career. Some younger people now prefer to work as part-timers or as contractors. They have learned that even if they worked full-time for a large company, their future is not guaranteed.

customer or a senior person named Tanaka may be addressed as Tanaka-*sama*.

- Following this custom, Japanese people may also attach '-*san*' to the family names of foreigners, or to their given names if the foreigners have invited Japanese counterparts to use the latter.
- It is best not to call Japanese counterparts by their given names unless they have invited you to do so more than once.

Women's lifestyles have changed dramatically in the past 20 years in Japan, especially in Tokyo. More women remain single by choice, and the average age for marriage as well as divorce rates have both risen. Some women who do marry decide not to have children; recent research indicates that the average number of children per household is less than two.

There has also been an increase in women who choose to continue to work after marriage, although many of them still quit once they become mothers. It is extremely hard for women to rejoin the workforce and rebuild their careers after spending several years taking care of their family. On the other hand, the number of married women who engage in part-time jobs is increasing, although these jobs may not lead to serious careers. Some work simply to supplement their overall family income or to seek a degree of financial freedom. Others work outside their homes in search of 'self-realisation'.

Despite these changes in women's lifestyles, there are still differences in the roles of men and women in Japanese society. In the corporate world, the number of women in managerial positions is still limited and women tend to engage in administrative or support work. In families, women assume most of the responsibility for housework and managing the education of children. Most male employees work long hours and it is virtually impossible for them to do anything at home but sleep.

Children in Tokyo

Raising children in Tokyo is an increasingly daunting task due to the escalating costs of education and a rise in crime among youths.

The cost of supporting a child from birth through university is now ¥ 10 million. Parents work hard and sacrifice much to send their children to tutoring classes or to hire private tutors to prepare their children for school exams. In order to be hired by the best companies, students must attend the best universities. To enter good universities, students must attend good senior high schools and to enter good senior high schools, they must go to good junior high schools. Stringent entrance exams must be passed at each step in order to enter good schools. The only way parents can help children avoid the stress of this series of exams is to enrol them in one of the elite primary schools, which offers the potential for continuous education all the way through to university. Children need only take an exam to enter the primary school, after which they can enjoy the rest of their school life. Competition to enter such primary schools is extremely stiff, however.

Another challenging factor of child-raising is that the crime rate among young people has increased dramatically in recent years. These crimes include robbery, assault, and

homicide. Of great concern to society is the fact that some students in Japanese schools tease and bully classmates for no obvious reason, with the bullying sometimes leading to actual assault. Occasionally, some youngsters who are the targets of persistent bullying even commit suicide.

Observers attribute the rise in youth crime to several factors. One is the stress from continuous educational pressure. Another is the sense of insecurity that young people feel regarding work, as during times of economic slowdown graduating from a good university does not guarantee lifetime employment or career success. Still another possible factor is that many children spend more time on their computers than with their friends or parents. Their inner worlds are greatly affected by the stories and characters that appear in computer games, some of which are extremely violent. It is suspected that children accustomed to seeing simulations of crimes in games have thus become desensitised to the seriousness of the crimes, and to the probable consequences to themselves and their families.

Elderly People in the Society

Japan is rapidly becoming an elderly society. It is expected that in the year 2015, the percentage of people older than 65 will account for 25 per cent of the entire population. With many older people collecting social security each month, reserving adequate funds for future payments is of great concern for the Japanese government. As interest rates in Japan have been kept low in recent years, older people who expected additional income from interest on savings are having a hard time.

For centuries, Japanese people, influenced by Confucian teachings, have believed that adult children are supposed to take care of their parents both physically and financially. Nowadays, many parents and children prefer to live separately even when the parents have grown old, partly because rents are so expensive in Tokyo it is difficult to find an adequately large yet affordable place to live with one's parents. In addition, the lifestyles of parents and adult children are generally so different that an unreasonable amount of tension can be expected if they live together. Finally, younger generations have been influenced by a more Western, independent mindset, with priorities shifting to the pursuit of individual rather than family goals.

Despite changes in people's mindsets and lifestyles, the belief that adult children are responsible for taking care of their parents is still strong, and most children feel hesitant to put their parents into external facilities such as nursing homes. Consequently, few of such facilities have been built.

Many Japanese people are still physically sound and energetic even after retirement (generally at age 60). Having a fulfilling life after retirement is a challenge for them, and creating stimulating opportunities for these valuable members of society is a challenge for the country.

A Tokyo Family

What is life like then for a typical Japanese family in Tokyo? The life of the fictional Yamada family provides some insight.

To reduce confusion, in this description family members are referred to by their given (first) names. In Japan, however, first names are used only among family members and close friends. (*Refer to the previous page for more details about Japanese names.*)

The head of the family is 43-year-old Takeshi Yamada. He was born in Sendai, in the northern part of Japan, and moved to Tokyo when he entered university. After graduation, he was hired by the headquarters of a bank in Tokyo and has been working there ever since. He is now the manager of the accounting department and has an annual income of ¥ 7 million.

Takeshi is married to 38-year-old Hiroko Yamada. Her parents moved to Tokyo when they were young and Hiroko was born and raised in the city. She met her husband at the bank, where she was also an employee. Like many Japanese women of her generation, she quit her job after getting married. Hiroko's parents built a house for the newlyweds in Toshima-ku, in eastern Tokyo, on land they had owned for many years.

Takeshi and his wife feel very fortunate to own a home so near the centre of Tokyo, as doing so is just a dream for many people. Most of Takeshi's colleagues live outside of Tokyo and commute more than one hour to work, but Takeshi's commute is only half an hour.

Takeshi wakes up at 7:00 am. He eats a traditional Japanese breakfast, consisting of rice, *miso* soup and a slice of fish fillet or some leftovers prepared by Hiroko, and leaves home around 8:00 am. He walks to the station to take the subway, which is tightly packed with people. When he arrives at his office, most of his colleagues are already there. They chat about the weather, last night's baseball game, and exchange information about ongoing projects. At noon, Takeshi and his colleagues usually lunch at the company cafeteria that has a reasonably priced set menu. Some of Takeshi's colleagues, mostly those who are single women, lunch at restaurants, but as Takeshi has two children to support, he does not have the luxury of splurging on lunch.

Takeshi and his department colleagues have been working on a quarterly financial report, so he has worked until 11:00 pm every day for the past week. The bank recently restructured to cut expenses and some employees were laid off, thus Takeshi feels great pressure to
(continued overleaf)

(continued from previous page)

work hard and perform well. He now feels insecure about his own position. He has been working for this bank for 20 years and does not know what he would do if he lost his job.

When Takeshi and other men of his generation started working, they believed that once they had a job at a major bank or manufacturing company, a stable income and lifetime employment would be guaranteed. But economic changes are forcing companies to change their employment policies, and typical Japanese families to restructure their expectations and lifestyles.

Concerned about Takeshi's job security, Hiroko has started working part-time at a small company, helping with the accounting. She did not delay looking for a job as her best friend's husband, who used to work for a big manufacturing company, was recently laid off during a corporate restructuring exercise. A couple of her friends have also taken part-time jobs to help cover rising expenses. Hiroko feels it is useful to have a second source of income in case Takeshi loses his job and also because the costs of their children's education are likely to increase. While Hiroko enjoys working again after spending more than ten years taking care of her family, she would not have thought about re-entering the workforce if the situation had not required it. She feels lucky to have her current job as it is generally difficult for women to re-enter the work-force once they have quit.

Kanami, age 14, is the oldest child in the family. She is in the second year of a public middle school located in her neighbourhood. She and many of her classmates are from the same primary school. Since entering middle school, their interests have changed to fashion and make-up. Some of Kanami's friends have dyed their hair and she wants to dye her hair too, but she knows her parents will disapprove. She always feels that she does not have enough money for socialising and shopping, so she wishes she could have a part-time job, but her school does not allow students to work. Her school requires all students to engage in some kind of extracurricular activity. Kanami is a member of the tennis club and practises three times a week. She enjoys going to fast food joints and family-type restaurants with her club mates after practice. On days when she does not have tennis practice, she attends tutoring sessions to prepare for senior high school entrance exams.

The youngest member of the family, Yuji, is 10 years old and goes to the same public primary school Kanami attended when she was younger. Yuji does not like studying, but his parents send him to a tutoring class after school because they want him to go to a private middle school. They believe that he will have a better chance of getting into a good university if he goes to a particular private school. He enjoys playing computer games with his friends, and has recently been trying to convince his parents to buy him new game software if he gets good grades on his next report card.

(continued on next page)

(continued from previous page)

The maternal grandparents (Hiroko's parents) live with Hiroko's younger sister, Kyoko, in the same neighbourhood. Kyoko is 35 years old and works in the marketing department of an apparel company. As she lives with her parents, she does not have to pay rent and can spend all the money she makes. She dines in trendy restaurants, purchases luxury goods and travels overseas at least once a year. Although her parents pressure her to get married, she prefers the single life. She does not envy her sister Hiroko, whose only concern is her children's education.

TRADITIONAL EVENTS IN TOKYO

Although Tokyoites' lives today are very Westernised, there are several traditional events that are important to punctuate peoples' lives, most of which are linked with seasons. Seasons are so important to Japanese people that when they write a letter, even a business letter, they customarily begin by mentioning something about the season.

Here are highlights of seasonal events that have been celebrated for hundreds of years and still play major roles in the Japanese people's lives. The **New Year** is the most important seasonal event for Japanese people. The official New Year holiday is from 1–3 January, and many companies close their businesses for a week, including the days before and after the holiday.

At the end of December, many people clean their houses from top to bottom to greet the New Year with a fresh mind and spirit. They also place special decorations inside and outside their homes, and prepare special foods to be eaten over the course of the holiday period, although this custom is being observed less and less among younger people. Everyone writes *nengajo* (postcards) to thank others for their support in the past year and to wish them the best in the new year. Most people feel rushed during December as they must complete many tasks to bring the current year to a close and to properly welcome the new year.

On New Year's Day, you can see many people wearing the *kimono* (Japanese traditional costume). The New Year holidays last until 3 January, but the holiday mood continues until mid-January and people still hold parties to celebrate the New Year.

On 3 March, families with little girls celebrate *Hinamatsuri* (**The Doll Festival**) to wish for healthy and happy lives for their daughters. To honour the occasion, they create arrangements of peach blossoms and display *hina-ningyo*, miniature dolls in traditional *kimono* costumes.

A big event during spring that people look forward to, since ancient time, is viewing the cherry blossoms. In Tokyo, many parks are graced with an abundance of cherry trees. Most of the flowers are pale pink but some are almost white, and the scene with hundreds of trees in bloom at once is just stunning. Towards the end of March, the television news gives forecasts of when the cherry blossoms will be at their peak (which in Tokyo is usually around the end of March or the first week of April), and people begin planning picnics and outdoor parties. The party-goers take food and drink, sing along with karaoke machines, and have fun under the canopy of blossoms.

In early May, families celebrate *Kodomo no hi* (**The Children's Day**). This is the holiday to wish for healthy and happy lives for their sons. Families with boys hang three carps (called *koinobori*) made out of cloth on a pole in the garden. The way the carps fly in the wind simulates the way real carps swim upstream—parents hope that their boys grow up with such strength.

In summer, many festivals and events are held at neighbourhood parks, shrines and school fields where stalls sell foods, crafts and small animals such as bunnies and chicks. Some festivals include folk dances and fireworks displays. The most famous fireworks display is held at the Sumida River near Asakusa. (If you plan to attend, reserve a spot early!)

In mid-August, there is the *Obon* festival. According to Buddhist teachings, this is the time when the spirits of the dead are believed to return to this life, so people gather with their families and visit their home towns to welcome their ancestors' spirits. Although *Obon* is not a national holiday, many companies and shops close for three to four days, and trains and planes are packed to capacity.

In November, families with small children celebrate *Hichi-go-san* (literally translated as 7-5-3): this is to celebrate girls who have become 3 years old and 7 old years old, and boys who have become 5 years old. Parents take children (usually wearing *kimono*) to a shrine to wish for their happiness.

The memories of these traditional events and memories of the season in which the event is held are inseparable. People recall their childhood memories when the season returns each year. (*Refer to* Chapter 7 *for a more detailed calendar of events.*)

JAPANESE CULTURAL VALUES

The Japanese culture emphasises some traditional values and beliefs that may seem different or unusual to foreign visitors (especially to Westerners). These values derive from historical, political and religious influences. For foreigners, understanding these values and beliefs is often the key to successful interaction with Japanese people, although the degree to which individual Tokyoites adhere to these traditional values varies. Acceptance of diversified values and beliefs are gradually increasing. In general, younger people fit less closely into the stereotyped view of Japanese people.

Group Orientation

The most prominent feature of Japanese culture is its group orientation; group goals, achievements and interests are emphasised in social and business situations. It is important for Japanese people to have a sense of affiliation with a group (such as a school, company or interest group) and they value collaboration and teamwork.

The importance of teamwork is taught to Japanese children from a young age. School children are encouraged to play and study in groups with other children, and to accomplish tasks together with other group members. Most junior and senior high schools require students to participate in group extracurricular activities (such as tennis, volleyball and theatre), so that they will learn how to organise and participate in group events. Teachers and parents believe that the students can nurture team spirit by working together towards a team goal, and that this team spirit will strengthen each individual's mental state.

Group lessons and activities are common in Japan, even among adults. Instructions in tennis, foreign languages, and flower arrangement are often provided to groups of people, and groups of friends, especially women, who tend to do many things together, for example, shopping, eating out, and going to movies. By doing things jointly, there is an increased sense of bonding. On the negative side, there is sometimes hidden pressure for continual group participation in order to maintain friendship.

Group Instinct

One reason for this focus on groups may partially be attributed to the country's geography and history. Japan is a small, mountainous country surrounded by water. As a result, mobility was low and many people remained in the same community throughout their lives. In addition, rice cultivation was historically an important industry in Japan. Successful rice cultivation required extensive, continuous care of the rice fields—the more effectively people worked together in groups, the more efficiently they could work the fields and achieve good annual harvests.

At companies, projects and tasks are often assigned to groups rather than to individuals, and group members help each other complete the task. Therefore, it is usually difficult to distinguish individual performance, and both rewards and punishment are typically given to a group rather than to an individual. Also, much of one's personal identity is derived from the groups one belongs to; people tend to be more concerned about the company they join than about the actual job itself. Because of this emphasis on the group, in situations where people introduce themselves, people often mention the name of the company they work for first, and then followed by their own name.

Harmony

Japanese people believe that in order for a group to function optimally, the maintenance of harmony and good relationships among members is crucial. Japanese people take great care to avoid hurting other people's feelings and, consequently, use a communication style that is indirect and relatively tentative.

Group members are connected to each other through a sense of interdependence and responsibility. They constantly monitor each other's well-being and try to offer help before others ask for it. Those who receive favours show appreciation by returning favours. In other words, people practise reciprocity in many aspects of life.

Japanese people also maintain group harmony by following protocol or rules. There are many formal as well as informal rules in Japan, and people generally follow them. For example, most people wait for the traffic signal to turn green before they cross the street, even when there are no cars coming. The Japanese feel most comfortable when everybody follows the same rules, and harmony and conformity are maintained.

> Japanese people usually return from vacation with souvenirs for neighbours and colleagues to show appreciation for work done during their absence and on their behalf. Japanese people usually bring gifts when visiting–even for very brief visits—to show appreciation for being hosted.

Another example of this preference for conformity can be observed in the Japanese tendency to follow what others do. As a result, when a particular style of clothing comes into fashion, everybody wears it, and Tokyoites often form long lines to buy a popular type of food, or to get seats in trendy new restaurants.

Hierarchy

Hierarchical differences are observed and respected in Japan because doing so keeps order. To show respect, Japanese people use special phrases and verb forms when interacting with people higher than themselves in the hierarchy.

In organisations, work titles are a reflection of the hierarchy; employees in Japanese companies often call their superiors by title instead of by name, and are reluctant to take on new responsibilities unless they have been officially given an appropriate title. As Japanese people tend to work for the same company for a long time and are generally

Japanese people form a line to buy a popular snack.

promoted on the basis of seniority, title and age often go hand-in-hand.

In social interactions, age determines one's place in the hierarchy. As people are expected to show respect to their elders, they want to know the ages of their acquaintances or neighbours so that they can use the appropriate language and behaviour.

Insider/Outsider (Uchi/Soto)

Because the sense of affiliation to a particular group is important to Japanese people, they tend to differentiate between members of their own group (insiders—*uchi*; literally, 'within' or 'home') and those outside of their group (outsiders—*soto*; literally 'outside') based on several factors, including the specific group people belong to (such as company or school), background (such as age or place of origin), and common interests. Different sets of behavioural and communication styles are applied depending on whether the person with whom one is interacting is considered *uchi* or *soto*.

With insiders, the Japanese discuss things relatively openly and share their true feelings directly. They believe that insider group members are mutually dependent, caring and supportive. In contrast, they often keep a certain distance from outsiders, treating them with what can seem like excessive politeness, but not openly disclosing their true feelings.

A significant insider-outsider differentiation frequently made is between Japanese and non-Japanese. Generally speaking, foreigners are considered outsiders. As a matter of fact, a popular—and often objected—to word for 'foreigner' literally means 'outside people' (*gaijin*). Keep in mind that this word does offend many foreigners. This differentiation is applied more strongly to Westerners and other foreigners whose cultural backgrounds are distinct from the Japanese, than to other Asians. Some expatriates feel that, even after having lived in Tokyo for a long time, the Japanese people have yet to fully accept them.

To add to the confusion, Japanese people sometimes adjust their attitudes towards insiders or outsiders according to the context. Because of the emphasis on group harmony and hierarchy, Japanese people are attentive to figuring out and engaging in the behaviour and communication style that is most appropriate in a given situation. And because what is appropriate depends on the context, such as the occasion and people involved, their perceptions of who is an insider or outsider are affected by who else is present.

For example, when alone, a Japanese person may treat a foreign friend as an insider and share confidential information. However, when other Japanese people are present, he or she may treat the foreign friend in a more formal and distant manner. When alone with the foreign friend, the Japanese feels it is appropriate to be open and casual. In other words to behave like insiders, as no one else is present. But when other Japanese people are present, the Japanese person may be more concerned about showing culturally appropriate behaviour, such as respecting hierarchy and maintaining harmony among those present. Out of such concern for others, the Japanese person now considers the foreign friend to be an outsider and treats him or her likewise.

This modification in behaviour and communication style often confuses foreigners and gives the impression that Japanese people are insincere or even dishonest. While it may sometimes be difficult to judge what factor caused the shift in attitude, it might be comforting to know that the behavioural changes were based on context, and not on how they actually feel about the foreign friend. It may also be comforting to know that this shift also applies to interactions with other Japanese people.

One way to reduce this gap between insider and outsider is to establish something in common with Japanese people. Having similar interests, sharing common experiences and spending time together can all serve to create more open and personal relationships with Tokyoites.

A view of the Tokyo Tower and the beautiful cherry blossoms. Each year, many Japanese enjoy the age-old tradition of sitting in groups beneath the trees to bask in the short-lived beauty of the cherry blossoms

A train passing through Akihabara train station. Akihabara is a major shopping area for electronic and computer products and it is aptly known as 'Electric Town'.

The modern and the traditional: The two ladies in their *kimonos* contrast with the modern attire of the other pedestrians.

Traditional food stalls and eateries have not lost their appeal in the face of competition from modern restaurants. Here, locals enjoy a hot meal after a day of work.

Purchasing your subway ticket at the ticket machine in the subway stations is convenient and simple. Tokyo has one of the most extensive and efficient subway systems in the world.

Changing Trends

Many young Japanese people identify more with the individualistic values of some Western cultures than with traditional Asian ways of thinking. For example, their individual goals and interests take priority over those of others, and they tend to assert their uniqueness and differences of opinion more openly in public than do older people. As a result, particularly in Tokyo, there is increasing acceptance of a diversity and variety in people's tastes, lifestyles and working habits.

As young people become more focused on personal interests, they seem to care less about other people's feelings and about following rules and social etiquette. This shift is particularly prominent in Tokyo where people are busy taking care of their individual lives. For example, some young people speak loudly on their cellular phones in public, and do not use the appropriate language to show respect when speaking to older people.

SOCIALISING WITH LOCALS

CHAPTER 4

'Ability in using language ambiguously while still
getting your point across remains one of the most
important social, business and political skills in Japan.'
—Boy Lafayette De Mente
(author on Japanese culture)

THE UNWRITTEN RULES OF A NEW CULTURE are rarely immediately apparent to newcomers. Rather, they are slowly revealed in the course of daily life. To give you some insights into ways of interacting with Japanese people, this chapter discusses the communication styles of the Japanese, as well as tips on socialising with people in your daily life.

Perceptions Towards Foreigners

Today, more than 300,000 foreigners are registered to be living in Tokyo. Among them, the largest numbers are from Korea (both North and South) and China. Many are descendants of people who moved to Japan before World War II, but the number of recent immigrants from China is also increasing. Newcomers from the Philippines, Thailand and other nations in South-east Asia also account for a large percentage of the foreign population; many came to Tokyo in search of jobs. Employment opportunities have also led to an increase in the number of Brazilians living in Tokyo.

In addition, there are a number of people from Western nations such as the United States, the United Kingdom, Australia and France, most of whom have been posted here to work for their employers in the Japanese subsidiaries of foreign firms.

People from the same countries or similar cultural backgrounds tend to live together in certain neighbourhoods. As a result, a few distinct foreign communities have developed in Tokyo. Many people from the Philippines live in Shinjuku-ku, for example; those from China live in Toshima-ku; and many Westerners reside in Minato-ku. In some of these places, it is possible to see more foreigners than Japanese people.

Tokyoites are generally gracious hosts, willing to help foreigners. When asked for directions, Japanese people not only suggest the best route, they might even accompany foreigners to their destinations. However, some Japanese people may seem hesitant to interact with foreigners. In many cases, it is because they lack confidence speaking in English. Although everyone studies the English language in high school, emphasis is placed on grammar and vocabulary rather than on practical conversation, thus many people are better at understanding written English than spoken English. Foreigners who feel that their spoken English is not being understood by Japanese people can often communicate successfully by writing down their requests or main points.

Japanese people have a tendency to prize and value anything from the West (including food, clothes and pop culture). This can be attributed to the nature of Japan's historical relationship with Western nations. Extensive contact with Westerners began in the middle of the 19th century when Japan opened its doors to foreign countries after more than 200 years of insularity. Japanese people were shocked to see the advanced technology, wealth and different

Topics for Conversation

Here are general tips for topics of conversation with someone you do not know well.
Topics to avoid
- Personal matters e.g. health, families, significant others
- Negative comments on the society and culture
- Asking personal opinions about something in front of others (*Refer to* 'Japanese Communication Style' *in this chapter*).

customs of these Westerners, and an attitude of 'learn from the West' emerged. This same pattern was repeated after World War II when Japan rebuilt under the leadership of the United States. During both periods, Tokyo was the locus of interaction with Westerners. Even today, after becoming one of the world's most advanced nations, Japan still tends to follow trends initiated in Western cultures.

Because of this strong preference for things Western, Japan is sometimes accused by other Asian nations of neglecting the fact that it is part of the Asian community. In addition, because during World War II Japan pursued a cruel military strategy of expanding its territory into other Asian countries, tensions remain. However, in recent years exchanges between Japan and other Asian cultures have increased. For example, popular music has been exported from Japan to other Asian countries and vice versa. In future, more understanding and collaboration can be expected between the Japanese and the inhabitants of other Asian nations.

Foreigners who have lived in Tokyo for long periods of time comment that the metropolis has become friendlier to foreigners. There has been an increase in the number of instructions and signs in foreign languages (mainly in English, but also in Chinese and Korean). Foreign products are more readily available in local supermarkets and at lower prices. Japanese people seem more open and willing to speak in English although their abilities may be limited.

Safe topics
- Food
- Weather
- Sports
- Seasonal events
- Places to visit
- Customs and traditions in Japan as well as those in your own culture

COMMUNICATING EFFECTIVELY WITH JAPANESE PEOPLE
Japanese Communication Styles

While the biggest challenge in communicating effectively with Japanese people would be the language differences, foreigners would realise that even when Japanese people speak in English, many Japanese people tend to use elements of their own communication style, which reflect their cultural values. Foreigners will find that understanding such a communication style will enhance their effectiveness in communicating in Japanese. (*Refer to* Chapter 8 *for peculiarities of the Japanese language.*)

Indirectness

Japanese people tend to avoid saying things directly, preferring to express opinions and feelings in an indirect manner. Because 'not hurting other people's feelings' and maintaining group harmony are their primary concerns, and direct statements or emotional outbursts are believed to interfere with smooth interactions.

When declining a proposal, for example, Japanese people might say "I'll think about it", instead of saying "It's impossible". They worry that if they say 'no' bluntly, their counterpart may feel hurt as well as shamed, and both parties will face an uncomfortable moment. The speaker will let the counterpart know that the proposal is being declined by using one of several different actions, depending on the situation—through body language or tone of voice, or by asking a third party to convey the message, or by simply not responding to further requests from the counterpart, hoping that eventually the counterpart will get the message.

Japanese people sometimes even show positive feelings indirectly because appearing to be happier than other people may jeopardise harmony.

Silence is a typical tool Japanese people use. They become silent when they do not understand the meaning of a message, because they do not feel comfortable asking for clarification. They worry that by doing so, they might appear unintelligent, or that they might make the speaker look unprepared. People are especially likely to remain silent if the speaker is of a higher status.

A popular saying in Japan is that 'silence is golden'. Japanese people feel that if they put everything into words, the value of the message will be lessened—as a result, many things are left unsaid. Instead of effusing over how much they appreciate a favour someone did, they may give that person an expensive gift to show their gratitude. Rather than praising a subordinate for good performance, a manager may just buy the subordinate a meal.

Avoiding Confrontation

Confrontation and argument are often perceived negatively because most Japanese people believe they harm relationships. Thus, direct confrontation in many situations is avoided. If conflicts are minor, issues may be ignored until they cause greater problems. If a conflict needs to be resolved, it may be settled indirectly. For example, a person who disagrees with a counterpart might say, "I like your idea but I would also like to examine other alternatives". If the conflict is serious, he or she might ask a third person to mediate, or remain silent and not say anything, delaying action so that the counterpart realises something has gone wrong.

It is difficult for Japanese people to separate differences in opinion from personal relationships. When someone disagrees with them, they tend to perceive the feedback as personal criticism and start wondering what they did to upset the other person. Of course, this is very different from some Western cultures where debate is considered stimulating and constructive. In some societies, people can still be friends and have no hard feelings after an intense debate. In Japan, people may become overly emotional if they experience direct confrontation and find it difficult to heal the relationship after a heated discussion.

Apologising

In an attempt to maintain harmonious relationships, Japanese people frequently apologise for what may seem to be trivial matters. Such apologies, however, do not always indicate an admission of fault. People usually apologise for the inconvenience caused but not necessarily for mistakes made. For example, after a car accident, one driver may apologise to the other, but this does not necessarily mean that the driver was at fault. Rather, it may mean, "It was very unfortunate that the accident happened. I hope we can discuss this calmly". Sales clerks will immediately apologise when a customer complains, regardless of the reason for the complaint, and even if they were not responsible for what happened. In other words, apologies are often used to sympathise and show sincerity towards those involved in the incident. In many cases, a word of apology soothes the negative emotions of all involved and makes problem-solving easier.

Humility
'The nail that stands up will be pounded down' is an expression that shows very clearly how important humility is in Japanese society. Because of the group focus and the emphasis on group harmony, people are constantly aware of mutual dependence and generally wish to avoid standing out from the group. Thus, they tend to attribute any success in performance to other people's support rather than to their own abilities.

For example, Japanese people frequently say *Okagesamade*, which means 'Owing to (all of) you'. When greeting each other, if a Japanese is asked how he or she is doing, that person might reply, "Owing to (all of) you, I am fine". Similarly, when praised, a Japanese may say, "It is owing to (all of) you. I did not do anything". It is rare to hear people say, "I think I did a good job. I am proud of myself", even if they actually think so. If one acknowledges one's own achievements without mentioning what is 'owed to others', one could be perceived as being arrogant.

Communicating with Japanese People in English
While some Tokyoites you meet or work with may speak English fluently, most people you interact with on a daily

basis will have limited experience in speaking English. Communicating effectively with them requires some effort and patience from both sides. (*Refer to* Tips for Communicating in English *on page 56*.)

English Language Education in Japan

Most Japanese people study English in school for at least six years (three years each in junior high school and in senior high school). Those who go on to university usually study English for an additional four years. Many children and adults also attend private English schools or hire tutors.

Japanese youths tend to develop greater proficiency in reading and writing, than in comprehension and speaking, for a couple of reasons. Firstly, Japanese schools emphasise the learning of correct grammar and sentence structure, and the memorisation of vocabulary and phrases. In general, a significant portion of the entrance exam for high schools and universities is devoted to the testing of students' mastery of those aspects of the English language. As a result, schools tend to teach *juken eigo* (entrance-exam English), focusing on drills and memorisation, while largely neglecting comprehension and practical application.

A second reason is based on cultural values and communication styles. Because of the focus on group dynamics mentioned earlier, Japanese people care greatly about what others think of them. In consequence, they speak cautiously to avoid making any mistakes. This attitude often hinders them from developing fluency in English or other foreign languages, as in order to improve one must practise and make mistakes. Many Japanese who can speak English fluently do so because they spent some years abroad when young. Children have fewer cultural filters and will try out phrases in a new language with less hesitation. This is one reason why Japanese schools are trying to implement English education in primary schools when children's learning styles are more flexible.

Tips for Communicating in English

Modify your English

- Simplify your English and try to put only one idea into a sentence. Avoid using too many pronouns, adjectives and adverbs.
- Speak slowly, pausing between sentences. Japanese people feel more comfortable when speaking in turns and will wait until you finish your sentence.
- Avoid negative questions. Japanese people tend to misunderstand negative questions. To avoid confusion, it is better to state questions in the positive. For example, to a question: "Didn't you know that there was a class this afternoon?" Japanese people who are not fluent in English would probably indicate they did not know by saying "Yes"(meaning, "Yes, I didn't"), which is a direct translation of how they would answer in Japanese. To avoid misunderstanding, ask in this manner: "Did you know that there was a class this afternoon?"
- Avoid tacking questions onto statements. For example, "You didn't know that there was a class, did you?" is difficult for non-native speakers to understand because they cannot tell if it is a positive or negative question. Again, use a simple direct question: "Did you know that there was a class?"
- Avoid idioms and colloquial expressions. For example, instead of saying "Shall I give you a hand?", say "May I help you?". Instead of saying "Are you all set?", say "Are you ready?" or "Have you finished?"

Check for understanding

- Do not assume that everything is understood if Japanese counterparts remain silent.
- Check frequently for comprehension. (The question "Do you understand?" is not effective for confirming comprehension because Japanese people often feel it

is rude to say "No".) Rephrase your statements and ask probing questions to confirm comprehension (such as asking for a specific date, figure or action plan).

Use documents to support your message
- Japanese people comprehend better reading English rather than listening or speaking it. Support what you say in writing.

Speak in small groups of people
- When several native speakers of English are involved in a conversation, it is extremely difficult for Japanese people to understand all that is said. Limiting the number of native speakers can slow the pace of the conversation and make it easier for Japanese people to participate.
- When Japanese people are in a group, they are expected to observe group dynamics and pay attention to what others might think about their comments. You will probably get more honest reactions when you interact with Japanese people one-on-one.

Be personal
- Having good relationships is important for Japanese people. They feel more relaxed when they speak with someone they know. Try to get to know them personally. Face-to-face communication is usually more effective than telephone conversations.

Be patient
- Modifying your English and checking frequently for comprehension requires energy and can sometimes be frustrating. Understand that your Japanese counterpart is equally frustrated. Effective communication depends on mutual effort.

SOCIAL CUSTOMS AND ETIQUETTE
Visiting a Home

Japanese people do not often invite others to their homes because most homes are not large enough to accommodate many people at once. A Japanese person who invites a friend, especially a foreign friend, to his or her home is showing a deep commitment to the relationship.

Unless specified otherwise, an invitation to someone's home is only for you; it does not include a spouse or other family members. Japanese people generally keep personal friends and family members separate and tend not to introduce them to each other (which is another reason why friends are not often invited to their homes). However, your family may be included if the person inviting you has already met them, or knows them well.

Arrive up to 5 minutes later than the specified time so that the host can relax a bit after completing preparations for your arrival. If the invitation is for dinner, you will probably be asked to arrive between 6:00 pm and 7:00 pm and will be expected to depart around 10:00 pm. (How late you stay depends, of course, on your relationship with the host.)

Always bring a gift when you are invited to the home of a Japanese person. You can ask what they prefer if you share a very close relationship with the host. Even if the host declines your offer, bring something anyway. Popular gifts are fruits, chocolates, cookies and flowers. If your host drinks alcohol, you can take a bottle of wine (beer may be considered too casual except for a barbecue party). You can also bring gifts such as small toys for any children in the house. The hosts might not open the gifts before you, but this is not because they do not appreciate your gift. Opening a gift and showing a reaction is considered too risky. (What if they do not like it?) They will open it after you leave and thank you later.

You are supposed to remove your shoes when entering a Japanese home, so come prepared and wear a clean, hole-free pair of socks! Most Japanese hosts will offer you a pair of slippers to wear inside their home. You should remove them when you enter a traditional *tatami* mat room or the bathroom. You usually will find another pair of slippers

A typical family dinner setting an expat will be invited to.

inside the latter, which should be used exclusively in that room. Some guests (not just foreigners) make the mistake of wearing these slippers out to other rooms and then feel very embarrassed!

Japanese people show their hospitality by putting a lot of time and effort into preparing a big meal for guests. Leave anything you cannot eat aside and untouched. Your host might notice and will not offer you the same thing again.

Your host will appreciate receiving a thank-you letter or a thank-you call the following day. When you see your host later, thank him or her again for the occasion even if you have already made a thank-you call or sent a letter. Japanese people like to experience continuity in relationships and reinforce them by referring back to past events. Additionally, they will feel happy to hear that you appreciated their efforts.

Hosting Japanese People in Your Home

If you have been invited to a Japanese friend's home, you may want to reciprocate the invitation. If you were the only guest at your friend's home, you might want to invite only your friend to your home. In general, Japanese people prefer to develop in-depth relationships with a small number of people rather than to meet many people at one time. In other words, they may feel more comfortable visiting you individually or as part of a small group rather than attending a large party with strangers. Their comfort level in speaking English will also affect their preferences.

Some people do not feel comfortable accompanying their spouses to a party if they do not already know the hosts. In Japan, husbands and wives tend to have different groups of friends and it is not as common as in the West to accompany each other to social occasions. Also, single people feel hesitant to bring dates unless they are engaged

Greetings

Japanese people bow when greeting
- Deeper bows indicate more respect.
- People bow more deeply the first time they meet and on more formal occasions (e.g. a college graduate at a job interview bows almost 90 degrees in front of the interviewers).
- People try to bow more deeply than their counterparts if the counterparts are more senior to them either in status or age (e.g. at a job interview, the graduate bows deeper than the interviewers to show respect, and the interviewers would probably just nod to acknowledge the candidate.).

People also bow when they depart, thank others, apologise and offer gifts, etc.
- Because bowing is a way of showing respect, those who do not bow are often considered rude or arrogant.

(a socially approved status). All of this, of course, depends on several factors including the nature of the relationship, English proficiency and past overseas experience.

When offering food or drink, make the offer a few times. Japanese people usually decline the first offer out of politeness. In Japan, people often feel that it is not polite to ask for a drink or an item, so they tend to wait until their host has offered a few times. Therefore, good hosts should be attentive to the needs of their guests.

Select the menu based on what you already know about the food preferences of your guests. They may not tell you what they like or dislike even if you ask directly, but in general, Japanese people tend to prefer hot meals over cold and prefer foods that are not greasy; some do not like cheese. Meat other than beef, pork or chicken is not popular in Japan (and are not readily available). These are just general guidelines; some people are more adventurous than others and love to try foods from other cultures.

Shaking hands is not common except on ceremonial occasions such as press conferences and meetings of political leaders.

- Some people offer to shake hands with Westerners, knowing that this is their custom, but Japanese people tend to bow even when shaking hands.

Exchanging business cards is the most important part of the greeting ritual among Japanese people.

- People exchange business cards the first time they meet in business situations as well as on non-business occasions. (*Refer to* 'Business Etiquette' *in* Chapter 9 *for more details on business card exchange*).

Gift-giving

Japan is a 'gift culture'. Gifts play an important role in building and nurturing relationships.

There are official gift-giving periods twice a year: one in mid-July (*ochugen*) and the other at the end of the year in December (*oseibo*). People send gifts to superiors, colleagues and neighbours, and to others who have done them favours. To show appreciation and nurture relationships, companies also send gifts to their clients and other business associates. Department stores and retail shops regard these gift-giving periods as sales opportunities and offer special discounts to attract customers. Food, wine and household goods such as towels and linens are popular gifts. The amount spent on each item varies depending on the relationship, but usually ranges from ¥ 3,000–10,000.

Japanese people generally do not expect foreigners to follow these formal gift-giving customs. Even among Tokyoites, gift-giving is becoming less popular. Few younger people practise the custom of ritualised, obligatory gift exchange, preferring more casual relationships. Some companies have discontinued the practice of sending gifts to other companies in order to reduce expenses, and others have banned gift exchanges among employees in order to abolish ritual formalities. But if you like, you can use these opportunities to deepen relationships and to show appreciation for the help your Japanese friends have given you. Be aware that once you have started the custom, it will be reciprocated and will continue over the years.

Another occasion when Japanese people give gifts is upon return from a vacation or a business trip. They bring souvenirs (*omiyage*) to colleagues, neighbours and friends. For a group of colleagues, people bring something inexpensive that can be shared (cookies, chocolates or finger foods). For colleagues who have done work for them while they were absent, they may bring specially chosen souvenirs. They also bring gifts to their neighbours, particularly if they have asked the neighbours for a specific favour (such as watering the plants or looking after the mail), or if the neighbours have previously brought them *omiyage*. (Reciprocation is important in Japan!)

Finally, they may also bring *omiyage* for close friends if they have received *omiyage* from them before or if they have found something that their friends would like. *Omiyage* do not have to be expensive, but should be reminiscent of the place the person has visited.

People often give farewell gifts when colleagues, neighbours or friends move to another location, or when colleagues leave the company or retire. Expatriates who leave Tokyo after their assignments are finished are likely to receive a lot of gifts from Japanese colleagues and friends. It is also common for people who are leaving to give gifts to those whom they leave behind to thank them for their support and companionship. When giving farewell gifts, people try to choose items that are reminiscent of the relationship or place.

Japanese people do not celebrate the anticipated birth of a baby by attending a 'baby shower' (a party for giving gifts before babies are born). Instead, they give clothes, toys or other baby-related items within a month after the birth.

Christmas and birthday gifts are only exchanged among adults if they are quite close. School-aged children may exchange birthday gifts and invite each other to birthday parties. The value of gifts varies by age and school, so if you have children you might want to check on this with other parents.

Japanese people have a tradition of giving *otoshidama* (pocket money) to children during the New Year. Adults are expected to give *otoshidama* to children present at New Year parties. The amount varies according to the age of the children and ranges from ¥ 2,000–10,000. The money is placed in small envelopes specifically designed for *otoshidama*. (Such envelopes are sold in stationery stores.) *Otoshidama* is a major source of children's savings.

Wrapping is another important aspect of gift-giving in Japan. You might be surprised to find that everything is neatly and sometimes densely wrapped in several layers. Actually, some shops have been criticised for using excessive wrapping. Nevertheless, the appearance of a package is as important as the contents. Japanese people tend to think that attention to detail (such as wrapping) reflects the degree to which a giver cares for or respects the gift recipient. Most department stores or large retail shops will gift wrap at no additional cost; the first thing a new department store clerk learns is how to wrap a gift! Even more attention is paid to the wrapping of gifts presented on formal occasions.

Weddings and Funerals
Attending a Wedding

Expatriates may be invited to wedding cocktail parties or receptions. This is especially true for expatriates who are managers of Japanese workers, as in Japan, the boss is often the most important guest at wedding parties.

Wedding receptions are usually held in the banquet rooms of hotels or at wedding convention halls. It has also become popular to hold wedding receptions at restaurants. You are likely to receive a written invitation from the bride and groom, and you are supposed to RSVP by sending a postcard back by a certain date. Unless it is specified otherwise in the invitation, your spouse is not invited. Sometimes you may also be invited to the wedding ceremony before the reception, but often invitations are issued only to relatives and very close friends.

Guests at wedding receptions generally give gifts of money. The amount depends on the guest's relationship with the couple and ranges from ¥ 20,000–50,000. If you have been invited to a wedding and do not know how much to give, consult your Japanese friends or colleagues. Guests put the money into special envelopes (*shugibukuro*) purchased at stationery stores, and take them to the reception. In return, guests receive souvenirs (such as plates, teacups, or glasses) from the bride and groom at the reception.

Wedding receptions are rather formal occasions. Men are expected to wear suits; preferably black ones. Women are expected to wear party dresses or suits of any colour except white, which is reserved for the bride. A full-course meal (usually Western food) is served at the reception. Guests begin eating and drinking only after a formal toast is made by one of the honoured guests. Pre-designated speakers give speeches and someone may sing a song during the meal to celebrate the marriage. If you are the boss of either the bride or groom, you will be asked to give a speech. The bride and groom usually leave to change their clothes once or twice during the reception. These days more couples prefer to wear Western wedding clothes, but some still wear traditional Japanese *kimono*. The reception usually ends with a speech by the newlywed couple and/or their parents.

Wedding cocktail parties, organised by friends of the bride and groom, often follow the formal wedding reception. While wedding receptions are for family members and close friends, cocktail parties are mainly for casual friends and colleagues. To attend wedding cocktail parties, guests are usually asked to pay an entrance fee, ranging from ¥ 5,000 –10,000. The dress style for a cocktail party is less formal than for a wedding reception; regular suits for men and dresses for women will suffice.

People who are not invited to either the reception or the cocktail party, but still want to congratulate the newlyweds, sometimes send the couple a gift with a value of ¥ 3,000–10,000. Some items, which are not appropriate as wedding gifts are scissors or knives (which can 'cut' the relationship) and anything in fours (because the pronunciation of the number 'four' is the same as 'death' in Japanese). People also often send telegrams to the place where the reception or party is held in order to pass their personal congratulations along to the bride and groom.

Going to a Funeral

Most funerals in Japan, except those for the followers of Christianity or other religions, follow Buddhist rituals. For Buddhist funerals, people mourn in two different days. The first day is called *otsuya*; it literally means, 'to spend a night' with the deceased. A ceremony is usually held the same night or the following night after the deceased has passed away. The second ceremony is called *kokubetsushiki* and is usually held the day after the *otsuya*. The purpose of the second ceremony is to say goodbye to the deceased; the body is cremated shortly after this ceremony.

Those who are not particularly close to the deceased attend only the second ceremony. However, there is no rule regarding who should attend a funeral. Japanese people often help out at the funeral ceremonies of their colleagues' close family members.

People give *koden* (condolence money) to express their condolences. The amount depends on the guest's age and relationship with the family. When close family members of colleagues or friends pass away, people may give ¥ 5,000–20,000. If you attend a funeral, it is always best to consult with Japanese friends or colleagues to determine the amount that is appropriate to give. The money should be put into a special envelope (*kodenbukuro*) and presented when you arrive at the funeral. Put your name, address, and the amount you enclosed on the outside of the envelope, as the family will need this information later when they send a gift to thank you for your generosity. The gift they return will usually be about one-third to half of the value of the money they received. This custom is called *kodengaeshi* (returning condolence money).

People should wear black clothing when they attend funerals. Men usually wear black suits (or dark grey suits if they do not have black ones) with a black tie. Many kiosks at train stations sell black ties for men who suddenly have to attend funerals. Women also wear black suits or black dresses; their handbags and shoes should be black, too. Pearl jewellery is the only type worn.

During the funeral, Buddhist priests recite a sutra while mourners listen, and towards the end of the ceremony mourners are asked to offer incense. It is best to observe what others do and to do the same. The entire ritual is conducted in silence and guests do not speak to family members during the ceremony.

SETTLING IN

CHAPTER 5

'A tip for a happy life in Japan is to go with the flow
and embrace the differences rather than fighting them.'
—An expatriate in Japan

SETTING UP A NEW HOUSEHOLD AND STARTING A NEW LIFE can be exciting but also overwhelming, especially in unfamiliar surroundings. This chapter offers a variety of information on day-to-day living in Tokyo.

VISA REQUIREMENTS

Foreigners of every nationality need a valid passport to enter Japan, and most also require a visa. To determine if you need a visa to enter Japan, contact the Japanese embassy or consulate in your home country.

Generally, foreigners do not need a visa if they meet the following criteria: 1) they are citizens of a country that has a reciprocal visa exemption arrangement with Japan; 2) they will not be earning money in Japan; and 3) they do not intend to stay in Japan beyond the period of time allowed under the visa exemption arrangement, which varies according to the country of origin. This exemption also applies to people who are visiting Japan for business purposes, such as attending business meetings, as long as they do not receive payment from any entity in Japan.

Immigration officials stamp the passports of arriving foreigners with the date until which they are allowed to stay in Japan. Occasionally officials will ask to see proof that visitors have a confirmed ticket to leave Japan.

Visas must be obtained by foreigners who plan to stay in Japan for a period of time longer than that granted upon entry, and by those who plan to work in Japan. The type of visa, application form and required supporting documents vary according to the purpose of the stay. A Japanese embassy or consulate can provide further details.

ARRANGING HOUSING
Choosing a Neighbourhood

When choosing a place in which to live, two important factors most expatriates consider are the location of their workplace and, if they have children, the location of their children's schools. People who will use public transportation to get to work generally prefer to live near public transportation stations. Families with children who will attend an international school generally prefer to live near a bus stop for the school's bus service. (Japanese private and public schools do not offer school bus services.)

In addition to the practical considerations mentioned above, many foreign residents consider the type of neighbourhood in which they would prefer to live: international, old-style Tokyo, quiet residential or suburban greenery.

International Neighbourhoods

Foreign residents who want to be immersed in an international environment often choose to live in one of the large expatriate communities that have developed in Minato-ku (areas such as Azabu, Aoyama, Roppongi and Akasaka), and in Shibuya-ku (areas such as Hiroo, Jingumae and Ebisu). Many embassies, foreign clubs, international schools and international supermarkets are located in these areas. Be forewarned that rents here can be very high.

Old-style Neighbourhoods

For those wanting to experience the flavour of old-style Tokyo, neighbourhoods such as Bunkyo-ku, Taito-ku and Toshima-ku in the eastern part of the city are ideal. They each have a small-town feel created by the many small wooden houses standing next to each other and the mom-and-pop shops that have been doing business in the same location for

Procedures for Obtaining a Visa

- In general, a visa applicant is advised to obtain a Certificate of Eligibility issued by the Ministry of Justice in Japan.
- In order to obtain the Certificate of Eligibility, a sponsor in Japan (e.g. employer, school, or spouse) must apply for the document on behalf of the visa applicant. Sponsors can call the Immigration Office in Tokyo at (03) 3213-8523 for more information.
- After obtaining the Certificate of Eligibility, the sponsor sends it to the applicant, who must then complete the visa application procedures specified by the Japanese embassy or consulate in the applicant's home country.
- Regardless of the type of visa, staying beyond the date of expiration is against the law, and those who do so can be fined or imprisoned.

generations. Housing here is reasonably priced compared to those in other areas of the city.

Quiet Residential Neighbourhoods

Foreigners seeking quiet neighbourhoods that are somewhat distant from expatriate communities often settle in the residential areas of western Tokyo, including Meguro-ku (Jiyugaoka, for example), Ota-ku (Den-enchofu, for example) and Setagaya-ku (Yoga, Komazawa and Seijo, for example). The rents in these areas tend to be high, especially for larger homes.

Suburban Neighbourhoods

Finally, foreigners who prefer to live in a suburban environment with attractive greenery often enjoy the neighbourhoods located further west. These include Musashino-shi, Mitaka-shi, Chofu-shi and some areas in Kanagawa Prefecture such as Kawasaki-shi and Yokohama-shi. Rents for apartments and houses are generally lower in these areas, allowing residents to lease larger places than they could in central Tokyo. One drawback, however, is the long commute into the city on crowded trains.

Choosing Accommodation

Three main types of accommodation are found in Tokyo: apartments, *manshon* ('mansion') units and houses. While these differ in terms of size and amenities, all three types are described using a similar 'code'—1K, 2LDK, or 3DK, for example. 'K' stands for kitchen, 'L' for living room and 'D' for dining room; the number indicates the number of bedrooms. Therefore, a 2LDK house or apartment has two bedrooms, a living room, a dining room and a kitchen.

The overall sizes of apartments, *manshon* units, and houses are indicated using square metres. However, the size of an individual room is usually indicated by the number of *tatami* (straw) mats that will cover the floor—*tatami* mats were, at one time, found in most rooms of Japanese houses. The size of one *tatami* is approximately 90 cm by 180 cm (3 ft by 6 ft) and a space equivalent to one *tatami* mat (about

A home in suburban Tokyo.

1.60 sq m/18 sq ft) is called a *jo*. *Tatami* sizes can vary; often one finds widths of 80 cm. Even though many modern Japanese houses are designed in a more Western style and some rooms do not have *tatami* mats, the same measurement system is used. The size of a room might be indicated, for example, as 8 *jo*, which means that the size is equivalent to eight *tatami* mats.

Apartments

Apartments are generally the smallest and least expensive housing option. Most apartment buildings are two storeys tall and made of wood, although some have exterior walls made of mortar. The most common floor plan for apartments is 2LDK (two bedrooms, a living room, a dining room and a kitchen). Bedrooms range from 4.5 *jo* (about 7 sq m/80 sq ft) to 6 *jo* (about 10 sq m/110 sq ft), and usually at least one bedroom is a *tatami* room. Very old apartments do not have showers or baths, so residents use public baths nearby. Renters may be required to pay monthly management fees for the maintenance of public spaces in the apartment buildings; these fees vary from building to building.

Manshon Units

The term *manshon* is used to refer to newer apartments that are made of reinforced concrete; most are higher than three storeys and some are taller than 10 storeys. These buildings started appearing in the late 1960s and were called *manshon* (meaning 'mansions') because they looked so luxurious compared to the old-style wooden apartment buildings. They are more durable than wooden apartment buildings, and as they generally have better facilities, such as lifts and garages, are more expensive than apartments. *Manshon* come in three types: regular, those catering to foreigners and those in which units can be rented by the week.

The smallest *manshon* unit is called a 'one-room *manshon*', which is basically a studio apartment with a small kitchenette attached to it. The largest *manshon* units are 4LDK or 5LDK (four or five bedrooms, a living space, a dining area, and a kitchen). The sizes and the types of rooms vary; the average bedroom size ranges from 6 *jo* (about 10 sq m/110 sq ft) to 8 *jo* (about 13 sq m/144 sq ft). The entire area of a typical *manshon* unit ranges from 30 sq m (about 330 sq ft) to more than 100 sq m (about 1,100 sq ft). Most have at least one *tatami* room; some have balconies or patios. Like apartments, most *manshon* require payment of monthly management fees.

In areas with high expatriate populations, there are many *gaikokujin-yo manshon* (meaning foreigner-style *manshon*). These *manshon* usually do not have *tatami* rooms and have an average bedroom size of 8 *jo* (about 13 sq m/144 sq ft) to 10 *jo* (about 16 sq m/180 sq ft). Appliances such as clothes washers and dryers, dishwashers and gas ovens are often already built in. Some buildings have separate living quarters attached for tenants' domestic helpers. Because these types of *manshon* are larger than the average apartments and *manshon* in Tokyo, they are one of the most expensive options. The majority of tenants in such apartments are foreigners, but some are Japanese people who prefer a Western-style and can afford the rent.

For temporary housing, there are also 'weekly *manshon*'. As the name indicates, units can be rented on a weekly basis. They are furnished and usually include basic items such as cookware and linens. Although rents are high, staying in a weekly *manshon* is generally much cheaper than staying in a hotel.

Finalising a Rental Contract

Once you have chosen a place to live, a formal contract must be signed with the landlord. Here are common processes in finalising the contract:

- The contract period is generally two years, although for some properties it is one year.
- Most contracts are renewable; however, the rent might change and tenants could be asked to pay a renewal fee equivalent to approximately one month's rent.
- Before signing a contract, check to see if it includes any penalties for early termination.

The following are required to finalise a rental contract:
- Foreign Resident Registration Card
- Income Statement
  You may be asked to show documentation that proves your income. Most employers in Japan are accustomed to issuing such documents.
- Guarantor (*Hoshonin*)
  In Japan, it is common practice to have a surety's (guarantor) signature to finalise a rental contract. The guarantor should be someone who has income and who can pay the rent in case the tenant is unable

Single-Family Houses

A single-family house is the third option for foreigners, although the selection in central Tokyo is limited. Some houses are built completely in Western style, similar to the foreigners' *manshon*, with large rooms and no *tatami* room. Rents for large houses can be very high.

Design Features

In all these types of housing, foreigners may notice some unique features in Japanese-style bathrooms. Most have a deep, square bathtub (though Western-style oblong bathtubs are the norm in apartment buildings designed for foreigners),

to. Ask your manager, a colleague or a friend to act as your guarantor.

Seal Registration Certificate

- Japanese people usually use seals when signing contracts. Signatures are often acceptable for foreigners. Ask your landlord what is required.
- Initial rental payments usually include the first month's rent, a *shikikin* (deposit), and a *reikin* (monetary reward). The *shikikin* is a deposit that is equivalent to two- to three-months' rent and is generally refunded when you move out. However, if there is any damage to the residence, the landlord will subtract from the *shikikin* the amount required to repair the damage. The *reikin* is a payment of one- or two-months' rent made to acknowledge the landlord for accepting the tenant. It is neither optional nor refundable. In addition, real estate agencies usually charge one-month's rent as their commission. Relocation companies often combine all such fees into a package.

and a separate adjacent area for washing; some have a showerhead on the wall outside of the bathtub. (Japanese people only soak in bathtubs—they do not wash their bodies or shampoo their hair in them.) While some residences have a bathtub that fills with hot water from the tap, others have bathtubs where cold water from the tap is heated by a gas heater attached to the tub.

Another design feature of Japanese bathroom facilities is the squat toilet, instead of the ceramic 'chair' on which people sit. This is most common in some older apartments, as well as in some public restrooms. Also, either type of toilet may have a water tank attached above or adjacent to it (in place of the toilet tank) in which one can wash one's hands; water automatically comes out of a spigot after the toilet has been flushed.

Finding a Home

The easiest way to find accommodation may be to work with a relocation company with offices in both your home country and in Tokyo. The Tokyo staff of the relocation company will pre-select a couple of places for you to view when you arrive in Tokyo. The staff will probably be fluent in English, so you will not have to worry about language issues.

In order to find a home without the services of a relocation company, you can work with a real estate agency. There are several such agencies in Tokyo that cater mainly to foreigners. They have English-speaking staff and understand foreigners' needs. Because they target expatriates, the places they show you will be mainly those built for foreigners, and thus, can be expensive. (*Refer to the* Resource Guide *for a list of real estate agencies servicing foreigners.*)

If you do not want to live in housing built for foreigners, you can work with a local real estate agency. Several agency offices are located near major train and subway stations. If you plan to visit these agencies, ask a Japanese friend or colleague to accompany you. People at local agencies generally do not speak English, and some may not feel comfortable communicating with foreigners, even if you do speak some Japanese. Also, you may discover that some landlords are hesitant to rent to foreigners because of limited experience in interacting with them. The Japanese person who accompanies you can help build your credibility and reduce the anxiety of the agent and potential landlord.

Another approach to gauging prices and finding a place is to check rental listings in housing magazines and to contact the designated real estate agencies for details. This approach has a couple of drawbacks, however. First, almost all of these magazines are written entirely in Japanese. Second, because the magazines are published weekly instead of daily, they seldom contain the most up-to-date listings. In most cases, by the time you contact the agencies, the properties listed are no longer available.

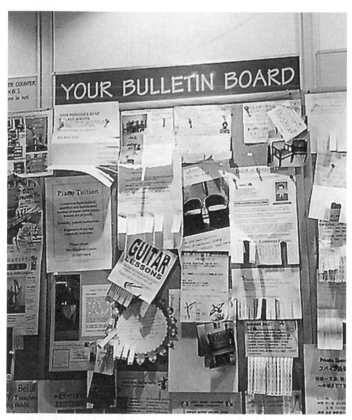

A bulletin board with English notices at an international supermarket.

Capsule hotels, a uniquely Japanese concept, rent out 'capsules' only to men at about ¥ 5,000 a night.

Finally, information available through informal networks may be a valuable source for finding a place to live. You can also check bulletin boards in places where foreigners are likely to gather (for example, international clubs, supermarkets and organisations), or the housing advertisement columns in English-language newspapers such as *The Japan Times*, magazines such as *Metropolis*, and the *Tokyo Notice Board*.

Arranging Utilities and Services
Gas
Many homes have gas ovens, stoves, water heaters, and room heaters. Gas distributed in the Tokyo area is primarily natural gas provided by the Tokyo Gas Company.

When tenants move out, gas service is discontinued. Therefore, prior to moving into a new home, you must call the nearest Tokyo Gas office and notify the staff of your moving-in date. Usually, instructions for new tenants (including the telephone number to call) are hung on the front door of the apartment or house. The instructions are in Japanese, however, and operators may not speak English, so it might be a good idea to ask your landlord or the real estate agent for assistance. After you make the call, a representative from Tokyo Gas will visit your home and make the necessary arrangements.

The gas meter will be checked once a month and you will receive a monthly bill. Most people pay their gas bills using the automatic transfer system at the bank with which they have a general deposit account. Payments for the monthly bills are then automatically deducted. Applications for enrolment in this system are available at all banks that offer the service. If you choose to enrol, make sure that your account contains sufficient funds on the monthly payment date. If you prefer not to use automatic debit, you can pay your bill in cash at a bank, post office or convenience store such as 7-11 (Seven-Eleven), Lawson or AmPm. These places serve as clearing agents for Tokyo Gas and no additional fees are charged.

Electricity

Electricity in the Tokyo area is provided by the Tokyo Electric Power Company (TEPCO). When you move into a new place, you will generally find a circuit-breaker box near the entrance to your home. Lift the circuit breaker (usually the biggest switch on the board) as well as the other small switches on the board, and you should have activated electricity. If there is no electricity, call the nearest TEPCO office. You should also send an application postcard to the company to notify them of your billing information. You will generally find the postcard on the circuit-breaker box or hanging on the front door of your residence. You can also find further information on the English website of TEPCO at *www.tepco.co.jp*

A person from the TEPCO will check the electric meter monthly, and you will receive a monthly bill. Payment of bills is similar to that for gas—by automatic debit, or by cash at a bank, post office, or convenience store.

Water

Water is supplied by the Tokyo Metropolitan Bureau of Waterworks. To get water running prior to moving into your new residence, contact the Tokyo Metropolitan Bureau of Waterworks Service Station or the Waterworks Section of your area's ward or municipal office. You should also send an application postcard to notify them of your billing information. Ask the landlord or real estate agency for the appropriate number to call and where to find the postcard, if it is not hanging on the main door. If you live in one of the 23 wards, you can also apply for water supply on the English website of Tokyo Metropolitan Bureau of Waterworks at *www.waterworks.metro.tokyo.jp*. You will receive a bill once every two months. The payment methods are the same as those for gas and electricity. Tap water in Tokyo is safe to drink but does not taste very good, so many people use water filters or buy bottled water.

Garbage Collection

If you live in an apartment, there will usually be a garbage disposal area in your building. If you live in a house, there will be places every few blocks to put garbage on the day of pick-up. Garbage should be separated into combustible materials and incombustible materials, and these should be disposed of separately. In most of Tokyo, combustible materials are picked up twice a week; they should be placed in paper bags or specially marked plastic bags (sold at supermarkets). Incombustible garbage is picked up once weekly.

Recyclable materials such as glass, aluminum and steel cans, newspapers and magazines should be gathered separately. These are picked up once a week.

To arrange for disposal of larger materials such as furniture and electrical appliances, call the ward or municipal office in your area. Special arrangements must also be made to dispose of air conditioners, television sets, refrigerators or clothes washers. Shops from which new appliances are purchased are responsible for recycling old items. If you do not know where to take old appliances, ask your ward or municipal office for recommendations. You will have to pay a fee to recycle or dispose of appliances (even if you are buying a new one from the shop).

Telephone

- Installing Telephone Line

  Most rental units already have a telephone line installed. If you have to arrange for instalment of a telephone line, you must submit an application to your area's Nippon Telephone and Telegraph (NTT) Corporation East branch office. When applying, you will need your passport or Foreign Resident Registration Card as well as documentation to confirm your address. You must pay the following: a contract fee, a telephone ownership fee, and an installation fee. Call the NTT Information Service [in English. tel: (0120) 364-463] for more information.

- Telephone Bills

  You will receive telephone bills monthly—one bill for dialling charges from each of the telephone carriers through which you made calls, and a separate bill from NTT for basic charges for domestic calls (because all telephone

Cellphones are everywhere in Tokyo.

carriers are required to use the network installed by NTT).
The payment methods available for telephone bills are the
same as for other utilities. You can also pay the telephone
bills by credit cards. Please find further information at the
English website of NTT East at *www.ntt-east.co.jp*

■ Cellular Phone
  More than 75 per cent of Japanese people now use cellular
  phones. Most cellular phones are equipped with a variety
  of functions such as email and internet access, plus music
  and video-playing capability, in addition to its primary
  phone function. You can buy cellular phones at retail shops
  operated by these cellular phone service companies or at
  large electronic shops.

Other Documents Needed

Foreign Resident Registration

- All foreigners who plan to stay in Japan longer than 90 days are required to register at the ward or municipal office of the area in which they live.

- You will need your passport and two photographs (4.5 cm by 3.5 cm, that have been taken within the last six months); photographs are not required for children under 16. Anyone aged 16 or older must apply in person; parents can apply for children younger than 16. If you do not read or speak Japanese, it is best to go to the ward or municipal office with someone who does, as many application forms are in Japanese and office personnel are not always fluent in English.

- After your application is processed, you will receive a Foreign Registration Card valid for five years. This card will serve as identification and, within Japan, is almost as important as a passport. All foreigner residents aged 16 or over are required to carry their card at all times. Foreigners are also required to report to the ward or municipal office closest to their residence within 14 days if changes are made to any of the following: name, nationality, occupation, status of residence, period of stay, name of employer, work address or home address. Foreigners who move to a new location during their stay in Tokyo are required to report to the ward or municipal office closest to their new address.

Re-entry Permit

- Foreign residents who want to travel overseas must obtain a re-entry permit prior to departure from Japan. A single permit allows the holder to make one trip out of Japan and to return with no change in visa status. A multiple re-entry permit allows the holder to make unlimited trips abroad until the date of expiration of the permit.

- To obtain a permit, apply in person with your passport and Foreign Registration Card at the following Immigration Bureau:

Tokyo Regional Immigration Bureau
5-5-30 Konan, Minato-ku, Tokyo
Tel: (03) 5796-7112

Seal Registration
- In Japan, people use seals (*hanko*) instead of written signatures when signing contracts or documentations. They usually have family names in Chinese characters on their seals. Written signatures are accepted from foreigners in most cases, but some expatriates make their own seals for convenience and as a memory of their stay in Japan.

- In particular, seals that are registered with ward or municipal office are required when signing important documents (for example, when renting or purchasing a house, or purchasing a car).

- If you need to register your seal, take it and your Foreign Registration Card to the ward or municipal office of your residence. You will receive a Seal Registration Certificate that proves that your seal is registered. Seals with names that are not recorded on the Foreign Registration Card cannot be registered.

THINGS TO TAKE AND NOT TO TAKE

The length and purpose of your stay, budget and lifestyle will determine what to take and what to leave behind. Some people prefer to live surrounded by familiar belongings, while others prefer to take as little as possible and buy whatever is needed in Tokyo.

Many expatriates recommend that newcomers leave large pieces of furniture and appliances back home, as most neither fit nor function well in Tokyo. Instead, they suggest bringing personal items such as family photographs and favourite books or videos—in other words, things that cannot be purchased in Tokyo.

Men's Items

In Tokyo, good quality men's clothes of both domestic and imported brands are available. However, if you are tall or larger than an American size 40, an English size 40, or a European size 50, you should bring adequate supplies as large sizes are hard to find in Tokyo. (*Refer to the size comparison chart in the* 'Resource Guide'.)

Tokyo has four distinct seasons and most people prefer to wear different sets of clothes for each season. Winter can be cold and windy with occasional snow, so you will need long-sleeved shirts, woollen sweaters, a rather heavy coat, a scarf or muffler and a pair of gloves. Spring and fall are more moderate, so you will need both short- and long-sleeved shirts, cotton sweaters and a light coat. Summer can be hot and humid, so bring plenty of T-shirts and cotton short-sleeved shirts. Most Tokyoites carry a handkerchief at all times, handy for wiping a sweaty brow.

Due to seasonal temperature changes, most Japanese businessmen have an array of business suits in heavy-, moderate-, and light-weight fabrics. Foreign executives working in Japan may wish to dress as Japanese businessmen do for the sake of comfort and image. (*Refer to 'Business Etiquette' in Chapter 9 for more suggestions.*)

Some foreign businessmen living in Tokyo order tailor-made suits from Hong Kong, as these are much less expensive and the service is fast. As Hong Kong is only a six-hour flight from Tokyo, it is possible to have suits made during your stay for business or over a long weekend. (Be sure to allow time for at least two fittings.) Also, several tailors from Hong Kong come to Tokyo regularly to take orders, mainly from foreigners. To find a good tailor, ask other expatriates for recommendations.

Shoes wear out quickly in Tokyo, as most people walk a lot getting to and from public transportation stops. If you wear shoes larger than an American size 9.5, an English size 9 or a European size 42.5, you will find only a limited selection for sale in Tokyo. Shoes that are easy to slip on and off are more convenient than shoes that must be laced, as it is a Japanese custom to take shoes off in homes, and before entering the restaurants and inns that have *tatami* (straw mat) floor coverings.

Women's Items

Many of the same guidelines on packing that apply to men apply to women as well. Japanese women tend to spend a lot of money on clothing, and there is a wide selection of fine apparel (both domestic and imported) available in Tokyo. Sizes, however, may pose a problem if you are tall or larger than an American size 10, an English size 12 or a European size 42, so bring along plenty. (*Refer to the size comparison chart in the* 'Resource Guide'.)

For the cold winter, you will need a heavy coat, warm sweaters, a muffler or scarf and warm gloves. For the hot and humid summer, take shirts and dresses made of fabrics that absorb perspiration and are easy to wash. As the temperatures in air-conditioned buildings can be low, light sweaters, jackets and scarves are useful. For the more moderate but variable weather of spring and fall, take clothes that can be worn in layers (sweater sets, comfortable suits, and dresses with jackets, for example). Those who anticipate size problems should also pack sufficient quantities of lingerie and hosiery.

Women who wear shoes larger than an American size 7, an English size 5.5 or a European size 38 are likely to have difficulty buying shoes in Japan.

In general, Japanese women dress very neatly, conservatively and, in most Westerners' eyes, rather formally. To make a good impression, foreign businesswomen may want to do the same. (*Refer to* 'Business Etiquette' *in Chapter 9 for more suggestions.*)

A variety of imported cosmetics are sold in Japan, but some of them are produced specifically to suit Japanese preferences as well as skin types and tones. Consequently, if you are partial to a particular brand or type of cosmetic, bring along a supply that will last until you can find a suitable substitute in Tokyo. Also worth noting is that feminine hygiene products available in Japan tend to be smaller in size than those made for Western women, so some foreign women prefer to take a supply from their home country.

Children's Items
Buying clothing and shoes for children in Tokyo may be much easier than for adults. They are available in a great variety of sizes, designs and colours. As children grow fast,

you might want to take only the essentials with you and then shop in Tokyo as your children need them. Although some expatriates find children's clothing rather expensive in Tokyo, it is possible to save money during seasonal sales or by buying used clothes. For children who have larger builds, however, it would be better take sufficient clothes from home, as it is not easy to find apparel for big-sized children in Tokyo.

High quality toys are abundant in Tokyo, although they tend to be more expensive than in other countries. Some parents have also noted the preponderance (to the exclusion of other types, in many stores) of 'character' toys, such as Hello Kitty or Anpan-Man.

Foreign books and videos are also expensive, so you may want to take a good supply. They can be great for consoling homesick children. Be sure to bring several copies of your children's school transcripts, as they will be required for admittance into schools in Japan.

General Household Items
Furniture
Whether you take large household items such as furniture may depend largely on the transportation costs and whether the items will fit into your new home. In general, homes in Tokyo are smaller than those in many countries (especially the United States, Canada and Australia). Therefore, unless you know the size of your new living area and that your furniture will fit, it may be safer to leave it behind. If you are taking your beds, pack also the bed linens as it may be difficult to find items in Tokyo that fit your bed size—Japanese beds are shorter than those found in many other countries.

Electrical Appliances
The electric power in Tokyo is 100 volts and 50 cycles (hertz). (Electricity in eastern Japan is 50 cycles, but in western Japan it is 60 cycles.) Small appliances such as radios and hair dryers that are 110 volts and 60 cycles (the standard in the United States and Canada) can be used in Tokyo, but might run a

little hot. Most portable computers are equipped with internal converters and should run with no problems, although some very early models might not have this capability. Electric clocks and other sensitive appliances may not work properly. It is generally better to buy large appliances such as television sets and refrigerators.

Not all foreign-made videos will work. Japan uses the NTSC video format, as do the United States and Canada, so videos made in those countries can be played on Japanese VCRs. However, the PAL video format used in most of Europe and Australia is not compatible with the majority of Japanese VCRs. In Tokyo, it is possible to buy VCRs that can handle multiple formats, but they are more expensive than single-format VCRs.

As for DVDs, regional codes are generally programmed into them in the countries in which they are released. The regional code for DVDs released in Japan and many European countries, for example, is 'two', whereas it is 'one' for DVDs in the United States and Canada. Most DVD players sold in Japan accept only DVDs with the regional code 'two'. Thus, if you want to watch DVDs with other regional codes, you will need a player that accepts multiple regional codes. Such players can be found in some shops in Akihabara.

The electrical plugs in Japan are flat two-pronged plugs, similar to the two-pronged plugs used in the US and Canada. Three-pronged grounded plugs will not fit into Japanese sockets. If necessary, take a supply of converter plugs or buy them after you arrive.

Medication

You can bring up to a month's supply of prescription drugs and up to a two-month's supply of non-prescription medications into Japan. If you are taking prescribed medication, you should bring a copy of the prescription and/or a letter from the prescribing physician explaining the nature of the medication. Most prescription drugs can be taken into Japan, including drugs that may not be available there.

Drugs that contain narcotic, psychotropic and/or hallucinogenic components will be confiscated unless pre-approval has been obtained. Also, some over-the-counter medications that are sold overseas are prohibited for sale in Japan because they contain some of the components mentioned above, e.g. Tylenol Cold, Nyquil and Sudafed.

Birth control pills can be prescribed by doctors in Japan, but to obtain refills, a doctor's visit is required. Therefore, many foreign women who use birth control pills take ample supplies with them.

Foodstuff

Japanese customs regulations do not allow people to carry most fresh fruits, vegetables and meat products into Japan. However, canned fruits, vegetables and prepared meat products are generally allowed. Dried meat, such as beef jerky, may be taken into Japan if it has been commercially prepared and packaged. Other dry products such as cookies, crackers, candies and cereals, as well as dried noodles, may be taken into Japan. Most types of nuts can also be imported if they are salted, dried or roasted, but walnuts are prohibited.

PETS

Upon arrival, all imported animals are subject to inspection by the Japanese Animal Quarantine Service. The time required for the inspection depends on the type of animal and the health condition of the pet. Health certificates are required for several types of animals.

For dogs and cats, the inspection period will be up to 12 hours if the animals enter from countries that are known as 'rabies-free', and if they are accompanied by a certificate issued by the government authorities of such a country. These countries include Taiwan, Australia, New Zealand and Britain. The certificate should state that: 1) the pet is free from rabies and leptospirosis (for dogs only) and any infectious diseases; 2) the pet was kept for at least six months or since its birth in one of these countries prior to transport; and 3) there has been no outbreak of rabies for the last six months in the country prior to shipment.

The quarantine period for dogs and cats from other countries (such as the United States) generally ranges from

12 hours to 180 days, depending on the condition of the animal. In order to qualify for the 12 hours quarantine period, dogs and cats must be accompanied by a certificate that states necessary information such as the microchip number for the individual identification and the dates of rabies vaccination.

For further details, please refer to the website of The Animal Quarantine Service at http://www.maff-aqs.go.jp.

RAISING CHILDREN IN TOKYO
Childcare

Leaving children in the care of others is not as common in Japan as in some Western countries. Therefore, it is difficult to find Japanese teenagers who want to do babysitting as a part-time job. However, you might be able to find foreign teenagers who want to earn some spending money. Locate them by asking other expats, by contacting the international schools, or by putting up bulletin board ads in places frequented by expats. An online source with a listing of babysitters along with recommendations from actual users is Tokyo with Kids (www.tokyowithkids.com). Some expatriates hire live-in

Young children wear bright yellow caps when out on field trips.

domestic helpers who are responsible for childcare as well as other duties.

As the number of Japanese mothers who work increases, so will the number of childcare facilities. Child-care facilities, called *hoikuen*, both private and public, are available; they usually care for children of working Japanese parents, but foreign working parents are also eligible to apply. Some of these facilities even accept children who are less than one-year old. Prior to accepting children, the *hoikuen* verifies the parents' employment status and income, and sets the fee accordingly.

Private childcare facilities are more flexible in their requirements for enrolment, as well as designated time for picking up the children, but they also cost more. Also, some private facilities are not adequately staffed because they are not inspected as stringently and as frequently as are public facilities.

The number of *hoikuen* is increasing, but not fast enough to support the needs of working parents in Tokyo.

Preschools

Tokyo offers a variety of educational opportunities, both international and Japanese, for children who are not of school age. (*Please refer to the* 'Resource Guide' *for a list of international preschools.*)

Unique Customs in Kindergartens

Parents who send their children to Japanese kindergartens may experience some customs and systems that are unique to Japan.

Renrakucho (daily communication notebook)

It is a common custom in Japanese kindergartens for teachers and parents to exchange notebooks, called *renrakucho*, on a daily basis. Parents are supposed to write down in the notebook things that teachers should know (health problems, for example). The teachers will write, in Japanese, about how the children behaved in class. Foreign parents who cannot read Japanese well can inquire if any teachers are able to write the notes in English (or the foreign language spoken by the parents), or request that the notes at least be written in simple Japanese.

Obento (boxed lunches)

Children may be asked to take boxed lunches on special occasions (such as field trips), a few days per week, or every day. Japanese mothers spend much time preparing, wrapping and arranging the contents of the boxed lunches for their children. They fill the boxes with several foods, such as sausages, small tomatoes, boiled vegetables, small hamburgers, etc., arranging the contents so carefully that the lunch sometimes looks like a piece of artwork.

The appearance of the containers is as important as the contents. Most children have cute containers that feature famous comic-book characters. There seems to be hidden competition among children concerning whose boxed lunches look best—it becomes the mothers' responsibility to prepare nice boxed lunches so that their children can feel proud. Not wanting their children to feel embarrassed about having 'substandard *obento*', foreign mothers do usually try to make their lunch creations look attractive.

Japanese kindergartens (*yochien*) can provide wonderful cultural experiences for both children and parents. Japanese kindergartens are of two types: private and public; but private facilities are more numerous. Many private kindergartens accept children as young as three, while most public kindergartens accept children four years of age. Fees for tuition are higher for private kindergartens.

Language is initially an issue for foreign children who do not speak Japanese, and the first couple of months can be difficult. However, most children pick up the language rapidly and soon adjust to the new environment. Language can also be an issue for parents struggling to communicate with their children's teachers. Be patient and expect some miscommunication periodically.

The Japanese Educational System

In Japan, the basic educational system consists of six years of primary school, three years of junior high school and three years of senior high school. Many parents also send their children to kindergarten and university. School attendance through junior high school is compulsory for all children.

Both public and private schooling are available for children at all levels. Tuition is free for public primary and junior high schoolchildren, and parents need only pay for textbooks, uniforms and additional expenses such as lunch fees. Tuition fees are charged for public kindergarten, senior high school and university, but the fees are generally less than half of that for private schools.

The school year starts in April and ends in March. In most primary, junior high and senior high schools, it is divided into three terms: term one from April to late July, term two from September to late December, and term three from January to late March. Between each term there are summer, winter and spring vacations, in addition to national holidays. No public schools hold classes on Saturdays and Sundays, but some private schools do on Saturdays.

Examinations are not necessary for entry into public kindergartens, primary schools, or junior high schools. However, examinations are required for entrance into public senior high schools and universities, as well as private schools at all levels.

Entrance examinations for the best schools are rigorous. As graduates of the top universities are prime candidates for jobs with the most prominent companies and government organisations, many parents want their children to enter these universities. Students from premier high schools have the best chances of entering top universities, so students feel the pressure to enter good high schools. The same principle applies to entrance into junior high schools, so competition starts at a very early age, just to ensure that children will have good careers!

Parents often send their children to tutoring classes to assist them in preparing for entrance examinations. Many children attend these classes almost every day after school. Consequently, life for junior and senior high school students is strenuous. Japanese people call this period *juken jigoku*, which means 'entrance examination hell'. Nowadays, many parents try to send their children to good private schools that provide continuous education from primary school through to university, so that their children do not have to take examinations to move up to senior levels and can thus enjoy their school life. As a result, competition for entry into these primary schools has become very intense and even small children must attend tuition to prepare for the exams.

Education for Foreign Children
Tokyo offers several options for the education of foreign children, and most expatriate parents are quite satisfied with the quality of education available.

Japanese Schools
Foreign children are eligible to attend Japanese public schools in the districts in which they reside. If you are considering this option, you can get detailed information by contacting the Board of Education at the ward or municipal office nearest your residence.

Language is an important issue to consider when choosing a school. Most Japanese public schools do not offer 'Japanese as a Foreign Language' classes, so if your child does not understand Japanese, keeping up with lessons and other activities can be extremely difficult, especially at the higher levels. In addition, as Japanese society is relatively homogeneous, teachers are not specifically trained to accommodate cultural diversity in their classes. Consequently, foreign children may not receive adequate assistance to help them adjust and thrive in the new culture.

As Japanese schools are now in the process of changing their curricula to support the goal of developing students to be successful in the global arena, they are gradually becoming more accepting and accommodating of foreign students.

While attendance at a Japanese public school can be a nearly insurmountable challenge for children from other countries, some foreign parents are pleased with the experiences their children have while attending Japanese schools. This is especially true for parents of young children as they tend to develop fluency in the Japanese language quite easily. Parents are also often impressed by how attentive and committed the teachers are to the students.

Unique Customs in Japanese Schools

Customs at schools in Japan include:

- students take off their street shoes and wear indoor shoes at school all day—usually there is a specific type of indoor shoes that should be worn and are sold at schools or designated shoe shops
- students are required to clean their classrooms—through this exercise students learn to take good care of what they use everyday and teamwork by working together with other students
- students stand up and bow when teachers enter the classroom—this is to show respect to the teachers
- preparing nice boxed lunches for the children when they are required to bring lunch (*obento*) to school as their children take pride in them.

International Schools

Tokyo has many international schools that serve the needs of the foreign community. In selecting a school, consider

High-school girls in typical attire—mini-skirts and 'loose' socks.

various factors such as academic standards, philosophy of education, level of discipline and facilities. It is strongly recommended that prior to enrolling your child, you should visit the school and speak with the staff—many schools welcome parents to tour the school. Some schools host official open houses or regular school tours.

Please note that in Tokyo, demand for places in international schools is greater than the supply, and at many schools, openings fill up far in advance of the beginning of the school year. Thus, the availability of an opening may actually be the most important factor in determining which school your child will attend.

Most international schools begin the school year in September and end in June. However, many schools will accept students at any time the school is in session if there is an opening.

The application process varies from school to school. Most schools ask applicants to submit application forms as well as official transcripts from previously attended schools; some schools require recommendation letters. After school officials review these documents, they may request that applicants attend an interview and/or take certain tests. Check with each school for specific application requirements and procedures.

Tuition for international schools is generally quite high, ranging from ¥ 1.7–2 million annually. Additional expenses can easily add up to ¥ 1 million, and typically include registration fees, building maintenance fees and school bus service fees. (*Refer to the* 'Resource Guide' *for a list of international schools.*)

Extracurricular Activities

Children in Japan are kept busy after school. This is especially true when they are young and have not yet begun intensive studying. Many of them engage in two or three extracurricular activities. Popular activities among Japanese children include ballet, piano and swimming lessons for girls, and soccer, baseball, and martial arts for boys. Japanese parents are enthusiastic about developing well-rounded children, and are willing to pay the fees for these extracurricular activities.

The number of extracurricular classes taught in English is increasing. Generally, more than half of the children participating in such classes are Japanese, because English-language instruction for young children is something which Japanese parents are very eager to pay for. Children tend to learn foreign languages relatively faster when the languages are combined with activities. Thus, many classes (including dancing, drama and gymnastics) are now taught in English; instructors of some of these classes are native English speakers. Fees for these classes are generally higher compared to similar activities taught in Japanese. Most international schools also offer a variety of extracurricular activities; once your child has entered school, finding appropriate activities should be easy.

A note about martial arts: studying martial arts can be a unique cultural experience for foreign children living in Tokyo because several popular martial arts (such as *judo, kendo* and *karate*) were developed in Japan, and many classes are offered. Although martial arts are more popular among boys, girls are also welcomed to participate.

Entertainment for Children

Tokyo and the greater Tokyo area offer many types of recreation for children. Both adults and children will be able to enjoy many popular recreation spots such as amusement parks, aquariums, zoos and museums. (*Refer to the 'Resource Guide' for a list of those places.*)

HANDLING FINANCES
Banking Services

Several types of banks and financial institutions operate in Japan that differ in size and the range of services provided.

Most expatriates will need to open at least one account with a Japanese bank, as salaries are usually deposited directly into employees' bank accounts, and various bill payments are often made through domestic bank accounts. Services include deposit accounts, savings accounts, automatic teller machine (ATM) cards, and foreign currency exchange.

Employees at large branches are likely to be more familiar with the kinds of services foreigners often need, such as overseas remittance and foreign exchange transactions.

Types of Bank Accounts
General Deposit Accounts (futsu yokin)

This type of account is most convenient for regular transactions, such as paying bills or receiving salary and other payments. Money can be deposited and withdrawn from this type of account at any time. The interest rate on general deposit accounts, however, is the lowest among the several different types of accounts.

Checking Accounts (*toza yokin*)

This type of account, which bears no interest, is not popular in Japan for personal use as personal cheques are generally not accepted for commercial transactions. Also, payment via transfer of funds between bank accounts has been common practice for some time. Checking accounts are mostly used by organisations for business transactions.

Time Deposit Accounts (*teiki yokin*)

For savings purposes, most banks offer various types of accounts, including time deposit accounts and long-term deposit accounts.

Opening an Account

In order to open a bank account:

- Complete an application form (available at the counter of the bank of your choice).
- Show proof of identification such as your Foreign Resident Registration Card, passport or driver's licence.
- Seals are required for Japanese people but written signatures are usually accepted from foreigners.

ATM Cards

City banks have ATM machines located in many places throughout Tokyo. When opening a general deposit account, you will receive an ATM card and a deposit notebook in which you record the transactions for your account. It is easiest to record transactions by inserting the deposit notebook into the ATM machine at the time of each transaction.

The hours during which ATM machines operate vary. Many of them close around 9:00 pm on weekdays and around 5:00 pm on weekends; some locations are closed on Sundays. The number of ATM machines in operation 24 hours a day is increasing, but most still operate a limited number of hours per day. Recently, several large convenience store chains have begun installing ATMs in their outlets, offering round-the-clock withdrawal, remittance and deposit services for many major city banks.

As major banks are part of a coordinated network, for a small fee you can withdraw cash from an ATM of any city bank in the network. You will find instructions in English posted on the ATM machines at most major banks. Foreign credit cards and cash cards can also be used to withdraw cash at ATMs which display the sign indicating which cards can be used.

Payment of Bills

The most convenient way to pay utility bills is by automatic deduction through the bank with which you have an account. Each bank has specific application forms to initiate automatic payment for utilities such as gas, water and electricity. Automatic payment is also used for other services such as for newspaper delivery charges, telephone and credit card bills; application forms are available from these service providers. If you have insufficient funds in your account by payment due dates, service providers will not be able to debit your account, and your bills will be overdue. Service providers may charge interest for any overdue amounts, and if the overdue status continues, service may be terminated.

For one-time transactions, it is possible to make payment by transferring money to a bank account specified by the potential recipient. You can make such transfers through bank tellers by depositing cash, or debit directly from your bank account at ATMs with a transfer function.

Currency Exchange

In Japan, only banks that are authorised to handle foreign exchange transactions can buy and sell foreign currencies. All city banks are authorised, but it is best to visit large branches for such services, as smaller branches might not carry large amounts of cash in foreign currencies.

Internet Banking

Major banks offer some services over the Internet. Popular ones include the transfer of funds, verification of balances and transaction records, and postings of current market rates (such as foreign exchange and interest rates). However, as instructions are provided almost entirely in Japanese, foreigners may not find Internet banking useful. Citibank Tokyo offers Internet banking in English and Japanese.

Foreign Banks

Several foreign banks operate in Japan, including Australia and New Zealand Banking Group, Barclays Bank, Citibank, Deutsche Bank, J.P. Morgan Chase and Lloyds TSB Bank. Citibank (http://www.citibank.co.jp) is probably the most popular among foreign residents as it offers a wide variety of retail banking services and has branches in all major Japanese cities. Customers can withdraw money from their local Citibank accounts by using Citibank ATMs or the ATMs of any of the Japanese city banks, as Citibank participates in the network of Japanese city banks. In addition, Lloyds TSB Bank offers overseas remittance services at a reasonable rate, while the Australia and New Zealand Banking Group also offers some retail services.

Financial Services at Post Offices

Financial services are also provided by large post office branches in Japan. There, you can open a variety of accounts including ordinary saving accounts, fixed-period saving accounts and long-term saving accounts.

Post offices generally offer slightly higher interest rates than do banks for equivalent accounts, but limit the total amount of deposits per customer to ¥ 10 million. Customers can withdraw money from ordinary deposit accounts using ATM machines located at post offices. Post office ATM service is also linked with the ATMs of other types of financial institutions so that people can withdraw money from their post office account through the ATM machines of other financial institutions.

Cash

Japanese people prefer to use cash for many daily transactions. This preference for cash in Tokyo and throughout Japan stems, perhaps, from the relatively low crime rate—people can still carry relatively large amounts of cash without worrying about theft. In Tokyo, cash is easy to obtain as ATMs are everywhere.

Many shops and service providers now accept credit cards and their use has increased dramatically in recent years. However, foreigners in Tokyo are advised to always carry a certain amount of cash as some services (including doctors, small shops and public transportation) generally accept only cash for payment.

Credit Cards

As Japanese people prefer cash transactions, the use of credit

Sending Money Overseas

Money can be sent overseas either from banks or at post offices.

Banks

Money can be sent overseas by making a direct withdrawal from a bank account or by presenting cash at a major bank. Some form of personal identification, such as a Foreign Resident Registration Card, passport, or driver's licence, will be required. Popular international remittance methods are:

- Telegraphic Transfers
  Money is wired to the recipient's bank account and is available within two to three days.

- Demand Drafts
  The bank issues a draft based on payment by the customer, and the customer sends the draft to the recipient. The recipient then brings the draft to a bank and exchanges it for cash.

cards has lagged behind that in some countries. However, people now enjoy the convenience of credit cards and their use is likely to increase, accompanying an increase in Internet shopping and other forms of electronic commerce.

Nowadays, a great number of stores, restaurants and other service establishments in Tokyo and other cities accept credit cards. However, you may not be able to use credit cards for public transportation or for some taxis, or in small shops, restaurants, hospitals or public offices. Also, some shops set a minimum charge for credit card use.

Major credit cards such as VISA, MasterCard, and American Express are the most widely accepted. If you use a credit card issued from your home country in Tokyo, the credit card company will convert any charges from Japanese yen to your home country's currency, and bill you in that currency. Thus you will face the risk of foreign exchange fluctuations.

Post Offices

Post offices also handle two types of overseas remittances. More information is available on the Japan Post Office website at: http://www.yu-cho.japanpost.jp

- Remittance to the recipient's address
  Post offices will issue a money order equivalent to the amount you want to remit and will send the money order to the recipient's address. The recipient then takes the money order to a local post office and exchanges it for cash. The fee for this form of remittance varies based on the urgency of the delivery and the amount.

- Remittance to the recipient's bank or post office account.
  Fees for this type of remittance also vary based on the urgency of the delivery and the value of the remittance.

In addition, most card companies charge a small fee for the conversion. You may want to get details from your credit card company and make sure that your card can be used overseas. For security purposes, some credit card companies ask customers to notify them before using their cards outside their home countries; others require a special personal identification number for withdrawing money from foreign ATMs.

As most foreigners in Japan will not have established credit histories there, obtaining a credit card may take some time. The easiest approach is to apply for a card with a bank or credit card company with which your employer has some kind of relationship.

Credit card bills are usually paid once a month by automatic debit from customers' bank accounts. Customers generally can choose to pay the amount in full or in instalments. You should ensure your account has sufficient balance by the payment due date or else you may be charged penalties for the overdue bill; if the overdue status continues, the card may be cancelled.

Taxes

Tax requirements in Japan are probably different from those in your country. You should contact a professional tax advisor for detailed information.

Consumption Tax

Consumption tax is imposed on most products and services in Japan. In many cases, this tax is included in the price tag and the price tag indicates how much of the price comes from the tax portion.

Income and Resident Taxes

All residents in Japan, regardless of their nationalities, are required to pay both national personal income taxes (levied by the national government) and local resident taxes (levied by the governments of municipalities and prefectures). Both types of taxes are calculated based on annual personal income earned between 1 January and 31 December.

For salaried employees, employers withhold and deduct estimated personal income tax from monthly salaries. Near the end of the calendar year, employers calculate any excesses or shortfalls in taxes deducted during the year and make corresponding adjustments to the December salary amount.

Employees do not have to file personal income tax reports unless they fall into one of the following categories:

- Salaried employees with an annual income of more than ¥ 20 million.
- Salaried employees with extra annual income amounting to more than ¥ 200,000.
- Salaried employees with incomes from two or more employers.

Local resident taxes are computed by the ward or municipal office of the area of residence of each employee on the basis of the income reported by the employer. These taxes are also deducted from monthly salaries in 12 instalments from June through May of the following year.

Non-salaried workers (such as the self-employed and part-time workers) must calculate personal income tax based on income during the year, submitting tax reports and making payments at local tax offices. Tax reports should be filed between 16 February and 15 March of each year. Non-salaried workers must also pay local resident taxes in four separate instalments in June, August, October and January. The ward or municipal office will send out notifications, and payments can be made through banks, post offices, or other financial institutions.

You may consult English-speaking representatives at the Tokyo Regional Tax Bureau for details (tel: (03) 3821-9070).

SHOPPING

Things tend to be more expensive in Tokyo than in other cities in the world, but the durability of products and the services included in the retail price often justify the additional cost. By comparing prices and shopping during sale periods, savvy shoppers can actually find very good deals. Bargaining is not a custom in Tokyo, except at some small shops and flea markets. Credit cards are accepted at department stores and large retail shops, but not at some small shops. Shopping hours are generally from 10:00 am to 7:00 pm. Many shops are open on Sundays; some shops close for one day each week.

Returning merchandise is not a common practice in Japan. In case there is a need, ask the sales clerk about the return policy when you make the purchase and retain the receipts, as they will be required when making the return. Sales clerks are more likely to accept a return for reasons such as malfunction or a size problem.

Shopping Districts
The Ginza
Ginza is the most expensive place to shop in Tokyo. The area around the 'Ginza 4-chome Crossing' (the intersection of Harumi Dori and Chuo Dori streets) hosts world-famous designer boutiques interspersed with traditional and exclusive Japanese shops. Merchandise from famous boutiques—Gucci, Chanel and Prada, to name a few—can cost one-and-a-half times the price of the same items in other countries. Such mark-ups reflect the Japanese preference for high-quality, luxury items, as well as Tokyo's high real estate prices. Young Japanese women are the best customers at these boutiques, as wearing and carrying designer goods is considered very fashionable. It can be fun to window-shop in this area, even if you do not purchase anything.

The traditional Japanese shops located here carry conservative, high-fashion items popular with older, well-to-do people. Many of these shops have been in the Ginza area for a long time and have established reputations as premier retailers of specialised goods, including tailor-made suits, shoes and *kimono*. The families of the shop owners and those of many of their clients have been doing business together for at least a few generations.

In an attempt to attract a wide variety of people to the area, the main street of Ginza, Chuo Dori, is closed to traffic during the day on weekends, and a few fast food joints have

Tree-lined boulevard in Harajuku.

opened among the finer restaurants and traditional shops. Although young people and families with children welcome the more casual atmosphere, many older people continue to resist moves to make the Ginza less exclusive. After all, the people who are attracted to this area enjoy the classy atmosphere that can only be experienced here.

Other Areas

People in search of trendy fashion frequent the fashionable boutiques in the **Aoyama** areas. There are many designer boutiques that sell more contemporary and less expensive clothes than those in Ginza. Also, **Daikanyama** and **Jiyugaoka** on the Tokyu Line and **Shimokitazawa** on the Keio and Odakyu Line are little neighbourhoods with clusters of small interesting boutiques.

Both **Shinjuku** and **Shibuya** are large shopping districts with department stores, 'fashion buildings' with small boutiques, discount electronics shops and major bookstores. With different kinds of stores conveniently located in one place, these areas are always crowded with young people and families. Those tired from shopping can rest in one of the many restaurants in the area. **Harajuku** is another place popular with young people; its tree-lined boulevard and adjacent side streets are lined with numerous shops selling inexpensive clothes, jewellery, and cosmetics. Several famous European brand boutiques have opened branches here to attract older and more well-heeled customers.

Types of Stores
Department Stores

Department stores are convenient places to shop because they carry a wide range of products (including clothes, household items, crafts, toys and food) and you can compare items of different brands in the same place. Also, most have special corners for extra small and extra large sizes, although the selections tend to be limited.

Regular prices of items in department stores tend to be high. However, they hold frequent discount sales (especially for clothing) due to intense competition. During sale periods, selected merchandise is often reduced by 30–40 per cent. Payment can be made with major credit cards.

Customer service in department stores is quite impressive. Customers arriving at a department store at opening time are greeted by a number of uniformed store clerks lined up at the entrance. The clerks bow and say *Irasshaimase*, which means 'Welcome'. As customers leave the store at closing time, the clerks bow to them at the exit and say *Arigato gozaimashita,* which means 'Thank you'. Some stores have girls who operate lifts; they will inform customers what products are sold on each level, as well as usher customers on and off the lifts. Many wear hats and white gloves.

Sales clerks are quite attentive. They will help you select merchandise by finding the appropriate size, colour and design. They will take your payment to the cashier and bring you back the sales receipt. And they will wrap up each purchase neatly for no additional fee.

Department stores also offer additional services that enhance the shopping experience. Most have restaurants and coffee shops, and some have small galleries exhibiting world famous paintings or cultural artefacts. Some offer childcare and roof garden amusement facilities for children. Most have

Busy shopping street in Shinjuku.

parking in the basement or in an adjacent building. (*Major department stores in Tokyo are listed in the* 'Resource Guide'.)

Large Supermarkets

There are several large supermarkets in Tokyo that are a cross between regular supermarkets and department stores. Most sell grocery items and a variety of products including casual fashion and household items. The quality of the products is often lower than that in department stores, but then, so are the prices. Many supermarkets belong to chains and are located in suburban Tokyo or just outside Tokyo in Chiba, Saitama and Kanagawa. Popular stores are Ito Yokado, Jusco, Seiyu and Daiei.

Flea Markets and 'Recycle' Shops

Flea markets and used-items ('recycle') shops have recently become popular in Tokyo. Japanese people used to be hesitant to wear clothing or buy furniture that had previously been owned by strangers, but now they seem to realise the practicality of recycling these goods. Items sold at flea markets or in 'recycle' shops tend to be in very good condition.

Several wards or municipal districts occasionally hold flea markets. You can obtain the schedule by checking with the ward or municipal office in your area. A few commercial organisations in Tokyo regularly hold large-scale flea markets in public spots such as Meiji Park in Sendagaya and Yoyogi Park in Harajuku. Check the website of the Tokyo Recycle Movement Association for upcoming flea market schedules: (www.trx.jp). You can also obtain information about flea markets and recycle shops in the book *Japan with Kids: A Guide for Parents*. Visit the website 'Tokyo with Kids' (http://www.tokyowithkids.com), or look for notices in English.

Visiting antique flea markets is also a way of finding unique antiques at reasonable prices. They are usually held at shrines on Sundays. (Check with each of the shrines for their schedules.) You can bargain at these flea markets. (*See the* 'Resource Guide' *for a list of antique flea markets.*)

Internet Shopping

Shopping online is increasingly popular in Japan. People who cannot find their clothes and shoe size in Japan can order from shops in their home countries via the Internet. Bear in mind, however, that shipping and handling charges can be quite high (sometimes higher than the retail price of the products).

Things to Buy
Clothes

Clothes sold in Tokyo are generally of good quality and can be pricey. You can find the latest styles because Japanese people are followers of world fashion trends. As young Japanese women spend a lot of money on clothing, many shops in Tokyo target them and selections are abundant. A large variety of men's casual wear, Italian fashions and conservative suits can also be found.

As mentioned earlier, foreigners may find clothes sold in boutiques and department stores rather expensive if there isn't a sale. However, less expensive items are available at individual shops in small neighbourhoods, large supermarkets and used-clothing shops, and the number of inexpensive domestic brands is also increasing in the city.

American casual apparel brands such as the Gap, Old Navy and Eddie Bauer are popular and are located throughout the metropolis, including Shibuya, Harajuku and Shinjuku.

Household Items

Most household goods (such as linens, tableware and bathroom items) are available at department stores, but you can probably save money by shopping at large supermarkets or neighbourhood shops. For a wide variety of reasonably priced kitchen utensils, go to Kappabashi (near the Asakusa area), where wholesale stores for kitchen items are located. You can even buy the plastic models of foods displayed at restaurant entrances—while expensive, the *sushi* samples make good souvenirs.

Tokyu Hands specialises in household goods and items for home improvement and repairs. Here, you can hire contractors to renovate your home for you. They also carry products for a variety of hobbies such as gardening, knitting and crafts.

Furniture

Nowadays, most Tokyo residents use Western-style furniture, or a combination of Western and Japanese styles. The designs and colours of the Western-style furniture sold in Tokyo may not suit Western tastes, however. Many Japanese people prefer furniture with simple designs and in bland colours, so that it will blend in with other items in their homes. Furniture sold in Japan is smaller and shorter than those manufactured overseas, to fit the smaller-sized Japanese and their cramped homes. Out of necessity, Westerners in Japan often buy imported furniture.

Some department stores have furniture corners. While their inventories may be limited, by visiting a few you can get an idea of design, size and price. There are also a few large furniture stores in Tokyo, of which IDC Otsuka (http://www.idc-otsuka.co.jp) has the largest interior showroom in Japan. It carries an extensive inventory of American, European and locally manufactured furniture. Considering the transportation and insurance costs of importing your own furniture, the imported furniture at IDC Otsuka is priced fairly reasonably. Several individual shops also sell specific brands of imported furniture.

Foreigners who are in Tokyo for only a short time can rent furniture through furniture leasing stores; most of these stores give customers the option of purchasing rented furniture at a reasonable price should they want to take it back to their home countries later. Relocation companies or real estate agents can often recommend leasing stores. Classified advertisements on furniture shops and leasing stores appear regularly in English-language newspapers and magazines, and in the NTT TOWNPAGE telephone directory.

Electronics

The quality and versatility of Japanese electronic appliances for the home is unbeatable. The high-tech appliances used in the course of daily life are amazing and include cordless irons and vacuum cleaners, and refrigerators that alert owners when the doors are open for too long. Like other products in Japan, electronic appliances cost more than in many other countries. Still, considering all the functions and the durability of the products, they may not turn out to be as expensive as they seem.

Akihabara is the place to go for reasonably-priced electronic appliances and computers. In this district, there are more than 600 shops selling a variety of electronic products. The prices are 20–30 per cent less than the suggested retail and you may be able to get further discounts by bargaining—unlike in other shops in Tokyo, you can and should bargain in the shops in Akihabara. Because this district is frequented by tourists, sales clerks are accustomed to dealing with foreigners and may speak some English.

There are discount electronics shops in major shopping districts (Shibuya, Shinjuku and Ikebukuro, for example). Shops such as Yodobashi Camera, Sakuraya Camera and BIG Camera, all carry a good variety of electronic products (not just cameras!) at prices which are lower than those in department stores.

Compact Discs

A boon for music lovers, large compact disc (CD) shops in Tokyo carry substantial collections of American, European and Japanese music in a variety of genres. A CD manufactured in Japan will cost about ¥ 1,500 for a single and ¥ 3,000 for an album. The prices of imported CDs are generally lower because they do not include the lyrics or comments about the music that are included in Japanese CDs.

You will find large CD shops in major commercial areas such as Shibuya, Shinjuku and Ikebukuro. Tower Records has a huge store housed in a seven-storey building in Shibuya as well as smaller branches elsewhere. Other large CD shops include HMV, Shinseido and Tsutaya; all have branches throughout Tokyo.

Toys

Most department stores have relatively large toy corners in which children enthusiastically congregate to play with the toy displays.

Pokémon, a story that had its origins in Japanese comics, is famous worldwide. The Pokémon Centre here carries a huge amount of merchandise and is a must-see.

Computer games and video games are very popular among Japanese children. In addition to department stores and individual toy shops, many stores in Akihabara and electronics shops around major stations sell electronic

Safety Tips

Here are some general tips to help you stay healthy:

- To adjust your temperature against the extreme cold of winter and the extreme air-conditioning in summer, wear layers of clothing in both seasons.
- To protect yourself from flu during winter, dress warmly, wash your hands frequently, gargle and consider taking flu shots.
- To avoid food poisoning in the heat of summer, keep your food cool in the refrigerator.
- If you have food allergies, guard against allergic reactions to foods by carrying a note in Japanese indicating what kind of ingredients you are allergic to and show it to servers and sales clerks.
- To prepare for emergencies, especially if you have small children, locate a hospital in your neighbourhood and visit it prior to any emergency.
- Tap water is safe to drink, but many people prefer to drink the foreign and domestic bottled waters that are available, as the taste is better.

toys. Kiddy Land in Harajuku has been a very popular toy store for a long time. It carries Japanese-made and imported toys for children of all ages. Giant American toy store, Toys 'R' Us (http://www.toysrus.co.jp), now has more than 100 outlets in Japan, including several in Tokyo. In addition to toys, they sell children's clothing and nursery items.

Japanese Crafts and Antiques

Japanese crafts make good souvenirs for friends and are nice to keep as mementos of your time in Japan. One interesting craft is *washi*, or Japanese handmade paper. Hundreds of different items can be made from *washi* and include lantern covers, umbrellas, notebooks and letter paper. Many little shops on the street (Nakamise Dori) leading to the Sensoji Temple in Asakusa sell such paper products and other crafts. Isetatsu in Yanaka (close to Asakusa) also carries a lot of paper products specially made with patterned prints. Kyukyo-do near the 'Ginza 4-chome Crossing' is an old store (founded in 1663) specialising in Japanese paper products such as postcards, stationery, calendars and folding fans.

Traditional Japanese toys make good gifts for children. Although Japanese kids nowadays play more often with computer games, they still play with some traditional toys. A popular one is *kendama*, a ball and wooden cup at the end of a handle. The cup and ball are tied together with string and children swing the ball and try to catch it in the cup.

Another traditional toy is the wooden top (*koma*) which children spin by hand or with a heavy string. They compete with each other to see how fast they can spin their *koma*. Kites are still popular among some children. In addition to modern kites made of plastic, there are traditional kites made from Japanese paper featuring *Kabuki* (traditional Japanese theatre) actors or other Japanese motifs. Some adults use them to decorate their homes, as they are too valuable to fly!

Like the colourful kites, Japanese paddle-shaped fans (*hagoita*) make wonderful household decorations; they are intricately crafted using quilted cloth and feature *Kabuki* characters. (Children used to play with plain wooden paddles during the New Year holidays.) A *hagoita* market is held in December at Sensoji Temple in Asakusa. The prices can be quite high, but the fans are beautiful. You can find all of these traditional toys in shops on Nakamise Dori.

The Oriental Bazaar in Harajuku also carries a variety of Japanese crafts. This is the largest craft shop in Tokyo. It carries typical souvenir items such as paper products and cotton robes, more expensive items such as swords, block prints, chinaware and antique furniture.

Some department stores also have a Japanese crafts corner, selling items such as accessories, paper products, *kimono* and table linen. Tablecloths and place mats made from Japanese fabrics are great for daily use and for souvenirs.

If you are into antiques, you will find many antique shops along Kotto Dori (meaning 'Antique Street') in Aoyama. Items sold here can be very expensive.

TAKING CARE OF YOUR HEALTH

Medical standards in Tokyo are very high, and up-to-date medical treatments are available at most hospitals and clinics; though some aspects of medical care may differ from that are found in other countries. One thing that might surprise newcomers about Japanese hospitals and clinics is that while much of the cost of health services is generally covered by one of two national health insurance plans, some payment is required upon services rendered, and most service care providers accept only cash. Thus, expatriates living in Japan learn to keep a certain amount of cash on hand in case of medical emergency.

The Health Insurance System

All residents of Japan, including foreigners, are required to join a public health insurance programme. To participate, people pay monthly fees (according to their income) and in return, receive coverage for a large portion of their medical expenses. Private insurance is also available, but serves primarily as supplementary coverage for complex treatments or luxury hospital rooms. The biggest advantage of public health insurance is that it can be used at any hospital or clinic, so patients are free to choose their doctors and to change hospitals. Public health insurance covers medical treatment and prescribed medicines, but not preventive care.

Although foreign residents are expected to enrol in the public health insurance system, some do not. Instead they buy foreign-based private insurance policies, especially if they are living in Tokyo for only a short period of time. The reasons: 1) people who are not fluent in Japanese and who are in Tokyo for short stays often prefer private clinics that cater to foreigners—some of these clinics do not accept Japanese public health insurance because they operate independently from the national health care system; 2) Japanese public health insurance is valid only in Japan— most expatriates need insurance that will cover treatment not only in Japan, but also in their home countries and other nations.

Expatriates with overseas-based private insurance are usually required to pay the full costs of any medical treatment or prescriptions provided. They then apply to their insurance companies for full or partial reimbursement. Foreigners who plan to visit a doctor, clinic or hospital in Japan may wish to inquire in advance about policies regarding insurance acceptance and billing, as some health care providers may be hesitant to treat patients who are not enrolled in one of the public health insurance programmes.

Japan has two types of public health insurance: Employees' Health Insurance (*Shakai Kenko Hoken*) and National Health Insurance (*Kokumin Kenko Hoken*).

Employees' Health Insurance

This type of insurance is generally provided to full-time employees and any of their dependents residing in Japan. It covers most basic and emergency health care at the rate of 70 per cent for employees and dependents. It also covers a portion of the cost for prescriptions, but not for preventive care, childbirth, cosmetic surgery or luxury hospital rooms.

Expatriates on assignment in Japan often qualify for this type of insurance. If you are eligible, your employer will ask you to complete an application form that will be submitted to the Employees' Health Insurance Office.

The insurance card (*hoken-sho*) is issued when people subscribe to the insurance, and this card should be presented when they see a doctor. Patients who visit a doctor in an emergency without their insurance cards must pay all fees in full. They can then submit receipts to the Employees' Health Insurance Office to request partial reimbursement. It is highly recommended that all family members carry a photocopy of the insurance card in case of an emergency; some medical institutions accept a photocopied version.

Insurance premiums are calculated based on the individual employee's standard income and are automatically deducted from the monthly salary. Many employers pay a portion of the premium on the employee's behalf. The premium remains the same no matter how many dependents an employee has.

National Health Insurance

This insurance is generally provided to residents of Japan who are not covered by other insurance plans. It covers most basic and emergency health care at the rate of 70 per cent for policyholders and their dependents. The insurance also covers a percentage of the cost for prescriptions, but not for preventive care, childbirth, cosmetic surgery or luxury hospital rooms.

Foreigners who are not full-time employees can enrol in the National Health Insurance programme if they meet one of the following criteria: they are residing in Japan for one year or longer; or they have resided less than one year, but can prove intent to stay one year or longer (for example, to students who are admitted to schools for one year or longer). If you qualify, submit an application to the National Health Insurance Section of your local ward or municipal office within 14 days of completing your Foreign Resident Registration. When applying, take your Foreign Registration Card, your seal (although your signature will be accepted if you do not have one), and a document that proves your stay will be one year or more (for example, a copy of your visa). The insurance card is issued upon enrolment and the card must be presented whenever you receive treatment. Insurance premiums are calculated according to income and the number of dependents covered. Payment can be made in instalments at banks, post offices, or local ward or municipal offices.

Health Care Facilities and Procedures
Hospitals and Clinics
Medical facilities with 20 or more beds are categorised as hospitals, and those with fewer than 20 beds are categorised as clinics. Hospitals vary greatly in size, areas of expertise and medical equipment available. Some large hospitals are affiliated with universities and serve as research and teaching facilities. There are also many small private hospitals. Some hospitals offer services in all major medical fields and others specialise in one particular field, such as oncology or cardiovascular medicine.

There are two types of clinics: those run by one doctor with expertise in a single field (paediatrics or dermatology, for example), and those run by a few doctors with different expertise. Patients have a choice of either seeing a doctor at a hospital or going to a clinic; both have advantages and disadvantages.

The advantages of visiting hospitals:
- Large ones, especially, have advanced medical equipment, enabling them to conduct complex examinations;
- Hospitals that provide services in various areas mean different specialists can be consulted under one roof.

On the other hand, the disadvantages are:
- At many hospitals, unless a patient's symptoms are life-threatening, the wait to see a doctor can be more than an hour—most hospital doctors do not accept appointments, especially for initial visits;
- Because hospital doctors see so many patients each day, they can seem rather impersonal and may not give patients their full attention; and

- In many hospitals, more than one doctor is assigned to see outpatients, so there is no guarantee that patients will be seen by the same doctor each time they visit the hospital.

The advantages and disadvantages of clinics are just the opposite of those for hospitals. As there are more clinics than hospitals, patients can easily find one near their home or office. The waiting time at clinics is usually shorter than at hospitals, and some clinics now accept appointments. The disadvantage is that clinics cannot usually afford to buy the most advanced medical equipment, and doctors may not be up-to-date in some fields.

Generally, people go to clinics when they think that their symptoms are not serious, and only when the symptoms persist do they visit a hospital. On occasion, clinic doctors will refer patients to hospitals when they think that further testing and more in-depth examinations are necessary.

International Clinics

Certain clinics in Tokyo serve the foreign community almost exclusively. They are popular among expatriates because the doctors as well as some staff members, including nurses and receptionists, speak English. Physicians in these clinics are usually either foreigners or Japanese doctors who have been educated abroad.

As previously mentioned, many of these clinics operate independently from the Japanese health care system and do not accept public health insurance. Thus, they are not bound by certain regulations stipulated by the Japanese government. For example, they are free to use medications that have not been officially approved for use in Japan, and to charge whatever fees the market will bear. Consequently, such clinics and the medication they prescribe tend to be more expensive than the regulated versions.

International clinics, are located primarily in Minato-ku and Shibuya-ku where many expatriates live. Foreigners living in other areas usually seek out a neighbourhood doctor on whom they can rely on in urgent situations. (*Refer to the* 'Resource Guide' *for a list of international clinics.*)

Doctors in Japanese Hospitals/Clinics

When symptoms warrant, many people go directly to a specialist. Others consult a general practitioner (primary care physician) first and then to specialists when referred. When consulting a specialist, especially one who is well-known or affiliated with a prominent hospital, an introduction or referral is very important. Without an introduction, patients often must wait several months for an appointment. Doctors sometimes charge patients a fee for writing a referral letter to another physician. If your doctor does not personally know a particular specialist whom you would like to see, ask colleagues and friends if they know someone who knows the specialist and who can make an introduction.

Approaching another doctor for a second opinion is rarely practised in Japan. Some doctors are reluctant to share data with other practitioners, so patients who seek another opinion may have to undergo duplicate medical testing. Nonetheless, this practice is becoming more widespread and is often worth the trouble, as it may result in valuable information on diagnosis and options for treatment.

Communicating with most Japanese doctors can be a challenge for those who do not speak Japanese. Although many doctors know certain medical terminology in English or German, they may not understand casual descriptions of symptoms. Doctors who have spent a couple of years in an English-speaking country, however, will probably have a good command of the language. The best places to find such doctors are at large hospitals and international clinics.

Japanese doctors tend to be authoritative, although their styles vary depending on personality and age. It is widely believed that doctors are experts who know what is best for patients; thus patients tend to follow the instructions of their doctors without asking many questions. The concept of 'informed consent' (that patients should be informed about options for and risks of treatment, and agree to a plan of treatment prior to implementation) is relatively new in Japan. Although the importance of such a concept is widely recognised, doctors are not required by law to discuss treatment options and risks with patients, and many physicians are still not used to doing so.

In dealing with Japanese doctors, be patient and persistent, and do not be discouraged from asking questions. Be prepared for initial resistance from them, however, or in some cases a continuing refusal to discuss your case to your satisfaction. You may decide that it is necessary to find a more receptive doctor. Although more doctors now think it is important to share information with patients, some still think that patients who ask too many questions are challenging their expertise and decisions.

Payment for Medical Services

Charges for tests, medical treatments, consultations, and prescriptions must be paid when services are provided. People who enrol in one of two public health insurance plans and who present their insurance card will be charged only their co-payment (30 per cent of the total cost). If they do not carry their insurance card (such as in cases of emergency), they will have to pay the full amount and then apply for reimbursement. People enrolled in foreign-based private insurance plans have to pay in full, and then submit an application to their insurance company for reimbursement.

Most clinics and hospitals do not accept credit cards, and as cheques are not widely used in Japan, all patients should carry cash when visiting any kind of health care provider.

Medication

Patients used to purchase medicines prescribed by doctors at the clinics or hospitals with which the doctors are affiliated, but an increasing number of doctors today just write prescriptions and ask their patients to purchase the medication at pharmacies. As public health insurance covers a large portion of the costs of prescribed medications, they are often cheaper than over-the-counter medications. Doctors usually prescribe a three- to four-day supply and ask patients to return if symptoms have not improved over that period of time.

Recommended dosages of both prescribed and over-the-counter medications (especially painkillers) are generally lower in Japan than in the West because the average body size of Japanese people is relatively smaller. Let your doctor know if the dosage of the prescribed medication seems ineffective. Prior to moving to Japan, it may be useful to obtain a note or a copy of your prescription from your previous doctor to show as reference to your doctor in Japan. Foreign prescriptions cannot be filled in Japan, so any prescriptions written by doctors in other countries must be rewritten by doctors in Japan. (*See the 'Resource Guide' for a list of pharmacies that carry foreign drugs.*)

Hospitalisation

Sometimes doctors prescribe a stay in the hospital for further examination, specialised treatment, or surgery. Patients of doctors who work at large hospitals are eligible to be hospitalised whenever a bed is available. Depending on the patient's condition, the waiting period can be more than one month.

The average length of stay in a hospital is generally longer in Japan than in many Western countries. This can be attributed to several factors: 1) there is an assumption that it is the responsibility of hospitals to see that patients have fully recovered before release; 2) as homes in Japan (especially in Tokyo) tend to be small, most families do not have private

Cultural Adjustment

Adjusting to life in Tokyo is not always easy. Initially, many people experience emotional stress. People sometimes feel isolated, lonely and homesick. Some even feel physical symptoms such as fatigue, stomach ache, or a lack of appetite. Such symptoms are natural reactions to adjusting to a new environment.

If you suffer any emotional or physical distress, do not be too hard on yourself, or be judgmental about things and people around you. It is a transitional phase and things will get better. However, if your physical symptoms persist for an unreasonable period of time, do check with a physician.

To cope with such stress, talk to others who are experiencing the same problem or have already gone through it. Seek support from members of international clubs or organisations; you can exchange experiences with others. Participate in cultural activities or study the Japanese language. Take short trips out of Tokyo to gain a fresh perspective. Eventually, you will begin to accept cultural differences and will be able to define a way of living that is fairly comfortable for you, even though it is a different feel from home.

rooms in which convalescing family members can rest; and 3) because public health insurance covers a large portion of the costs of hospitalisation, it is not overly expensive for patients to stay in hospitals for extended periods.

During hospital stays, patients usually share their room with a few other patients. Private hospital rooms are available, but these are not covered by public insurance and patients thus have to pay a rather substantial fee per day for such rooms.

Health Examinations

Companies in Japan are required by law to provide free annual health check-ups for their workers. The standard procedure includes chest X-rays, a blood pressure test and blood tests to check cholesterol levels and liver function. Schools also offer students basic annual health check-ups (such as blood tests, eye and dental examinations and examination by a doctor).

Each ward or municipal district in Tokyo offers free or low-cost basic health check-ups for residents who are self-employed or unemployed, including foreigners. These check-ups are conducted at public health centres and at designated clinics or hospitals. Check with your ward or municipal office for information about dates and locations. Thorough physical examinations are also available at designated clinics and hospitals at relatively low charges for people with some form of public health insurance.

Children's Health Care

Parents whose children will be accompanying them to Tokyo should look for a good paediatrician (*shonika*) soon after their arrival. One way of finding a paediatrician is to ask friends, neighbours and the parents of your children's classmates; another is to check the international clinics mentioned earlier; and yet another is to ask staff members at the international schools for a list of English-speaking paediatricians. The books *Japan Health Handbook* and *Japan for Kids* also list paediatricians who speak English.

When contacting these doctors, check whether they will see patients after hours, as many Japanese doctors will not.

Parents who choose a paediatrician who does not offer after-hour care should identify a hospital or clinic that will accept children in case of emergencies.

Vaccinations

While no longer compulsory in Japan, certain vaccinations are strongly recommended and are provided free of charge at designated clinics, hospitals and public health centres. Shortly after registering your residence with your local ward or municipal office, you will receive a notification letter indicating the dates and places that vaccinations will be administered (contact your local ward or municipal office for more details). Recommended vaccinations include the following:

- Polio
- DPT (combined triple vaccine for diphtheria, pertussis, and tetanus)
- Measles
- Rubella
- Japanese Encephalitis
- BCG (tuberculosis)

Other vaccines such as those for influenza, chicken pox, mumps and hepatitis B are available at clinics, hospitals and public health centres for a fee.

Women's Health Care

Women go to either a gynaecologist (*fujinka*) or an obstetrician-gynaecologist (*sanfujinka*) when they want to consult a doctor on female health matters.

However, few Japanese women go for routine check-ups by a gynaecologist, because this type of preventive care is not covered by public health insurance. Also, some Japanese women are psychologically resistant to an internal examination gynaecologists typically conduct. For many Japanese women, the first time they visit a gynaecologist is when they become pregnant. The importance of early detection of breast and uterine cancer is increasingly publicised, and some doctors now encourage women to receive routine gynaecological checkups. In Tokyo, ward and municipal districts offer female residents (generally only to those over 30) free examinations for both uterine and breast cancer at designated clinics, hospitals and public health centres.

Gynaecologists will generally accept public health insurance for check-ups if patients claim that something is wrong with them, even if the problem appears to be minor. The routine exam is similar to that conducted in most other countries; however, a mammography is conducted only if a doctor finds some abnormality.

Family Planning

Condoms are the most popular form of contraception and are sold at drugstores and supermarkets. In 1999, the Japanese government officially approved the birth control pill as a contraceptive, but public health insurance does not cover the cost of the pills. The pills can be obtained only with a doctor's prescription, and a doctor's visit is required each time a refill is needed.

As Japanese doctors usually only prescribe up to a three-month supply of the pills, and because the variety is still small compared to some other countries, many foreign women who use them bring an ample supply to Tokyo and get refills when they travel back home. Other forms of contraception available in Japan (although not popular) are spermicidal jellies, intrauterine devices and diaphragms.

Many couples in Japan struggle with infertility problems, and the number of clinics and hospitals that specialise in infertility has been increasing. Several advanced treatments have become available, including medication, surgery, artificial insemination and invitro fertilisation. Infertility treatments can be quite expensive, as they can continue for long periods of time and are not covered by public health insurance.

Abortion is legal in Japan, and can be performed if a woman has the nominal consent of her partner. Doctors seldom ask many questions and the paperwork is minimal. Fees are not covered by public health insurance if the abortion is done by choice rather than due to health considerations, but the cost is relatively low.

Having a Baby in Tokyo

Some foreign couples decide to have a baby while living in Tokyo. Factors to consider are the quality of health care and the fact that accompanying spouses may not be able to find work. It can also be useful to know how pregnancy and childbirth are handled in Tokyo.

■ During Pregnancy

Pregnant women in Tokyo regularly see obstetrician-gynaecologists for check-ups. Note that in Japan, doctors calculate the human gestation period as ten months (in 28-day increments since the last period), whereas Westerners generally calculate it as nine months (in 31-day increments since the last period). Thus, in Japan a typical pregnancy is said to last ten months.

After a pregnancy is confirmed, a woman is expected to register her pregnancy at the ward or municipal office where she lives. She will then receive a booklet called *Boshi Kenko Techo (Mother and Child Health Handbook)*. This booklet should be taken to every doctor's visit before and after delivery, in order for doctors to record the mother's and baby's health information and immunisation histories. The booklet also contains the schedule and coupons for vaccinations as well as coupons for regular check-ups.

Some wards and municipal offices carry free copies of bilingual handbooks. The booklets can also be ordered at a small charge from the Mothers' and Children's Health Organisation. Bilingual editions are available in eight different languages: English, Thai, Spanish, Chinese, Korean, Tagalog, Portuguese and Indonesian.

Japanese doctors are concerned about difficult deliveries and various diseases (such as diabetes) associated with weight gain during pregnancy. Consequently, they are strict about weight gain and recommend that women limit the gain to between 8–10 kg (about 16–20 pounds).

Because the body sizes of many foreign women and Japanese women are different, doctors may adjust their standards for foreigners. Genetic testing is not routinely performed unless the family has a history of some congenital disorder. However, such testing can be performed if requested by the patient.

■ Giving Birth

Usually women give birth at the same medical facility where they have received pre-natal care. There are many options, ranging from small clinics to large hospitals. In general, clinics are more personal and open to accommodating individual needs, whereas hospitals tend to abide by rules and are less likely to make exceptions or cater to individual requests. One benefit of large hospitals, however, is that they are capable of handling complicated births and have access to a wide variety of drugs.

Additional issues to consider when choosing a place for delivery are the availability of pain relief medication, rules regarding the presence of the father at delivery and the length of the recommended post-natal stay.

In Japan, it is quite common for women to give birth without taking painkillers, as people are concerned about possible side effects on both mother and baby. Also, there is a fundamental belief that giving birth is a natural human process that should not be interfered with. Nevertheless, as it becomes more evident that the appropriate administration of pain medication is unlikely to have negative consequences, more doctors are willing to agree when patients request such medication. Hospitals are more likely than clinics to have several pain relief options available.

Many hospitals in Japan do not allow fathers to be present during the delivery. This may be due to a general assumption that delivery is a woman's job. Actually, many Japanese women do not want their husbands to see them at the delivery scene and as more than one woman is likely to be undergoing labour in the same room, the lack of privacy could be a factor. However, the trend is slowly changing and it is becoming more common for fathers to participate in pre-natal care and childbirth.

In Japan, new mothers and babies are kept in the hospital longer than in some other countries. Generally, mothers stay in the hospital at least five days to one week. If they have given birth by Caesarean section, they may need to stay longer. Some Japanese women who give birth overseas are surprised at how quickly they are sent home when they would prefer to stay and rest a little longer. In contrast, some foreign women in Japan feel that they are confined to the hospital for an unnecessarily long period of time. (Some hospitals are open to negotiation concerning the length of stay in hospital after childbirth.)

After delivery, babies are usually kept in a central nursery monitored by nurses and are brought to mothers, or the mothers go to them, only for breast-feeding. The main reasons for this separation are to protect babies from exposure to a plethora of germs and to allow mothers to recuperate. Some Western mothers dislike being separated from their babies, so they look for a hospital with which they can room with or negotiate the length of time they spend with their infants.

Midwives play an important role in the delivery of babies in Japan. Depending on the hospital or clinic, it is often the midwives, rather than the doctors, whom women consult for pre-natal advice. Midwives assist in deliveries at clinics and hospitals and some will also assist with home delivery, especially if no complications are anticipated.

Costs associated with normal pregnancy and childbirth are not covered by public health insurance. However, people enrolled in public health insurance can apply for a Lump-Sum Childbirth Subsidy of ¥ 300,000–350,000 when a child is born. The amount is roughly equivalent to the cost of hospitalisation and delivery. Expenses for medical treatment related to any complications of pregnancy and childbirth (such as Caesarean section delivery) are, however, covered by public health insurance. (*See the* 'Resource Guide' *for support groups for new parents.*)

Dental Care

Japanese dentists (*shika* or *haisha*) perform all regular dental care procedures, including fillings, root canals and cleanings, but they do not perform orthodontics.

As not all dentists have the same knowledge or use the same techniques, Japanese people often ask friends and colleagues for recommendations. For routine treatments, Japanese people visit dental clinics; for complex procedures, they sometimes go to dental hospitals affiliated with dental universities. Dentists, unlike other doctors, usually take appointments.

Basic dental procedures are covered by public health insurance, so insured patients should take their insurance cards with them to dental appointments. Optional treatments and better quality crowns are not covered by insurance and can be quite expensive.

The notion of preventive dental care (for example, regular teeth cleaning) is not yet widespread in Japan. Theoretically, public health insurance is accepted only for necessary procedures and not for preventive care so most dentists do not accept insurance for simple check-ups and cleaning. However, when patients claim that 'something is wrong', dentists will often accept the insurance. Some Japanese doctors who have received training overseas are more aware of the importance of preventative care and are more open to accepting public insurance for regular check-ups.

Orthodontic treatment has recently become popular in Japan, mainly as a result of influence from the United States. More parents are having their children's teeth straightened for health reasons, while many young women do so for aesthetic purposes. Orthodontic treatment is not yet covered by public health insurance and can be expensive.

> Previously, people considered certain teeth misalignment (such as crooked teeth) to be charming. As a result, few children and almost no adults wore braces. Now, the benefits of tooth alignment on health and beauty are being emphasised.

Mental Health Care

Although it is not common for Japanese people to seek mental health services such as psychiatry or counselling, in Tokyo these services are readily available, and some are geared towards the foreign community.

Counselling

When experiencing symptoms of stress, or more serious emotional or relationship problems, many Japanese people are reluctant to visit a mental health professional. There are two main explanations: firstly, people are not comfortable expressing feelings and emotions to a third party whom they do not know well; and secondly, among Japanese people there is still a negative bias attached to mental illness, so people are concerned about how they will be perceived if others learn that they are being treated for mental problems. As a result, in Japan, the field of counselling is still immature. However, the need for professional treatment and the number of counsellors are increasing, especially in Tokyo where people experience a great amount of stress due to busy lifestyles and the hectic pace of work. *(Refer to the* 'Resource Guide' *for a list of organisations that offer counselling in English and other languages by counsellors who had overseas training. The* Japan Health Book *provides further options.)*

Alternative Health Care

Although mainstream Japanese medical procedures are similar to those practised in the West, a wide variety of alternative medical treatments have been used in Japan for centuries. Many people today rely on these alternative treatments to help them relax and reduce the effects of work stress, or to treat chronic pain and diseases that Western medicine can't seem to cure. A growing number of doctors now regard alternative treatments as complementary to their allopathic treatments.

There are numerous practitioners of alternative medicine in Tokyo, although finding one who can alleviate specific symptoms may require some time and experimentation. Also, as not many such practitioners accept public health insurance, the cost of seeing them regularly can be high.

Acupuncture (Hari)

Acupuncture was introduced from China early in Japanese history, and was used as a basis for developing a unique set of techniques and tools for treatment. Acupuncturists stimulate specific points (tsubo) along body meridians by inserting fine needles through the surface of the skin. Sometimes these needles are removed after brief stimulation, and sometimes they are left there for several hours. Discomfort is usually minimal. Different tsubo are related to various areas or functions of the body, and inherent healing powers are activated by the stimulation. Among other benefits, acupuncture treatments can contribute to the relaxation of muscles, an increase in circulation, the stabilisation of blood pressure and an improvement in the functions of the immune system.

Acupuncturists must pass a national licensing examination. Traditionally, many professionals in this field were blind people with an acute sense of touch that enabled them to easily locate tsubo. Although blind acupuncturists contributed greatly to the development of the field, today they make up a small percentage of acupuncturists in practice.

Public health insurance covers acupuncture treatments prescribed by medical doctors, but some acupuncturists do not accept insurance.

Massage

There are three different types of massage available today in Tokyo: anma, European-style massage and shiatsu. In each of these types of treatments, practitioners directly stimulate certain parts of the body with their hands to relax muscles and improve blood circulation. Massages are known to help stabilise blood pressure, increase immunity and relieve pain.

Anma was introduced centuries ago from China and has the longest history among the three styles. Practitioners mainly knead muscles, moving from the centre of the body outwards.

In Japan, practitioners of European-style massage (typically referred to simply as 'massage') lightly stimulate the skin surface, moving from the outer extremities of the body towards the centre (the heart). This is believed to improve the circulation of blood and lymphatic fluid.

Shiatsu combines techniques from a variety of treatments including *anma* and chiropractic, and even includes elements from *judo*. Practitioners mainly apply pressure to *tsubo* with the fingers with the goal of relaxing muscles and adjusting the function of the nervous system.

Practitioners of all three types of massages must pass a common national licensing exam. As with acupuncture, many early practitioners of massage were blind. Public health insurance covers massage treatments for certain types of illnesses if prescribed by doctors; however, some practitioners do not accept insurance.

Chiropractic

Compared with other alternative healing methods, chiropractic was made available in Tokyo only fairly recently. Practitioners adjust the alignment of a patient's spine to release healing powers. Chiropractic care is believed to be effective in lessening the symptoms of spinal misalignment such as headache, stiff shoulders and back pain.

Although chiropractic has been approved as a medical practice in some countries, it has not yet been approved by the Japanese government. Therefore, there is no formal certification procedure for practitioners. Some of them are graduates of chiropractic schools in the United States or other countries, and others studied at one of many private chiropractic schools in Japan. When looking for a chiropractor, it is a good idea to research carefully— some practitioners have limited training and experience. Because chiropractic care is not officially approved by the government, public health insurance does not cover this type of treatment.

Herbal Medicines

Many of the formulas used in modern-day Japanese herbal medicines (known as *kanpo yaku*) have their roots in medical concepts first encountered centuries ago by Japanese people through contacts with China. These herbal remedies are believed to enhance the harmony of the entire body and to increase natural recuperative powers. Various clinical studies have shown the efficacy of *kanpo yaku* in helping to boost the immune system, alleviating menopausal symptoms and improving nervous disorders and ailments of the elderly. Some people have reported cases in which *kanpo yaku* is believed to have cured cancerous growths.

The Japanese government has approved more than 100 herbal medicine formulas, and public health insurance covers the cost of these formulas if they are prescribed by medical doctors.

TRANSPORTATION IN TOKYO

Trains and Subways

Most people in Tokyo take trains or the subway to work; they avoid driving because of traffic congestion and high parking fees in business areas. As a result, the distance from a residence to the nearest station is a key factor in determining property value; the shorter the distance, the greater the value. Real estate advertisements commonly show the number of minutes it will take residents to walk from a home to the closest station.

Train Lines

Several different train lines cover Tokyo and also extend out to greater Tokyo. Major train lines in Tokyo are categorised into two main groups: those operated by the East Japan Railway Company (JR), including the Yamanote, Chuo and Keihin-Tohoku Lines; and those operated by private companies such as the Odakyu, Keio, Seibu and Tokyu Lines. All lines intersect with other lines at major junction stations such as Shinjuku, Shibuya, Tokyo and Ikebukuro. Railway maps (sometimes in *romaji*) are available free of charge at major train stations, and major hotels often carry railway and subway maps in *romaji*.

Tickets, Passes and Prepaid Cards

To enter the boarding platforms, passengers must present either tickets, passes or prepaid rail cards to be examined by automated machines or by station officials. It is important to always keep tickets, passes or cards with you after presenting them, as they will be examined again when you exit the train.

Thousands of people ride the trains into Tokyo every day.

You can buy tickets at the automatic vending machines located in all stations. Above the machines, there is usually a large board that shows the train system and the fare to each station. At many stations, names are written in both Japanese and *romaji*. You can buy your ticket using coins or bills, but not credit cards.

If you commute to the same destination regularly, purchasing a pass may be more convenient and less expensive than buying single tickets. The pass shows your original station and the destination, and allows you to get on and off at any station in between without buying additional tickets. Monthly, quarterly and semi-annual passes are usually available, and are sold at most large stations. Ask station officials for more detailed information. It is also possible to buy prepaid rail cards. Different kinds of rail cards are available that can be commonly used among different types of trains and subways. The convenience of using cards is that you do not have to check fares or wait in line to purchase tickets.

Taking the Right Train

Most lines offer both regular (local) trains that stop at each station, and express trains that stop only at major stations. Foreigners (and even Japanese people at unfamiliar stations) initially find it challenging to find which train stops at the destination they want to go. Here are some tips:

- Study the train map on the platform to find out whether a local train or express train stops at your destination station.
- Announcement boards indicate the service each train provides, and there is usually an audio announcement as to which type of train is approaching the platform.
- Be careful to check the train to find out whether it is a local or express train before jumping onboard.

Surviving Rush Hours

Rush hours are from 7.30 am to 9:00 am and from 5:00 pm to 6.30 pm in the evening. Surviving crowded stations and trains at these hours requires determination and certain skills. People normally wait in lines at platforms, but at rush hour the lines merge into a stream of people. When the train comes, just swim with the stream and jump into the train; otherwise you will never be able to board.

It is when boarding trains that some Tokyoites, normally polite and considerate, seem to take on a different persona as they push and shove to squeeze themselves in. The busiest stations even have railway officials who help to push in extra people, much like packing sardines into a can. Be careful when carrying purses or briefcases with thin straps or delicate handles, as they may break in the squeeze. After riding the same train several times, you will learn which section of the train is less packed, and board that section from the appropriate location on the platform. If you are travelling with small children or are not feeling well, it

- If you cannot figure out whether a particular train stops at the station you want to go, you can ask other passengers for assistance by stating the name of the station, pointing to the train and raising your eyebrows. People may nod (indicating 'yes'), or wave one hand side to side in front of their faces (indicating 'no') to let you know whether the train stops at the station mentioned.
- While on the train, prior to arrival at each station you will hear an announcement stating the name of the station. Even if you miss the announcement, when the train arrives at the station you will see the name of the station on the platform signs in both Japanese and *romaji*.

may be best to avoid riding on trains during the intensity of rush hour.

Another busy hour occurs around midnight, when trains can be crowded with people who have worked late or enjoyed dinner and drinks. It is quite safe to ride the trains at this time, even if you are alone. The only hassle you may encounter is someone who has had too much to drink and wants to practise his English. In that case, walk away from him (it is usually a 'him') and go to another section of the train. Usually he will not follow you, but in case he does, you can complain to the conductor when the train arrives at the next station.

Subway Lines

Subway lines are concentrated in central Tokyo. Main lines include the Ginza, Hibiya, Chiyoda, Hanzomon and Marunouchi Lines (all under the Eidan Group), as well as the Toei Lines (including the Toei Mita, Toei Oedo, Toei Shinjuku and Toei Asakusa Lines) operated by the Metropolitan Transit

Bureau. The ticketing system for subways is the same as that for trains. Unlike trains though, most subways offer only regular, local service (no express service), so there is less risk of missing your station.

Amazingly, the number of subway lines continues to increase in already crowded Tokyo. Each new line is built deeper underground, necessitating the use of long escalators to transport passengers to the surface or to other subway platforms. Foreigners not used to riding on subways have claimed that they sometimes feel claustrophobic in subway stations. However, most foreigners find the subways convenient, especially when it is raining or cold, because it is possible to get to so many points in Tokyo without having to step outside. Some subway stations are even located in the basements of large buildings or shopping complexes.

Buses

Riding buses may be a little more intimidating than using trains and subways until you become familiar with the bus routes and the neighbourhoods they cover. It can be difficult to tell where bus stops are located and to decipher the names of the stops as they are seldom written in *romaji*. Still, buses offer convenient transportation to points not covered by trains or subways. Bus services are operated by the Metropolitan Transit Bureau and other private companies. They cover separate routes and fares vary slightly, but other than that, there are no major differences.

Between many points in central Tokyo, the fare is a fixed rate regardless of the distance travelled. Generally you enter the bus by the front door, and pay the fare by putting coins or inserting a bill into a machine located beside the driver. Alternatively, you can pay the fare with a prepaid card (which you can buy on the bus) or by showing a pass (sold at major bus terminals).

When the bus approaches a stop, you will hear the driver or an automated tape announcing the name of the stop. To get off, alert the driver by pushing one of the buttons located beside the windows.

In suburban areas, the fare is based on the distance travelled. Generally, you enter the bus through the back door and take a numbered ticket from a machine located near the door. The number indicates the zone in which you entered the bus. When the bus approaches a stop, you will hear the driver or an automated tape announce the name of the stop. If you want to get off, alert the driver by pushing one of the buttons located beside the windows, make your way to the front door and put your fare into the machine next to the driver. In most buses, there is a board posted in the front indicating the fare from each zone; find your zone number on the board and pay the amount indicated under it.

Taxis

Getting around Tokyo by taxi can be rather expensive, so it is not recommended for travelling long distances. However, taxis can be convenient and economical for short distances, especially when travelling with a few friends. If you travel only a few blocks, the taxi fare will be comparable to the total amount of the bus fare for the same number of people. Every taxi has a meter with a minimum charge and the fare increases by distance and time. Taxis also charge extra fees for reservations and for rides between 11:00 pm and 5:00 am. The number of taxis that accept credit cards is increasing, but many still do not.

In most locations, taxis stop when you wave your hand, but in some locations (in Ginza, for example) taxis stop only at taxi stands. These stands are also located at large train and subway stations. At midnight, the lines at the taxi stands at train stations can be long as bus services usually end at that hour.

You will arrive at destinations more quickly if you can provide taxi drivers with exact addresses, as well as with information such as major cross streets, well-known landmarks or nearby train stations. It is highly recommended you have a map in Japanese showing this information and your destination. As many streets in Tokyo do not have names, so drivers may need to consult maps to go to places unfamiliar to them. As most taxi drivers do not speak English well, be sure to have addresses, directions and landmarks written down (preferably in Japanese).

Automobiles

Convenient and efficient public transportation makes owning a private car unnecessary, especially for people living in the central part of Tokyo. Many Tokyo residents with cars use them mainly for out-of-town trips, for moving heavy items or, in the case of mothers with small children, for carrying grocery shopping bags.

Drivers' Licences

You may be able to obtain an international driver's licence in your home country that will allow you to drive in Japan for up to one year. An international driver's licence can only be renewed in your home country. Those who have a driver's licence from a foreign country can usually convert it to a Japanese licence. This type of conversion will exempt foreigners from having to take intensive written and driving exams, but sometimes, short tests will be conducted to confirm driving skills and knowledge.

A foreign driver's licence can be converted to a Japanese one at any of the following Driver's Licence Testing and Issuing Centres of the Metropolitan Police Department:

Samezu Driver's License Testing and Issuing Centre
(Samezu Jidosha Shikenjo)
1-12-5 Higashi-Oi, Shinagawa-ku, Tokyo
Tel: (03) 3474-1374

Fuchu Driver's License Testing and Issuing Centre
(Fuchu Jidosha Shikenjo)
3-1-1 Tama-Cho, Fuchu-shi, Tokyo
Tel: (042) 362-3591

Koto Driver's License Testing and Issuing Centre
(Koto Jidosha Shikenjo)
1-7-24 Shinsuna, Koto-ku, Tokyo
Tel: (03) 3699-1151

Documents Required to Obtain a Licence
- Your Foreign Resident Registration Card
- A photograph (3 cm by 2.4 cm)
- A certified translation of your driver's licence into Japanese from your embassy, consulate or the Japan Automobile Federation
- Your passport
  For additional information in English regarding the application process, call either (03) 5463-6000 or (042) 334-6000. Automated information is available 24 hours a day.

If you do not have a driver's licence from your country and want to acquire one in Japan, you must pass two written tests and two driving tests conducted at any of the Driver's Licence Testing and Issuing Centres mentioned earlier. As tests are stringent and thorough preparation necessary, most Japanese people attend driving schools to acquire driving skills and knowledge of both driving rules and automobile mechanics. In addition, graduates of certified driving school are exempted from having to take the driving tests at a Licence Testing and Issuing Centre. Not many driving schools in Tokyo conduct lessons in English or other languages, so first-time foreign drivers often find it difficult to obtain a Japanese driver's licence.

The minimum age for obtaining a driver's licence is 18 (16 for a motorcycle licence). A Japanese driver's licence is valid until the driver's third birthday after its issue.

Traffic Rules
Driving in Tokyo requires some preparation and caution. Japan uses the international traffic sign system, so foreigners understand most signs without extensive study. However, as not all traffic signs are written in English, important Japanese signs must be memorised. The Japan Automobile Federation (JAF) issues a booklet called 'Rules of the Road' that explains traffic rules in Japan in five languages: English, Spanish, Portuguese, Chinese, and Hangul (http://www.jaf.or.jp). Here are the basic rules.

Continued from previous page

- Drivers from countries in which vehicular traffic flows on the right-hand side of the road (the United States, for example) should drive with extra caution because in Japan (as in Britain), traffic flows on the left-hand side of the road. People from these countries are advised to practise in areas in which there is little traffic and to use extreme caution when making turns (as the opposite lanes must be checked for cars and pedestrians).
- In principle, bicycles are supposed to travel on the left-hand side of roads designated for cars. As roads in Tokyo can be narrow, bicycles travel in close proximity to cars, so drivers must watch carefully for bicycles, particularly when turning.
- Seat belts must be worn by drivers and front seat passengers. If either drivers or front seat passengers do not wear their seat belts and are caught by the police, the drivers will be fined and penalty points recorded on their driving records. Drivers who accumulate excessive penalty points must surrender their licences. While it is not mandatory for back-seat passengers to wear seatbelts, child car seats are mandatory for children under six; violation of the latter will result in penalty points for the driver.
- Using a cellular phone while driving is also banned by law; using a cellular phone with a hands-free device is permitted. Violation of this law will result in either a fine or a sentence (less than three months), as well as penalty points on the driver's record.

Purchasing a Car

Many expatriates decide to buy cars in Japan, as importing cars into Japan can be expensive and time-consuming. Car dealers sell both new and used models of Japanese- and foreign-made cars. In general, the price of Japanese-made cars is about the same in Japan as in Europe or the United States, while new European or American cars cost much more in Japan than in the country of manufacture. Before visiting a car dealer, check the Internet and car magazines for typical prices of the models you like. Car dealers may offer discounts if you can negotiate skilfully.

Used cars can be purchased from departing expatriates. Advertisements for such potential sales appear regularly in English-language newspapers or magazines, newsletters of foreign social organisations and on the bulletin boards of international supermarkets.

Registering Your Car

After purchasing a car, you must register your car at one of the following locations: 1) ordinary cars at the District Land Transportation Office or automobile inspection and registration office administering the area you reside in; 2) light three- or four-wheeled cars at the Light Car Inspection Association or branch office administering the area you reside in; and 3) motor scooters at the ward or municipal office nearest your residence.

To register, you will need a Parking Space Certificate issued by a police superintendent, providing evidence that a parking space has been secured; in other words, you should secure a parking lot before buying a car. If your apartment or house does not have parking space, you can rent one near your home. You will also need your Seal Registration Certificate and Foreign Registration Card.

Maintaining a Car

In order to maintain your car, you will need car insurance, check-ups, and perhaps roadside assistance.

Car Insurance

Car owners are required to buy compulsory insurance. The application can be handled at insurance companies, car dealerships or repair shops. Compulsory insurance provides compensation for bodily injury only for victims and passengers and not for drivers, and the amount covered is quite low.

As the coverage of compulsory insurance is limited, buying supplementary insurance is strongly recommended. Supplementary coverage typically includes additional amounts for victim and passenger bodily injury liability, bodily injury to the driver, as well as collision coverage, property damage liability and other expenses such as medical payments. Such additional insurance coverage is offered by Japanese insurance companies, as well as several American and European insurance companies with operations in Japan. Contact information for these companies is available in the English-language directory, NTT TOWNPAGE.

Regular Check-up

Private passenger cars registered in Japan must undergo an inspection in the third year after the purchase of a new car, and once every two years for a used car. The inspection can be done by the dealer from whom the car was purchased or at certified repair shops or garages. On the windshield of used cars, there is generally an inspection sticker printed with the next inspection date. To receive an inspection, the owner must show proof of payment for automobile tax. Tonnage tax and compulsory insurance must also be paid to the inspector at the time of inspection. After a car is inspected, the owner receives a new inspection sticker to place on the windshield of the car.

Roadside Assistance

If you drive in Japan, you might want to join the **Japan Automobile Federation** (JAF; http://www.jaf.or.jp). You will pay an annual membership fee and receive roadside assistance in case of emergencies.

Parking

Finding a parking spot in Tokyo is extremely difficult and parking fees are high. As streets are narrow, most cars parallel park. Many large buildings, such as hotels and department stores, offer space for parking, and hourly parking spots are sometimes available on the street. But finding a spot is such a nightmare that many people just give up and park illegally.

The fines for illegal parking are quite high, however, and illegally parked cars may be towed. If you find a parking ticket on your windshield, take it to the police station specified on the ticket for payment instructions, then pay the fine at a designated bank or post office branch. If your car is towed, go to the police station specified at the place you parked your car, pay the fine and the towing expense, then pick up your car from where it has been towed (usually a different spot from where the police station is located). In addition to the fine, illegal parking also results in penalty points on drivers' records.

Highways

The highway that connects key points in Tokyo is called the Shuto Expressway; this highway makes several loops within Tokyo. Highways in Japan are not free, and the charge to use the Shuto Expressway is ¥ 700 regardless of the distance driven. Drivers usually avoid getting on the congested highway during rush hour. Highways that go to other parts of Japan (including the Tomei, Chuo and Kan-etsu Expressways) can be accessed from several locations in Tokyo.

Reading Japanese Addresses

The format used in Japan to address letters and parcels is different from that used in many countries. In Japan, addresses are written from general to specific, beginning with the postal code, administrative region, numbers, building name, company and department name, and finally the intended recipient.

The following is an example of how an address in the Tokyo metropolitan area is written and a brief description of its components:

> 777-8888
> Tokyo-to, Minato-ku, Akasaka, 10-20-30
> General Office Building 3rd Floor
> Service Company Accounting Department
> Mr Ichiro Suzuki

- **Line 1**: Postal code.
- **Line 2**: The first item on this line is the largest administrative region contained in the address; '-*to*' indicates the capital. The second-largest area is usually indicated by either '-*ku*'' (ward) or '-*shi*' (city). Next is the neighbourhood, followed by three numbers separated by hyphens. The first number is the '*cho-me*' (block), the second the '*ban*' (lot number), and the third the '*go*' (building number).
- **Line 3**: Building name and floor number.
- **Line 4**: Company and department names, sometimes written at the end of Line 3.
- **Line 5**: Name of the intended recipient.

When Japanese people write addresses in other languages or in *romaji*, especially when sending mail overseas, they usually switch the sequence (writing from the recipient's name or smaller entity first) to match other systems.

When you write addresses in Japan using *romaji*, you can use either system; if you write them in Japanese, it is better to follow the Japanese way. Please note that when Japanese people write their names in Japanese, they usually write the family name first followed by the given name.

In Case of an Earthquake

Earthquakes are one of the natural disasters Tokyo is prone to and its residents have become accustomed to feeling periodic tremors. As a new resident of Tokyo, you should familiarise yourself and your family members with the procedures to follow in case of an earthquake, some of which are outlined here.

Evacuation

In case evacuation is necessary, there are areas throughout Tokyo designated to accommodate refugees. These places are usually large open spaces such as parks or fields. Ask neighbours to show you the designated area nearest your home. Then visit the area with your family and identify a point where you will all meet in case you are separated. If you have young children, test them to make sure they know where to go.

Earthquake Kit

Prepare an earthquake kit that includes a minimum supply of items necessary for the first few days after an evacuation. Place the kit in a location in your home that allows easy access, and make sure everyone knows where it is. Suggested items include:

- First-aid supplies and any prescription medicine you may need;
- Enough bottles of water to last for two or three days;
- Instant and dried foods such as crackers, chocolate, and noodles;
- A portable, battery-operated radio and light;
- Copies of the Foreign Registration Cards and the main page(s) of the passports of all family members.

Information

In the event of a major earthquake, NHK (Channel 1) on TV will broadcast information and instructions in English. Tune your radio to NHK at 594 AM or the English-language channels AFN (810 AM) or InterFM (76.1 FM).

Steps to follow during an earthquake

The Tokyo Metropolitan Government suggests residents take the following 10 steps in case of an earthquake:

- Secure your safety as well as that of your family's. During a major tremor, hide under a solid table so that your head is protected from falling objects.
- Turn off all sources of heat. If a fire breaks out, extinguish it immediately.
- Do not panic and do not rush outside. Leaving a room or building is not necessarily safer than staying inside. Check the situation first and act calmly.
- Secure an exit. Tremors may warp doors and you could be trapped inside, especially in concrete buildings. Keep at least one door open by putting something (a shoe, for example) between the door and the doorframe.
- If you are outside, watch out for falling objects and loose electric wires. Stay away from buildings and evacuate to an open space.
- If you are in a department store or theatre, follow the instructions of the personnel in charge.
- Park your car on the left-hand side of the road if you are driving when an earthquake occurs.
- Move away from cliffs and the seashore, as landslides and tidal waves may occur.
- Evacuate on foot, and keep the belongings you bring with you to a minimum.
- Never be influenced by rumours. Act on accurate information only.

EXPLORING TOKYO ON FOOT

As residents of Tokyo use public transportation often, they spend a lot of time walking to and from train, subway and bus stops. People may initially feel fatigued by the incessant walking, but most will eventually get used to it and value the opportunity for exercise; some are also pleased to find that they have lost weight!

By walking, Tokyo residents discover the intricacies of various neighbourhoods. Busy side streets have developed around most train and subway stations, and here one can find major supermarkets and grocery stores, coffee shops, bookstores and other small shops carrying a variety of goods. These shopping streets are usually narrow and parking places are rare, so the best way to explore them is on foot.

One potential hazard is that bicyclists often use the same pavements as pedestrians do. They are allowed to walk their bicycles on pavements when riding on the roads may seem dangerous. The problem is that instead of walking, many bicyclists run. In addition, some pavements are designated for use by both pedestrians and bicyclists. The fact is, bicyclists are likely to use virtually any sidewalk and there is no police enforcement on bicycle laws. As speeding bicycles can be hazardous to pedestrians, both bicyclists and pedestrians should be careful before changing course.

Foreigners from countries in which vehicle traffic flows on the right-hand side of the street should be careful when crossing, because in Japan, traffic flows on the left-hand side. Tokyo streets can be narrow and winding, so drivers may have difficulty spotting pedestrians. If you have small children, you must remind them repeatedly to watch for cars and to never rush out onto the street.

From the perspective of personal safety, walking around Tokyo is generally safe. However, not all areas are equally safe so unfortunate incidents do happen from time to time. It is generally advisable to avoid walking alone in parks or other quiet places after dark, especially for women and children. Late night encounters with drunken men are not unheard of, but usually no harm will come to innocent bystanders. Walking on busy streets should be fine both day and night.

Shinjuku lights up at night. It is a major commercial and administrative centre and houses many offices, department stores and hotels.

A busy street in the Asakusa District. Asakusa has a more traditional Japanese atmosphere than some other neighbourhoods of Tokyo and is well-known for its temples and older buildings.

Traditional eateries and shops in little alleys offer authentic Japanese food and a unique taste of local life.

井上寿司

Despite its reputable as a modern city of high-rise buildings and offices, Tokyo has many lovely parks and gardens which offers a respite from the bustle of the city.

The Kannon Temple in Asakusa is quiet in the early morning, but attracts large numbers of worshippers and visitors later in the day.

FOOD AND ENTERTAINING

CHAPTER 6

TRIGG.

'If the containers are dull, the food will be dull.'
—Kitaoji Rosanjin, ceramist and a known gourmet

THE TRADITIONAL JAPANESE DIET is very healthy. It includes a lot of vegetables and features fish and soybean products (both of which are low in cholesterol) as the main sources of protein. In addition, the popular Japanese cooking methods of boiling, steaming and grilling require little use of oil. A typical dinner served at a Japanese home includes cooked rice, *miso* soup (broth seasoned with *miso*, a fermented and salted soybean paste), an entrée (fish or meat) and steamed or cooked vegetables.

The Japanese diet has been influenced by Western tastes, and in the past couple of decades, people have increased their consumption of meat, dairy products and oily foods. Traditional Japanese cuisine is regaining popularity, however, especially among health-conscious people and women who want to stay slim.

Certain Japanese foods seem unusual and, in some cases, even unappetising to many newcomers to Japan. Over time, however, many foreigners grow to enjoy Japanese cuisine.

JAPANISED FOODS

Japanese people like to modify foods imported from other countries to suit their own tastes. One example is *ramen* which is egg noodles in soup, a dish which was originated in China. Now there are many Japanese versions of this dish. Japanese people like curry so much that they have

An *itamae-san*. or *sushi* chef.

created many different curried dishes, including *karé* rice, (curry sauce over rice), *karé udon* (curry sauce over broad wheat noodles) and *karé pan* (deep-fried bread rolls stuffed with curry sauce). For another culinary adventure, Italian pasta is mixed with Japanese ingredients to make *natto* spaghetti (fermented soybeans seasoned with soy sauce and served over pasta) and *tarako* spaghetti (pasta with fish eggs and olive oil). Finally, Japanese people are very creative with breads and have popularised *an-pan* (buns filled with sweet bean paste) and *yakisoba-pan* (buns containing fried noodles!).

Typical Japanese Dishes

- **Sushi**

  A typical type of *sushi*, called *nigiri-zushi*, is a pressed oval of rice covered with a piece of raw fish fillet. Popular toppings include tuna, yellow tail and flounder, but other types of fresh seafood can be used as well. To eat a piece of *sushi*, dip it lightly in soy sauce and eat it in one bite (not always an easy task!). Other kinds of *sushi* include *maki-zushi* (*sushi* rolls) and *gomoku-zushi* (*sushi* rice covered with bits of seafood and vegetables).

- **Tempura**

  Tempura is seafood and vegetables dipped in batter and deep-fried. Large prawns, aubergine, sweet potatoes and asparagus are popular choices. The batter is made from flour, water, and egg. *Tempura* is usually eaten dipped in salt, or in a broth flavoured with soy sauce and a small amount of grated Japanese radish. It is sometimes served on top of noodles or over rice.

- **Sukiyaki**

  Sukiyaki is prepared by cooking thinly sliced beef and vegetables such as *shiitake* mushrooms, bamboo shoots and Japanese leeks, along with other ingredients such as *tofu*, in a large iron pan. The ingredients are seasoned with soy sauce, rice wine (*sake*) and sugar. *Sukiyaki* is usually prepared at the table–diners take the cooked food directly from the pan, dipping them in beaten raw egg before eating them.

(continued on next page)

Typical Japanese Dishes

(continued from previous page)

- **Shabu-shabu**

  Shabu-shabu is Japanese-style fondue. Thinly sliced beef is dipped and cooked briefly in a boiling broth flavoured with seaweed. *Tofu* and vegetables such as Chinese cabbage, Japanese leek and *shiitake* mushrooms are added to the broth. After the ingredients are cooked, they are dipped in a sauce made from either soy sauce and Japanese lime or from sesame paste. Like *sukiyaki, shabu-shabu* is generally shared by parties of four to five people.

- **Yakitori**

  Yakitori is skewered grilled chicken. Small chicken cubes are skewered onto a thin bamboo spike (sometimes alternated with small pieces of Japanese leek), seasoned with salt or glazed with a special sauce, and then grilled on a gas or charcoal grill. Old *yakitori* restaurants use their own secret sauce recipes that have been passed down through several generations. The smell of sauce that has dripped onto the grill can really stimulate one's appetite!

- **Ramen**

  Ramen is thin egg noodles in soup. Originally a Chinese dish, Japanese people modified the recipe, resulting in hundreds of versions of *ramen* made from different ingredients and soup bases. Ingredients added to ramen include corn, boiled egg, and sliced pork. The soup is made from pork, beef, or chicken broth, or a combination of these; some chefs even use fish broth.

- **Karé Raisu**

  Karé raisu (curry and rice) is meat and vegetables in curry sauce served over rice. This dish was imported from India, and then modified to suit Japanese tastes. Compared to Indian curries, Japanese curries are less spicy and the sauces are thicker because flour is usually added. There are hundreds of different recipes for *karé raisu* in Japan.

JAPANESE FOOD
CHALLENGES FOR FOREIGNERS

For many foreigners, especially Westerners, sampling certain Japanese foods for the first time requires courage. The most famous challenge is *natto* (fermented soy beans). *Natto* smells a bit like strong cheese and is gooey; the taste, however, is not so bad—it simply tastes like beans. Once you have acquired a taste for *natto,* you cannot live without it! The best thing about it is that it is full of protein and calcium and therefore, very nutritious.

Anko, or sweet bean paste, is used frequently in Japanese confectionery. The paste is made from cooked red beans and sugar. Some foreigners object to the idea of adding sugar to beans, because in many countries beans are supposed to taste salty. Others say that the look of particularly dark *anko*, which can be almost black, does not seem appealing.

Finally, although *sashimi* and *sushi* are probably the foods for which Japan is most famous internationally, foreigners are often reluctant to try them. Many are squeamish at the thought of eating fish raw and some are concerned with the freshness of the meat. It may be reassuring to know that Japanese restaurants usually cook any fish not fresh enough to eat raw. Give *sashimi* and *sushi* a try— you may become a connoisseur!

TABLE ETIQUETTE

In earlier times, Japanese people followed a detailed set of table manners carefully, but many now prefer to enjoy eating in a more casual setting. Foreigners are not expected to follow all the rules of traditional Japanese table etiquette, which is fortunate because Japanese people do not like to embarrass foreigners by letting them make a faux pas; but foreigners who do follow some of the traditions demonstrate respect for Japanese culture, and thus make a good impression.

For many foreigners, the most difficult part of eating the Japanese way is learning to use chopsticks *(hashi)*. Japanese people use chopsticks for most meals at home, in

The proper way to hold a pair of chopsticks.

restaurants that serve Japanese food and many other Asian food restaurants. At home, family members each have their own chopsticks. One form of chopsticks, known as *waribashi,* is made from a long piece of wood that is partially split; users complete the split when they want to eat. *Waribashi* are often provided at restaurants or given to dinner guests in homes. You might see people rubbing the two sticks together to remove tiny splinters, but this is not considered good manners.

When using chopsticks, hold one (by the thick end) at the base of your thumb, steadying it with your ring finger. Hold the other one (also by the thick end) in between your index finger and middle finger, supporting it with the tip of your thumb. Use the first chopstick as a stable base, and move the second chopstick toward the first as necessary to lift or cut foods (*see the above photo for proper way of holding chopsticks*). Use the thin ends to carry food to your mouth.

Chopsticks (the thin ends) are customarily placed on a chopstick rest in front of you before and after meals. When no rest is provided, people sometimes fold the piece of paper in which the *waribashi* was wrapped to make an instant chopstick rest.

When using chopsticks, certain movements should be avoided. First, do not stick your chopsticks straight up in your rice bowl, as this reminds people of how Buddhists make offerings to the deceased. Also, do not give another person food by passing it from your chopsticks to their chopsticks, as this resembles the Buddhist funeral custom where two people use chopsticks to hold a piece of bone from the cremated body (instead, place the food item on their plates). Finally, do not use your chopsticks to move plates or bowls, do not wave your chopsticks in the air while you speak and do not hold chopsticks in a fist.

There are some rules of dining etiquette that Japanese people still follow. In formal Japanese restaurants, dishes are served one after another, with rice, *miso* soup and pickled vegetables served at the end of the meal. In regular restaurants, rice and soup are served together with the entrée and vegetables. When foods are served simultaneously, it is good manners to eat them in an alternating fashion rather than to finish one dish first and then move on to the next one. When eating rice or *miso* soup, it is better to lift the bowl up to one's mouth than to lean toward the table; it is also customary to place the rice bowl on the table in front of the diner and put the *miso* soup bowl to the right of the rice bowl. Pouring soy sauce over rice is considered exceptionally bad manners. It can also make the rice very difficult to eat with chopsticks!

When eating noodles, Japanese people make a slurping noise. This is surprising to some foreigners, but they soon learn that such noise is not only appropriate in Japan, it is recommended. Noodles are supposed to be eaten quickly before they get soggy, especially when they are served in soup. Making noise while eating noodles indicates that one is enjoying the experience. Incidentally, some people also make noise when sipping soup or even coffee, but then, in Western etiquette, this is not considered good manners.

Japanese people usually begin eating only after everyone at the table has been served. To be polite, people who are waiting to be served invite those already served to begin eating. The people who have been served may then begin to eat, or they may continue to wait, especially if they are younger or of lower status than other diners. When people are about to begin eating, they say *Itadakimasu*, which is loosely translated as, 'I humbly receive the meal.' After the meal they say *Gochiso sama deshita*, which means 'Thank you very much for the meal'.

Japanese people like to make toasts when they drink, especially at parties and formal occasions. People usually begin drinking only after the glasses of all guests have been filled and someone has made a toast. Occasionally, a senior person or host will make a short speech, followed by everyone saying *kanpai* (meaning 'dry your glass'). It is customary for people to fill the glasses of the people sitting next to them. To show that they are paying attention to the needs of others, they try to pour refills before the glasses are empty. People do not fill their own glasses.

Japanese restaurants usually do not provide napkins, so many women carry nice handkerchiefs to place across their laps while they dine. Many restaurants provide diners with hot towels (*oshibori*) to clean their hands; some men use them to wipe their faces, but this is not considered to be the best of manners.

Seating arrangements at meals, especially formal meals, are an important consideration. (*Refer to* 'Seating Arrangements' *in Chapter 9.*)

SHOPPING FOR FOOD

Groceries can be purchased at Japanese supermarkets, small shops and department stores; convenience stores also carry basic food items. Expatriates often rely on international supermarkets when looking for imported products. Regardless of where you shop, a consumption tax is usually added to the stated price of food.

Supermarkets

People in Tokyo buy most of their groceries at supermarkets, and prefer to shop for a few necessities each day rather than buying in large quantities every few days. Over time, as people grew to prefer the convenience of finding a wide variety of foods in one place, supermarkets have overtaken small shops selling meat, fish and vegetables. Major supermarket chains include Ito Yokado, Jusco and Seiyu; in addition, there are many small local supermarkets.

Small Shops

There are still many reasons to shop at small stores, however. While small shops may not offer as large a selection as supermarkets, the products they sell may be fresher and the prices lower. Also, once the clerks get to know you they may give you a special discount or let you know the best buy of the day. For foreigners, communicating with store clerks may require extra effort, but establishing relationships with them is a great way to learn about Japanese culture, and you will feel that you are part of the community.

Department Stores

A third popular venue for grocery shopping is the basement of department stores. Most department stores dedicate the lower levels to selling foods of all kinds, including fish, meat, fresh fruits, and vegetables. Confectionery counters feature sweets and chocolates. The selection is large and upon

Japanese people pay exorbitant prices for exotic fruits. The famous South-east Asian durian fruit retails at ¥ 6,000, about US$ 50 a piece!

request, purchases can be artistically wrapped. Delicatessen sections offer cold cuts and prepared foods. Aisles can get crowded in the late afternoon when people shop for ready-made entrées and side dishes for dinner. By the way, if you purchase ready-made foods, it is best not to eat them on the street, as doing so is not common in Japan.

Convenience Stores

Convenience stores (called *konbini*) are very handy for last-minute shopping. They are usually open 24 hours a day, and sell basic food items such as salt, sugar and milk, as well as necessities such as batteries, stockings, toiletry products and first-aid items. They also sell ready-made and instant meals popular with people lacking time to cook. Convenience stores also offer a variety of other services. Here you can send faxes, make photocopies, pay utility bills and withdraw or deposit money using ATMs. Some convenience stores even sell train, airplane, and concert tickets.

International Supermarkets

Foreigners who have lived in Tokyo for a long time are pleased to find that the availability of imported foods is ever increasing, paralleling the growth in the foreign population and the diversification of the tastes of Japanese people. Many medium- and large-sized supermarkets have 'International Food Corners', and several supermarkets specialise in selling imported products. (*Refer to the* 'Resource Guide' *for a list of international supermarkets.*)

FOOD SELECTIONS
Vegetables and Fruits

Most common vegetables (such as lettuce, cabbage, onions, aubergine, mushrooms, tomatoes, cucumbers, potatoes and green peppers) can be found throughout the year in ordinary supermarkets and grocers. Some of these vegetables may look and taste a little different than those in your home country. Japanese eggplant, cucumbers and green peppers, for example, are thinner and shorter than those generally found in Europe and the United States, and are more flavourful.

Some vegetables are unique to Asia, such as *gobo* (burdock root), *daikon* (long radish) and *takenoko* (bamboo shoots). Japanese cookbooks written in English are available at major bookstores and feature a variety of recipes using these vegetables.

Fresh herbs have recently become popular in home cooking. Increasing numbers of supermarkets sell herbs, such as basil and mint, but the larger or international supermarkets offer the best variety.

Fruits are abundant in Tokyo and are best when purchased in season. Strawberries are tender and sweet in winter and spring. Cherries are luscious in early summer. Japanese cherries are a real treat but are incredibly expensive; a box may cost ¥ 3,000! Less expensive American cherries are also available. Watermelons and melons as well as peaches are sweet and juicy in mid-summer. Persimmons, Asian pears (*nashi*) and grapes are at their peak in fall. Apples and tangerines ripen just in time for winter. Japanese people tend to prefer sweet over sour when selecting fruits; as a result, farmers put much effort into creating sweeter fruits.

Vegetables and fruits are generally priced and sold in packages or piles and rarely by weight. Some supermarkets and independent shops sell smaller portions to meet the needs of small families and single buyers.

Meat

Pork, beef, and chicken are available at most meat shops and supermarkets. Japanese people buy pork and chicken more often than beef because they are cheaper. Japanese beef is very expensive, one reason being that farmers take extreme care in raising their cattle. It is said that some farmers feed beer or wine to cows to make the beef tender. Less expensive, leaner beef from places such as the United States and Australia has become available since the liberalisation of beef imports in 1990; consumption of beef has since increased. However, as many popular Japanese recipes call for the more fatty and tender beef that is produced domestically, Japanese cooks still spend a lot of yen on their beef.

Other meats such as veal, lamb, and turkey are not popular and are generally available only at international supermarkets. Japanese people prefer to purchase meat in slices rather than in large chunks. If you want to buy meat for a roast, for example, you will probably have to buy it at an international supermarket or ask a butcher in a meat shop to cut it specifically for you. While supermarkets generally sell meat in packages, individual shops usually sell it in units of 100 g (about one-quarter pound).

Fish

Fish shops and the fish sections of supermarkets are usually lively places. To attract customers, fish is nicely displayed and store clerks try to create an energetic and vibrant ambience through their interaction with customers, who are welcomed by shouts of 'Irasshai!' which means 'welcome'. (Sushi chefs and waiters in restaurants will often say this as well.) When hearing this forceful greeting for the first time, some foreigners feel like they are being scolded and wonder what they have done wrong!

A wide variety of fish is available throughout the year. Fall and winter are the best times to purchase certain kinds of fish, including Pacific saury, sardines and mackerel. Large fish are usually filleted and sold in packages or piles containing two or three fillets. Smaller fish are also sold in packages or piles. Fish for *sashimi* are often cut into small pieces and sold in packages, or, sometimes, in large chunks so that people can slice them at home.

In order to choose the freshest fish, people check the colour of the fillets (the brighter the better), the colour of the scales (the shinier the better), and the colour of the eyes (clear eyes are better than cloudy or red eyes).

Bread

Surprisingly, Japanese people are bread lovers, although their staple food has traditionally been rice. Many prefer bread for breakfast, and some restaurants offer customers the choice of rice or bread as a side dish. Fresh bread and pastries are sold at bakeries and in the basement grocery sections of department stores. People often stand in long lines to get bread hot from the oven.

In accordance with Japanese preferences, many bakeries in Tokyo produce soft, sweet white breads, but there are an increasing number of bakeries specialising in French, German and Italian style breads. Chains such as Kobe-ya and Andersen offer breads that are every bit as good as anything you can find in Europe! Japanese people can be very creative with breads and have invented interesting pastries containing Japanese ingredients.

EATING OUT

People eat out often in Tokyo and there is no shortage of restaurants serving Asian foods, such as Japanese, Chinese and Korean, and Western foods, especially Italian and French, as well as American. Some are world-class restaurants in terms of quality, atmosphere and prices. However, there are also many inexpensive places with good food. Foreigners

Plastic food displays at Japanese restaurants look like the 'real thing'.

are surprised to find that the portions of food served in restaurants in Tokyo tend to be generally smaller than those to which they are accustomed.

For foreigners who are unfamiliar with Japanese food, deciding what to order at a Japanese restaurant can be an intimidating experience. Fortunately, many Japanese restaurants feature menus with pictures to which you can point. Also, many display plastic models of meals in glass cases near the entrance. It is fascinating to see how closely these plastic models resemble the actual dishes served. Even if you cannot read the names of the dishes, you can order by motioning to the server to accompany you to the window where you can simply point to the model.

After your food has been served, a server will place the bill on your table; you should pay at the cashier counter as you leave the restaurant. In fancy restaurants, the bill will not be provided until you request it; you should pay at the table. As many smaller restaurants still do not accept credit cards, you need to carry sufficient cash. A consumption tax is added to the total price of your meal. While tipping is not required at restaurants in Japan, restaurants in hotels, as well as relatively expensive restaurants, automatically add a service fee of 10 per cent to the bill.

Smoking is permitted in most restaurants, although some have designated non-smoking areas.

Breakfast

Japanese people generally eat breakfast at home. Consequently, most restaurants are open only for lunch and dinner. Hotel restaurants do serve breakfast, but a glass of freshly squeezed orange juice alone can cost a whopping ¥ 1,000 and a full breakfast can set you back ¥ 3,000 or more. After adding taxes and service fees, a breakfast in a nice hotel in Tokyo could well be the most expensive breakfast in the world!

A more reasonably priced option is breakfast at a coffee shop. Some coffee shops located near train or subway stations or in commercial areas of Tokyo offer a breakfast menu called 'Morning Set' for around ¥ 500. It comes with a thick slice of toast, coffee, and a small side dish such as a hard-boiled egg or salad. 'Morning Set' is usually served from 7:00 am–9:00 am.

Lunch

The standard lunch hour in Japanese companies is from 12:00 pm to 1:00 pm. Everybody goes out for lunch at the same time; thus, restaurants near office buildings can be extremely crowded during that one-hour period. People who can avoid the rush hour will have a more relaxing lunch.

In order to serve many customers in a limited time, restaurants in business districts generally serve various set meals (*teishoku*). In Japanese restaurants, a set meal usually includes an entrée (grilled fish or sautéed meat, for example), a vegetable dish, rice and *miso* soup. In Western restaurants, a set meal might include soup or salad, an entrée, and rice or bread. The price of a set meal ranges from ¥ 700–1,500. If the restaurant is crowded, customers may be asked to share a table with others.

Noodle shops are popular places for lunch. *Ramen* shops often serve side dishes such as fried vegetables, dumplings, or fried rice, in addition to noodles. Other noodle shops offer both buckwheat noodles (*soba*) and/or wheat noodles (*udon*). These are usually served hot in a broth seasoned with soy sauce and various other ingredients, or cold with a soy sauce-based dip accompanied by a small amount of Japanese horseradish (*wasabi*) and finely-chopped scallion. Noodles shops charge between ¥ 600–1,000.

People who have time to enjoy a nice, leisurely meal often choose an upmarket restaurant, many of which offer lunches at reasonable prices. Full-course meals might include an appetiser, one or two entrées, and desserts for ¥ 2,500–5,000. Many famous Japanese restaurants also serve similarly-priced boxed lunches. If you order a boxed lunch, you can enjoy small portions of various Japanese dishes (such as *sashimi*, *tempura* and cooked vegetables), all artistically arranged in a lacquered box.

Dinner

In Japan, the largest meal of the day is dinner. When selecting a restaurant, Japanese people look for one with an atmosphere that complements the occasion.

Casual Dining

Italian restaurants are popular for dining with friends or colleagues. Tokyo is home to hundreds of Italian restaurants ranging from high-end establishments to pizza houses. Many offer high quality full-course meals for ¥ 5,000–10,000. Some boast Italian chefs who prepare authentic dishes and Italian servers to wait on you, so you can almost imagine that you are in Italy.

When cost is not an issue, *sushi* restaurants are a favourite among Japanese people. When dining in large groups, they often choose Chinese or Korean barbeque restaurants where they can share the food. People who like culinary adventures can try food from different parts of the world such as Thailand, India or Mexico or they might try 'fusion', a type of cooking that mixes the styles and ingredients of different cuisines.

Family restaurants (*famiri resutoran*) are places where families with children can enjoy food in a casual atmosphere at reasonable prices. Many of them are open 24 hours a day, and are located in the suburbs where they can provide ample seating and parking spaces. Popular family restaurants include SkyLark, Denny's and Jonathans. They can also be found within Tokyo itself, and often feature a wide selection of both Japanese and Western-style cuisine.

Restaurants for Special Occasions

Several Italian and French restaurants in Tokyo offer elegant settings and excellent food and wine. Dinner at these places may cost ¥ 20,000–30,000 per person or more, if wine is ordered.

After-Work Socialising

When people go out with colleagues they often choose *izakaya*, which are casual places serving drinks such as beer and *sake* (rice wine) along with lots of appetisers. The typical menu includes *edamame* (boiled soy beans), *tofu*, fried fish (*yakizakana*), and fried chicken. Most dishes are easy to share, so people order several for the group. Many *izakaya* offer *nomi hodai*, or 'all you can drink' at a fixed price. These *izakaya* are very popular with young people.

When paying the bill, co-workers often divide the total by the number of people and everyone pays the same amount (usually around ¥ 3,000). Some foreigners are surprised by this custom, called *warikan*, as it may be more common in other countries for people to pay only for what they have consumed. When a manager or older person accompanies the group, it is common for that person to pay a larger share, or even the entire bill.

After-work gathering spots also include *yakitoriya* and *odenya*. *Yakitoriya* are restaurants that serve *yakitori* (skewered grilled chicken) and drinks (mainly beer and *sake*). *Odenya* serve *oden*—a dish of stewed fish cakes and vegetables in soup that is especially good for staving off the cold winter and drinks (beer and *sake*).

Business Entertainment

Japanese food restaurants called *ryotei* are formal places for entertaining important customers. They serve traditional Japanese multi-course menus that were originally served at tea ceremonies, and the portions are tiny. The courses usually include appetisers, grilled or steamed fish and vegetables, rice and *miso* or clear broth. Considered a refined version of Japanese cuisine, great attention is paid to the appearance of the food as well as to the taste.

Many of these *ryotei* restaurants look like old Japanese houses and diners customarily remove their shoes when they enter. The food is served in private rooms, so *ryotei* are good choices for closed-door meetings. In fact, senior government officials use *ryotei* for their meetings so often that some joke that important Japanese political decisions are made at *ryotei* and not at the Diet building! Many *ryotei* only accept new customers with referrals. The price of entertaining here is beyond imagination; famous *ryotei* may charge more than ¥ 100,000 per person.

If *ryotei* are beyond your budget, Japanese restaurants that serve *sukiyaki* or *shabu-shabu* are also good places for entertaining. For those whose clients are wine connoisseurs should consider expensive French and Italian restaurants.

Fast Food Shops

Western fast food is popular in Japan, especially among the younger generation. Most major American fast food establishments have branches in Japan, among them McDonald's, Burger King, Wendy's, Kentucky Fried Chicken and Subway. In addition, there are several hamburger shops run by Japanese companies, such as MOS Burger—in addition to conventional burgers, they serve Japanese versions such as *teriyaki* chicken burgers and rice buns.

Pizza, too, is popular and shops that deliver are many. What is 'pizza' to Japanese, however, may not look like 'pizza' to foreigners. Japanese versions include toppings such as seafood and *teriyaki* chicken, and sauces such as mayonnaise and curry paste. Although some foreigners grow to enjoy these variations, at times they crave 'regular pizza' with cheese and pepperoni! Do not worry, the regular version is also available at most places.

There are also several kinds of Japanese fast food outlets. One type serves *gyu-don,* a bowl of rice topped with cooked sliced beef. Noodle stands, known as *tachigui soba* (literally meaning 'stand while eating noodles'), are also popular. These stands are located primarily at train stations. Most stay open all day and people stand there for lunch, snacks, or after-work drinks.

Coffee and Tea Shops

Coffee shops are everywhere in Tokyo and some are quite luxurious. Some Japanese are coffee connoisseurs and very particular about the kinds of coffee they drink. Because of the high cost of importing quality beans coupled with the high cost of rent, the price of a cup of coffee can reach ¥ 1,000! Many coffee and tea shops serve a variety of cakes and pies; these shops are especially popular with young women. Casual coffee stands have become an alternative to the more expensive coffee shops. Branches of the American-based chain Starbucks are prevalent.

EXPLORING TOKYO AND BEYOND

CHAPTER 7

'Tokyo offers a lot of great opportunities,
so go out and try everything at least once!'
—An expatriate in Japan

A GREAT ADVANTAGE ABOUT LIVING IN TOKYO is that there are plenty of options for leisure: exploring historic sites, trying out the latest electronic gadgets and enjoying a Kabuki performance are just a few. Weekend trips outside of Tokyo also will be good opportunities to see places that have different distinct characteristics from Tokyo.

PLACES TO VISIT IN TOKYO

In addition to places mentioned here, there are numerous interesting neighbourhoods waiting to be discovered.

Old Tokyo

Asakusa and its surrounding areas such as Nezu and Yanaka are the best places to experience the ambience of old Tokyo. Asakusa was developed in the 17th century (Tokugawa Period) as the commercial area of the capital (then called Edo). The old buildings and traditional atmosphere reflect the area's historic past. The main landmark is **Sensoji Temple**, the oldest temple in Tokyo. Kaminarimon, the main gate to the temple, features a huge red lantern and is a favourite spot for taking photos. **Nakamise Dori**, the street connecting the gate to the temple, is lined with hundreds of small shops offering a variety of souvenirs. Deep inside the temple's Main Hall is an original statue of Kannon, the Buddhist Goddess of Mercy. Although tourists are no longer allowed in that part of the temple, they toss coins as offering

Kaminarimon gate at Sensoji Temple in Asakusa.

into a box outside the Main Hall and pray to the goddess for their happiness. Several festivals are held in Asakusa throughout the year—the most famous is Sanja Matsuri, held each May. Try to catch this festival, during which portable shrines are carried within the Asakusa district by groups of people in traditional costumes.

The many temples and shrines scattered throughout Tokyo also provide glimpses of the past. Generally, temples are Buddhist structures and shrines are Shinto (*Refer to* 'Religion and Beliefs' *in Chapter 2.*) Occasionally, you will find them where you least expect to, such as between, or even on top of, tall buildings. Their traditional architecture will take you back in time. In addition to Sensoji, interesting temples include **Kiyomizu-do Kannon** in Ueno, **Kan-eiji** in Uguisudani and **Zojoji** in Hamamatsu-cho.

The **Meiji Shrine** in Harajuku, built in honour of the Meiji Emperor, is the most famous in Tokyo and the most visited on New Year's Day. The gate to the shrine is the largest wooden

The lively Sanja festival in Asakusa.

gate (*torii*) in Japan and the main building is an example of refined Shinto architecture. Although Harajuku tends to be noisy and chaotic due to its large concentration of youths, once you enter the shrine you will feel insulated from the outside world—dense woods around the shrine block out the sound of traffic, and the only 'noise' to be heard are that of birds singing and footsteps on the stone-paved path. Other famous shrines include **Nezu Jinja** in Nezu, **Yushima Seido** in Yushima, and **Sanno-Hie Jinja** in Akasuka.

Tokyo's most prominent historical landmark is the **Imperial Palace** (*kokyo*), located near Tokyo Station. It was at one time, much larger and called Edo Castle and served as the headquarters of the Tokugawa Shogunate (1603–1868); today it is the residence of the imperial family. The palace itself is new. Remnants of the old castle, including a few towers, gates and part of the foundation, are still visible in Higashi Gyoen, a garden on the east side of the palace. The surrounding stone walls and moat, built to protect the castle

The skyscrapers of the Tokyo Metropolitan Government Office in Shinjuku as seen from a children's park.

from potential attacks, are also original. The palace is open to visitors only on New Year's Day and on the Emperor's birthday. On both days, the imperial family stands on the balcony to greet people. Standing in the centre of the business district, the old stone walls provide a contrast to the modern office buildings, a reflection of Tokyo culture where the old co-exist with the new.

A comfortable way to visit many of Tokyo's landmarks is to take a **Hato Bus** tour. Hato Bus offers a few different guided tours in English, covering major sights in Tokyo, including historical sites. Check their website (http://www.hatobus. co.jp) for more information.

Vista Points

The observatory deck of the **Tokyo Metropolitan Government Office** in Shinjuku offers spectacular 360-degree views of Tokyo and the surrounding area; on a clear day you can even see Mount Fuji. (The Metropolitan Government

Office buildings were designed by the world renowned architect Kenzo Tange.) This part of Shinjuku, with its magnificent skyscrapers, is the centre of modern Tokyo. The observatory deck on the top floor of the 60-storey **Sunshine City 60** in Ikebukuro, with its shops, restaurants and a magnificent vista of the city, is also worth a visit. Before these superstructures existed, the **Tokyo Tower** in Shibakoen was the most popular observation spot. Built in 1958 and modelled after the Eiffel Tower in Paris, it is still included in city tour itineraries and is usually crowded with tourists. Nearby Tokyo Tower, **Roppongi Hills** in Roppongi also offers a 360° panoramic view of the city.

Tsukiji Fish Market

This wholesale fish market is the largest of its kind in Japan, where fish from all over the world gets auctioned off. Although visitors cannot join the auction, they can observe the auctioneers running through the market stalls that overflow with the day's catch. Bidding begins around 3:00 am and most activities end by 5:00 am.

Many restaurants in the market's vicinity serve breakfast to those attending the auction (including tourists). This is probably the only place in Tokyo where you can have *sushi* for breakfast, and the experience is well worth rising early. You can also buy fresh seafood at the fish shops located here; while the retail price is not much different from that charged elsewhere, the quality is better. This is a fun place to take visiting friends and family.

Waterfront Area

Odaiba is a new area developed on reclaimed land in Tokyo Bay. In addition to the office buildings, which themselves are worth seeing for their contemporary designs, Odaiba offers various attractions for both adults and children: the boardwalk that runs along the bay and an amusement park for kids. Several good restaurants are located in the shopping complexes and nice hotels overlook the bay. One indoor mall, Venus Fort, gives shoppers the impression that they are outside, because the ceiling is painted to resemble the sky,

Rainbow Bridge over Tokyo Bay.

complete with clouds. Visitors driving to Odaiba at night will cross a vividly illuminated **Rainbow Bridge**.

Shopping Districts
(Refer to Chapter 5 *for information on shopping districts.)*

Parks and Gardens
Tokyo has several parks and gardens where residents can escape from the crowds and the hustle and bustle of the city.

Ueno Park in the Ueno area is one of the Tokyo's largest parks and is famous for its breathtaking blooms of cherry blossoms in spring. During this season, people enjoy picnics both day and night in the park. It also offers other attractions such as a zoo (famous for its giant panda) and museums. **Yoyogi Park**, located next to the Meiji Shrine in Harajuku, has a nice picnic area and a large field where children can play ball games. It features a jogging track and a bicycling course, and has bicycles for rent. **Shinjuku Gyoen Garden** and **Shinjuku Central Park** are two oases found in the midst of the busy Shinjuku area. **Hama Rikyu Garden** in Shimbashi and **Koishikawa Korakuen Garden** in Koishikawa are beautiful Japanese-style gardens. **Higashi Gyoen** in the Imperial Palace consists of a Japanese style garden and a Western-style garden filled with beautiful flowers such as irises and azaleas.

Entertainment Spots
Art Museums
(Refer to the 'Resource Guide' for a list of some of the most prominent art museums in Tokyo.)

Movies
Major movie theatres offer Japanese films as well as American movies subtitled in Japanese. Popular American movies are released in Tokyo at the same time as in the United States; others are shown a few months later. Several smaller theatres specialise in presenting movies from Europe and other parts of the world.

Movie-going in Tokyo is rather expensive—adult admission to most theatres is ¥ 1,800, but discounts are often available for students, children and senior citizens. Every Wednesday is 'Ladies' Day' when women can watch movies for ¥ 1,000. Also, the first day of every month is 'Movie Discount Day', when admission is ¥ 1,000 for all adults. Advance tickets are also sold at a discount, and these are obtainable at the theatre ticket office, network ticket counters and some convenience stores.

Theatres and Concerts
Tokyo has more than 150 theatres and concert halls showcasing domestic and foreign performing arts, including operas, ballets, modern dance performances as well as modern and classical concerts. Large concert halls, such as the Tokyo Dome, Budokan and Tokyo International Forum, host the big names in popular music. Mid-sized venues

(capacity of 1,000 or so), including the Liquid Room in Ebisu and On Air in Shibuya, entertain domestic and foreign pop or rock acts. Classical concerts, operas, and dance performances are often held at the Orchard Hall, Suntory Hall, Tokyo Opera City and Ueno Bunka Kaikan.

Jazz is performed at the Blue Note, a branch of the famous jazz club in New York, and at numerous less expensive jazz clubs around the city, notably the Shinjuku Pit Inn, where one can often hear more cutting-edge jazz and improvised music. Otherwise, there are countless small venues (called live houses) featuring live music of every type scattered throughout the city, with large concentrations of them in Shimokitazawa and Shinjuku.

News on upcoming concerts and performances are published in English-language newspapers and magazines such as the *Tokyo Metropolis* (http://www.metropolis.co.jp) and the *Tokyo Journal* (http://www.tokyo.to). However, these listings are relatively brief and generally cover only the biggest attractions. Many people interested in the local music scenes get their upcoming concert information from flyers or posters (called *chirashi*) which are usually distributed at live houses and music stores throughout the city. Tickets for many performances are sold at outlets such as Ticket Pia, Lawson Ticket and CN Playguide. Unfortunately, most of these outlets offer information in Japanese only, over the phone. Try visiting their offices instead, some employees may be able to assist non-Japanese speaking patrons.

TRAVELLING BEYOND TOKYO

Areas outside of Tokyo offer a respite from the busy city life and a different perspective of the country. There are plenty of distinct and interesting places to visit, the most famous of which, for both Japanese people and foreigners, is the historic city of Kyoto. In addition to old cities, Japan also has beaches (Okinawa), summer hideaways (Hokkaido) and winter fun (Nagano, Niigata, etc.), hot springs (*onsen*) and other exciting places.

Travelling outside of Tokyo can be an eye-opening and educational experience: there are fewer signs or information boards in English than in Tokyo; Japanese people outside of Tokyo interact less frequently with foreigners and may be less proficient in English, so they might initially be reluctant to interact with you and may wave their hands in bafflement; and you may also find some people staring openly at you, usually out of a naive curiosity. Nevertheless, you will probably find that most people are polite and hospitable and willing to offer you assistance when you need it.

Travel Seasons

The busiest periods for travelling are: the New Year holidays (end December to early January); Golden Week (end April to early May); and the *Obon* Festival (middle August) when many people return to their hometowns. In addition, people like to take short trips during the period between mid-September and early November when the weather is nice. If you plan to travel during any of these times, to avoid disappointment, make reservations for transportation and accommodations far in advance; tickets sell out quickly and accommodations increase in price. If you are planning to travel by car, keep in mind that major highways will be so congested that you may get stuck in traffic for several hours. (Take along beverages, snacks, toys, and games for children.)

Transportation

The public transportation system is generally well-developed throughout the country; most people prefer to take public transport than to endure driving in heavy traffic and high petrol prices.

Trains

Trains are by far the most popular mode of transportation for domestic travel. Most long-distance trains are operated by the Japan Railway (JR) Group. In addition to regular trains, JR operates *shinkansen* (bullet trains), which rank among the fastest trains in the world. *Shinkansen* routes connect most major points in the country. The Tokaido & Sanyo

Shinkansen Line covers routes west and south of Tokyo; from Tokyo Station, it runs through Nagoya, Kyoto, Osaka, Okayama, Hiroshima and on to Hakata and Kagoshima on Kyushu Island. The Tohoku/Yamagata/Akita Shinkansen Line covers the northern parts of Japan. From Tokyo Station, it goes to Fukushima, Zao, Sendai, Morioka, Yamagata and Akita, while its Jyoetsu/Nagano line covers Nagano and Niigata. *Shinkansen* trips can be rather expensive, but to many people, the time saved travelling and comfort are worth it.

One pleasure of train travel is the *eki ben*, or boxed lunches sold in the stations. (*Eki ben* literally means 'station boxed lunch'.) Different stations sell different types of boxed lunches featuring local food. People buy *eki ben* when the train makes a stop, or on the train itself (especially on *shinkansen* or express trains).

Tickets for bullet trains and other local trains can be purchased at Midori no Madoguchi ticket windows operated by JR. As the staff may not speak English, it is a good idea to ask a Japanese friend to assist you with the process, or ask a Japanese friend (or hotel concierge) to write down the details of your journey (date, destination, class of service, number of tickets, etc.) in Japanese and present them to the JR staff. A third option is to write down the details in English, as many Japanese people who do not speak English can read it relatively well. Midori no Madoguchi offices are located in major JR stations in Tokyo (such as Shinjuku, Shibuya and Tokyo). You can also purchase tickets through travel agencies.

Airplanes

Flights are available to major cities and towns throughout the country. Flying to distant points such as Hokkaido or Kyushu is faster than taking the *shinkansen*, although the cost is usually higher. However, competition on some routes have led airline companies to offer discount prices that are cheaper than *shinkansen* tickets. Tickets can be bought through airline companies and travel agencies. Domestic flights from Tokyo depart from Haneda Airport as well as from Narita Airport.

The major airlines are Japan Airlines (JAL) and All Nippon Airways (ANA).

Long-Distance Buses

JR and other railroad companies such as Tokyu, Keio and Odakyu offer long-distance bus services. These used to be limited to night travel but some companies now offer day services. The popular Tokyo to Osaka route takes about eight hours (as opposed to three hours by *shinkansen* and one hour by plane), but the cost is about one third that of the *shinkansen*. The good news for budget-seekers is that the buses have reclining seats and the ride is quite comfortable. Several buses run to ski resorts in northern Japan and are frequently used by young people. Buses leave from major stations such as Tokyo, Shinjuku and Ikebukuro, and tickets are available at bus companies or travel agencies.

Accommodations

Various types of accommodations are available to suit different needs and budget, although the cost is generally quite high in Japan. Beware that prices are usually quoted per person and not per room and do not include tax (and sometimes service charges).

You can find Western-style hotels in major tourist destinations; many offer both Western-style and Japanese-style rooms. In Japanese-style rooms, straw mats *(tatami)* cover the floor and guests are supposed to remove their shoes when they enter. Guests sleep on the floor in Japanese-style bedding (generally consisting of a padded mattress, a down cover and a pillow) stored in the closet during the day. When making reservations, specify whether you want a Western room or a Japanese room. The price per person starts at around ¥ 10,000; the nicer hotels often cost more than ¥ 30,000. Breakfast is sometimes included in the price.

All the rooms in traditional Japanese inns, called *ryokan*, are Japanese style, and as they generally do not have restaurants, meals are served in the guest rooms. Menus feature typical Japanese food made from local produce. Guests are provided with *yukata* (simple cotton *kimono*) which most people wear as pyjamas and when walking around the hotel. You will find *ryokan* mainly located near hot springs (*onsen*). The prices are similar to that of hotels, but the total cost of a night in a *ryokan* may be less because breakfast and dinner are generally included in the price.

For budget accommodations, try Kokumin Shukusha, or government-sponsored lodgings located across the country. They are not luxurious, but are quite comfortable. The price is around ¥ 5,000 per night and usually includes breakfast. Reservations can be made through travel agencies. Youth hostels are yet another budget option. Some require membership in the International Youth Hostel Federation. You can become a member in Tokyo—contact the Tokyo Youth Hostel Federation for membership and reservations [http://www.jyh.or.jp].

You can also save money by staying at *minshuku* (boarding houses) or pensions run by private owners. Staying at a *minshuku* is like staying in the spare room of a Japanese home. Housekeeping service and sometimes meals are not provided, but prices can be as low as ¥ 3,000 per night. More upmarket than *minshuku* are pensions, which are Western-style petite hotels—many offer recreational facilities such as tennis courts, and most serve homemade breakfasts and dinners. The price (including the two meals) ranges from ¥ 5,000 to over ¥ 10,000, depending on the facilities. Both *minshuku* and pensions can be booked through travel agencies. For more specific information about *minshuku,* contact the Minshuku Network [http://www.minshuku.jp].

Travel Agencies

Travel agencies offer a variety of packages that include both transportation and accommodations. Tell the travel agent where you want to go and your hotel of choice, and ask if a package deal is available. If not, they can book transportation and accommodations separately. Travel agencies in Japan are very influential and it is often easier to book a popular hotel through an agency than to do so on your own.

JTB (Japan Travel Bureau) and Kinki Nippon Tourists are major Japanese travel agencies with experience in servicing foreigners. Both have many offices in Tokyo.

- **Japan Travel Bureau (JTB)**
  http://www.jtb.co.jp

- **Kinki Nippon Tourist**
  http://www.kintetsu.com

In addition, there is a company called HIS that is known for offering discount tickets and packages. Agents may not be fluent in English, but they are still worth a try.

The website of the Japan National Tourist Organisation (http://www.jnto.go.jp) also offers travel information and useful tips for foreign travellers. Travel agencies that serve the foreign community can be found in classified advertisements in English-language media and also in the phone directory NTT TOWNPAGE. (*Refer to* 'English-language Resources' *section of the* 'Resource Guide'.)

ONE-DAY TRIPS FROM TOKYO

In the vicinity of Tokyo are cities and towns with distinctive characteristics that make wonderful weekends getaways.

Yokohama

The city of Yokohama is located just to the west of Tokyo, less than an hour's train ride away. The JR Keihin Tohoku, JR Yokosuka and JR Tokaido Lines, as well as the Tokyu Toyoko and Keihin Kyuko Lines, all run to Yokohama from Tokyo. Many Yokohama residents commute daily to their Tokyo work places.

Yokohama's ambience and culture are very different from that in Tokyo. Facing the Pacific Ocean, Yokohama has been the country's most important port for international trade since the start of the Meiji Period (mid-19th century), when Japan opened its doors to foreigners after more than 200 years of isolation. As such, Yokohama was influenced by the West and at one time hosted a large foreign community.

Mount Fuji towers over the quiet hills of the Shizuoka Prefecture, a few hours' train trip from Tokyo.

Consequently, the city is more open to other cultures and has a cosmopolitan atmosphere.

A place you should visit is the **Yamate** area, which used to be a settlement for foreign residents—the exotic charm of days gone by still lingers. Several churches and Western-style buildings used by the foreigners still exist, as does a foreigners' cemetery in which more than 4,000 people were buried. **Motomachi** Street, the fashion street that used to serve the foreign community, still has many boutiques carrying imported goods. You will also find several European bakeries and coffee shops in this neighbourhood. Another area that contributes to the city's exotic flavour is **Chinatown**. With hundreds of shops and restaurants, this is the largest Chinatown in Japan.

The city continues to evolve. As part of an urban development project called **Minato Mirai 21** (usually translated as 'Future of the Port 21'), the city has built new office buildings, hotels, museums, a convention facility, shopping malls and an amusement park, all on reclaimed land. The project is ongoing and the city's goal is to build a multi-faceted, international city of the future for business, culture and leisure.

At the centre of the district is Landmark Tower. The tallest building in Japan, it has 70 floors and is occupied by offices, a hotel, conference halls and shopping areas. From the Sky Garden observatory on the 69th floor, you can enjoy a splendid view of Yokohama, Tokyo, Miura Peninsula, Boso Peninsula and, on a clear day, even Mount Fuji. The night view of the surrounding areas is breathtaking. Other attractions in this area are **Yokohama Cosmo World** amusement park, the **Maritime Museum**, and the **Yokohama Museum of Art**.

The port and waterfront add to the city's lively atmosphere. You can stroll along the waterfront in **Yamashita Park**, watching the sailboats and enjoying the fresh sea breeze. The view of Yokohama Port from the **Bay Bridge** observatory is spectacular. This bridge, modelled after San Francisco's Bay Bridge, is the gateway to Yokohama Port. The observatory is part of a pedestrian walkway spanning the bridge. You can enjoy a view of the Bay Bridge itself from Yamashita Park and from **Harbour View Park** in the Yamate area.

Kamakura

Kamakura is an old city that flourished as the *shogun's* capital from 1192 to 1333. (*See* 'The Feudal Period' *in Chapter 2*.) Today, 69 temples and 20 shrines built during that period remain. Kamakura is only an hour's train ride from Tokyo on the JR Yokosuka Line. Upon arrival, you may feel that you have been transported back in time; Kamakura derives its charm not only from its history but also from nature—mountains on three sides and the sea on one.

The major tourist attraction in Kamakura is the **Great Buddha**. This statue is 13 m (37 ft) tall and has been in existence for more than 500 years. The face of the statue is very calm and divine, seemingly unaffected by the centuries of human activity.

Near the Great Buddha is the **Hase Temple** housing the

11-faced wooden Kannon (Goddess of Mercy) statue. At about 9 m (30 ft) high, this is the tallest wooden statue in Japan. The temple was built in the 8th century and the statue is believed to have been carved even earlier. The temple is located on a hill and offers a sweeping view of the sea.

After visiting these sites, take a ride on the **Eno-den**, a mini-tram that leaves from Kamakura Station. It runs on a very narrow track and passengers feel as if they are riding a miniature train in an amusement park. It is, however, actively used by local people, and there are many nice coffee shops and restaurants hidden in quiet residential areas along the line.

The **Tsurugaoka Hachiman Shrine** is also popular with tourists. It was built in 1063 by Minamoto Yoritomo, the head of the Minamoto clan that governed one of Japan's earliest shogunates. The path that leads to the main building is called Wakamiya Oji, and was selected as one of the '100 best pathways' in Japan. Cherry trees line this narrow lane, making it a great place to enjoy cherry blossoms in spring. Many shops along the way sell souvenirs and local crafts. One of the most famous souvenirs from Kamakura is *Kamakurabori,* a style of woodcarving used to create items such as trays, boxes and mirror frames.

Nikko

Nikko is located to the north-west and is about a two-hour train ride from Tokyo; take Tobu Line's Limited Express that leaves from Asakusa. The city is famous for the **Toshogu Shrine,** which is the mausoleum of Tokugawa Ieyasu, who unified Japan and founded the Tokugawa Shogunate in 1603—it reigned for over 250 years. Tokugawa Ieyasu is considered one of the most important people in Japanese history. Tokugawa Iemitsu built Toshogu Shrine in 1636 to deify his grandfather.

Unlike most other shrines, which are simple in design and plain in decor, the Toshogu Shrine features a flamboyant architectural style and elaborate ornamentation. More than 15,000 craftsmen and artists were employed to create the carvings that decorate the shrine, many of which

An outdoor *onsen* (*rotenburo*) in Nasu.

are colourfully painted and gold-leafed. Among the most famous is the 'Three Monkeys' on the door of the stable. These monkeys are believed to protect the white horse, considered to be sacred, housed in the stable. One monkey has his hands covering his eyes, another has his hands on his ears, and the third has his hands over his mouth; the carving depicts the old saying, 'see no evil, hear no evil, speak no evil'.

Traditional Inns

In order to enjoy a total Japanese vacation, try staying at a *ryokan* (traditional inn) instead of a Western hotel when you visit an *onsen*. Meals featuring local ingredients will be served in your room, and both men and women wander around all day in *yukata* (simple cotton *kimono*) provided by the hotel. How more relaxing can life be?

There are about 2,800 *onsen* areas in Japan, including several (such as Hakone, Nikko, Atami, Izu and Shimoda) that are within two to three hours' journey from Tokyo. Be sure to try an *onsen* at least once during your stay in Japan.

The shrine is located in a grove of ancient Japanese cedars. The cedar-lined road continues for 37 km (about 23 miles) and today, 13,000 of the original trees, planted when the shrine was built in 1636, still stand.

Hakone

Located to the south-west of Tokyo, Hakone is a popular weekend getaway with its many attractions for people of all ages, including hiking, boating, golfing and museums. Above all, many people go to Hakone just to enjoy the clean air and relax in the hot springs.

The most popular way to get to Hakone is to take the Odakyu Express Line, also called the 'Romance Car', from Shinjuku—alight at the final station, Hakone Yumoto. You can also take the JR *kodama* bullet train from Tokyo Station and get off at Odawara, then change to the Odakyu regular line and get off at Hakone Yumoto. The whole trip takes about a one and a half hours.

From Hakone Yumoto, take the **Hakone Tozan Railway**, which climbs the hill up to Gora. The journey is about 15 km (about 9 miles) long and takes about 50 minutes. The ride through the mountains and forests is quite enjoyable—the view from the train is particularly lovely in June when the hydrangeas are in bloom and in fall, when the leaves change colours.

There are a couple of places to visit on the way to Gora. You will find several nice hotels, *ryokan* (traditional inns) and places to eat around the Tonosawa and Miyanoshita stations. If you are interested in the arts, the Hakone Open Museum, with about 700 sculptures by Rodin, Moore, Miro and other 20th century artists, is a great place to spend a few hours. In addition, the Picasso Pavilion features more than 200 of the artist's works, and the Picture Gallery has paintings by Miro, Renoir and other artists.

From Gora, the **Hakone Tozan Cable Car** will take you to the top of the mountain known as Sounzan. On the way, you can visit the **Hakone Art Museum**, which features collections of Japanese pottery and ceramics, and a beautifully landscaped Japanese garden that is especially attractive in fall when the maple leaves change colours. A little teahouse in the garden offers Japanese tea and sweets.

To get up close and personal with nature, visit **Owakudani,** (literally, 'big boiling valley'), where you can observe volcanic activities first-hand. To get there, take the **Hakone Ropeway** from Sounzan. When getting off the ropeway at Owakudani, you will notice a strong sulphur smell. Follow the short trail through the lava rocks and you will see steam erupting from deep in the ground.

If you have time, go further on the Hakone Ropeway to **Lake Ashi.** If the weather is clear when you descend the mountain on the ropeway, you may get a spectacular view of Mount Fuji. Lake Ashi was created by volcanic activity more than 2,000 years ago, and it has a circumference of approximately 19 km (about 12 miles). Cross the lake on a Hakone Sightseeing Ship, from which the view of Mount Fuji can be magnificent.

Onsen (Hot Springs)

Onsen literally means 'hot springs', which are veins of natural spring water that have been warmed by underground volcanic activity. Because Japan still has active volcanoes, thousands of hot springs are found across the country. The water of these springs contains minerals that are good for health; thus, in the past, people drank and soaked in *onsen* waters to cure diseases. Nowadays, people go to *onsen* for relaxation and recreation—there is nothing like soaking in a hot tub at the end of a day in the woods.

For Japanese people, who are accustomed to taking baths every night and love the moment when they dip themselves into hot water (especially during winter), *onsen* resorts and hotels are probably the most popular destination for domestic travel. They are favoured not only for the hot mineral water but also for their many other attractions such as golfing, hiking and skiing.

Almost all hotels in *onsen* areas offer large communal baths (separate ones for men and women) filled with hot spring water. When using the communal baths, you have to follow protocol.

Take towels, clean underwear and whatever else you need when you shower. In the common space, take off your clothes and place them and your other belongings in the baskets provided. Next, take a small towel (or washcloth) and enter the bathing room. (Japanese people, especially women, use a small towel to hide their private body parts.) Here, you will find showers and several small stools and washbowls. Sit on a stool, fill a washbowl with hot water from the nearest faucet, soak your towel in the bowl, and wash yourself with it or by splashing water from the bowl. Only then can you soak in the large tub. Although you can stay in the tub as long as you like, to avoid getting overcooked, you might want to get out after a few minutes, wash your body and/or shampoo, and then return to the tub. Most communal baths are open from very early in the morning until very late at night. Many people take several baths during the course of a day.

There are also outdoor baths at some *onsen* sites. These are usually hidden from public areas so that bathers do not need to worry about being watched by others. It is a wonderful experience to immerse in an outdoor tub under a starry sky.

EXPERIENCING JAPANESE CULTURE

Organisations catering to expatriates, such as the American Club [http://www.tokyoamericanclub.org] and the Tokyo Union Church [tel: (03) 3400-0047], host various cultural activities, many of which are open to non-members as well. In addition, many wards and municipal districts sponsor cultural events and classes for foreigners on subjects such as Japanese language, cooking and dancing.

Calendar of Public Holidays

1 January	New Year's Day
Second Monday of January	Coming of Age Day
11 February	National Foundation Day
21 March	Vernal Equinox Day
29 April	Greenery Day
3 May	Constitution Memorial Day
4 May	People's Day
5 May	Children's Day
20 July	Marine Day
Third Monday of September	Respect for the Aged Day
23 September	Autumnal Equinox Day
Second Monday of October	Health Sports Day
3 November	Culture Day
23 November	Labour Thanksgiving Day
23 December	Emperor's Birthday

If any of these dates falls on a Sunday, the following Monday will be a holiday.

Japanese Festivals and Events

1–7 January	**Hatsumode** **(First visit to shrines and temples)** People pay visits to famous shrines and temples to pray for health and happiness in the new year.
2 January	The Imperial Palace opens to the public and the Imperial Family receives greeting from visitors.

Young people in their best kimono attend
a Coming of Age Day ceremony.

3 February	**Setsubun** **(The Coming of Spring)** At shrines and temples (and at homes) people throw beans to expel demons.
14 February	**Valentine's Day** Women give chocolates to men to express love.
3 March	**Hinamatsuri** **(Doll Festival)** Families with girls wish for healthy and happy lives for their daughters by decorating miniature dolls in *kimono* costumes.
End March– Early April	**Cherry Blossom Viewing** Many events are held so people can enjoy the cherry blossoms.
5 May	**Kodomo no hi** **(Children's Day)** Families with boys wish for healthy and happy lives for their sons by hanging three carps (called *koinobori*) made out of cloth on a pole in the garden.
Mid-May	**Sanja Festival in Asakusa** One of the biggest festivals in Tokyo. People in *kimono* costumes carry *mikoshi* (portable shrines).
July–August	**Summer Festivals and Fireworks** Many festivals and events are held at neighbourhood shrines and temples to embrace the summer.
Mid-August	**Obon** **(Buddhist festival of the dead)** Spirits of the dead are believed to return to this life, so people gather with their families in their hometowns to welcome the spirits of their ancestors.
November 15	**Hichi-go-san (7-5-3)** Girls at age three and seven and boys at age five go to shrines to pray for good health. They are often dressed in *kimono*.

December 25   **Christmas**

Although Japan is not a Christian country, streets and shops are decorated for Christmas. Young people and families celebrate the holiday by exchanging gifts and having parties.

Sumo

This unique form of wrestling has been around in Japan since ancient times and is the official national sport. *Sumo* is a professional sport and wrestlers fight in tournaments held six times a year. Wrestlers are divided into several ranks; the highest is called *yokozuna*, and wrestlers are promoted based on their tournament records.

All *sumo* wrestlers are men and, by Japanese standards, extraordinarily large in both height and weight. Most wrestlers are taller than 180 cm (just under 6 ft) and easily weigh over 100 kg (about 220 lbs). Their attire and the rituals followed have not changed much since ancient times. They grow their hair long and tie it into a topknot (*mage*) and wear a belt called *mawashi* when they wrestle; in daily life, they wear *kimono*.

The rules of *sumo* are easy to understand. Wrestlers fight by slapping, pushing, or throwing; a wrestler wins if his opponent steps out of the ring or puts his hand on the floor. A match lasts only one to two minutes, and often only a few seconds!

Sumo wrestlers follow several rituals before and after fighting, and every move has a certain meaning. They repeatedly raise their legs and stamp the ring in a ritual to crush evil spirits that may exist around the floor. They also throw a handful of salt into the wrestling area to cleanse the ring and eliminate bad spirits. These various rituals add to the enjoyment of watching *sumo*.

Sumo tournaments are broadcast on television in English on Channel 1 (NHK) and NHK satellite (for television sets with a bilingual function). For a real thrill, watch a tournament live at the Kokugikan (stadium) in Tokyo where three of the six tournaments take place (the other three are held in other parts of Japan). You can purchase tickets directly at the Kokugikan ticket office, or from ticket agents such as Ticket Pia and Lawson Ticket. The most expensive seats, called *masu-seki*, are those closest to the ring. These tickets can be difficult to obtain because they are usually purchased by companies or patrons of the *sumo* wrestlers. Prices for ringside seats include food and drinks (served at the seats), as well as tournament souvenirs. Friends and colleagues in Tokyo will envy you greatly if you receive an invitation to sit near the ring during a *sumo* match.

Kabuki Theatre

Kabuki is a famous Japanese traditional theatrical performance in which both male and female roles are performed by men. The actors' names are hereditary and in order to play major roles, actors must be born into certain.families. Boys in Kabuki families are trained from a very young age by their fathers and grandfathers. The female roles have a peculiar charm and eroticism that female actresses might not be able to express. Kabuki actors study every detail of a woman's movements and may be more sensitive to some aspects of female behaviour than women themselves are.

Kabuki performances depict stories about ordinary people, members of the court and *samurai* in old Japan. The dialogue is in a form different from that currently used in daily life, and is spoken to dramatic effect. Consequently, it is sometimes difficult even for Japanese people to understand. To help the audience follow the story, theatres rent out headphones and tape players with recordings in Japanese or English summarising the plot. The colourful, elaborate costumes are also fascinating to watch.

Kabuki is mainly performed at Kabuki-za, a theatre used exclusively for Kabuki performances. The theatre is only a short walk from the Ginza area. Kabuki is also performed at the National Theatre (*Kokuritsu Gekijo*). Ticket prices vary greatly, from around ¥ 1,000–16,000, depending on seat location. Tickets can be purchased at the theatres or from ticket outlets such as Ticket Phone Shochiku, Ticket Pia and CN Playguide. For people who just want a glimpse, Kabuki-za offers tickets for one act at reasonable rates; seats are on the third floor and offer a relatively good view.

Flower Arrangement (Ikebana)

The Japanese style of flower arrangement, known as *ikebana*, was developed in the 16th century and symbolises harmony between nature and people. Because Japanese society appreciates the four seasons, flowers that best represent each season are used in the arrangements.

Currently, there are about 3,000 different schools of *ikebana*, the most famous are Ikenobo, Ohara and Sogetsu. Each school has its own arrangement style and is very particular about how stems are cut, the kind of vases used and the angle of the arrangement. Thus, in class, students are expected to follow the model arranged by the instructor rather than express their own creativity. After students master various styles created by the instructor, who is certified by an *ikebana* school, they are allowed to take that school's certification exam. Students need to pay to receive the certificate—a major source of funding for schools.

Japanese flower arrangement gives you an insight into Japanese culture, which values both patterns and forms. Japanese flower arrangement has gained popularity in the West and some *ikebana* schools have branched successfully overseas. At the same time, Western methods of flower arrangement with its fewer restrictions have become popular in Japan.

Several *ikebana* schools offer classes in English. Each class lasts approximately one to two hours and the fees are about ¥ 4,000–5,000, including the cost of materials needed. Contact the individual schools for more details: Ikenobo (http://www.ikenobo.jp); Ohara (http://www.ohararyu.or.jp); Sogetsu (http://www.sogetsu.or.jp).

Tea Ceremony (Sado)

Introduced from China around the 12th century, the Japanese version of the tea ceremony was developed in the 16th century. During a tea ceremony, known as *sado*, the host or hostess follows an elaborate, prescribed ritual of pouring hot water over tea powder, stirring it and then offering it to the guest, who then ceremoniously receives the cup, rotates it and drinks the tea. The essence of the tea ceremony is philosophical. Through the rituals, people aim to achieve inner harmony, appreciate the beauty of their surroundings and show care for others. In order to foster a relaxed inner state, talk is discouraged during the ceremony.

Teacups and other tea-making equipment, as well as flowers and pictures in the room, must be carefully selected based on the season, occasion and guest preferences. Tea ceremony hosts must master the rituals and develop an acute ability to show attentiveness to guests' needs. They must also acquire knowledge of and develop a discerning eye for many aspects of Japanese art and culture including flower arrangement, calligraphy and pottery. Guests are expected to demonstrate understanding and appreciation of the ambience created meticulously by their hosts.

There are several *sado* schools in Japan. One of the most famous, Ura-senke, has been encouraging the practice of *sado* overseas and welcomes foreigners. Information is available in English through the website (http://www.urasenke.or.jp). Other famous schools include Omote-senke and Mushanokoji-senke.

Martial Arts (Budo)

Many martial arts such as *judo*, *kendo*, *karate* and *aikido* had their origins in early Japan. Their purpose is not to defeat opponents, but to develop self-discipline that will contribute to mental and physical strength. All forms of martial arts stress highly on following decorum and showing respect for opponents.

Judo, a type of wrestling, is now famous worldwide and an Olympic sport. Judo players are ranked on ten levels (*dan*) according to their strength; the highest level is ten *dan* and the lowest one *dan*. Kodokan Judo Hall is the headquarters of the All-Japan Judo Federation. Here enthusiasts can receive instruction and watch others practise.

Kendo is a form of Japanese fencing using bamboo swords. It was originally a form of training in swordsmanship for *samurai* (warriors). Nowadays, it is practised by many schoolboys (and an increasing number of schoolgirls) to enhance their mental and physical strength. Visit the website of the Japan Kendo Foundation (http://www.kendo.or.jp).

Karate, a form of unarmed self-defence, originated in Okinawa (the southernmost island of Japan); it was developed after Okinawan people were not allowed to bear weapons. Masters of *karate* can break a stone block with only their bare hands. It is now an international sport. The Japan Karate Association (http://www.jka.or.jp) offers classes.

Aikido was developed in the early 20th century and combines the principles of *judo*, *kendo* and *karate*. In *aikido*, *ki* (usually translated as 'spirit' or 'energy') plays an important role; players use *ki* rather than strength to throw opponents. The headquarters of the International Aikido Federation is Aikikai (http://www.aikikai.or.jp).

Check the English-language phone directory NTT TOWNPAGE for information on private martial arts classes (some of which are taught in English).

Karaoke

Karaoke (literally 'empty orchestra') began in Japan and has recently become popular in other countries. Groups of friends or colleagues often go to *karaoke* spots after dinner. The experience encourages interaction in a casual atmosphere and allows individuals to express their hidden talents. People are often surprised to find a quiet colleague transformed into a great singer!

There are two types of *karaoke* clubs: *karaoke* boxes and *karaoke* bars. The former type are private rooms with *karaoke* equipment that can be reserved by a group of people, and allow friends and colleagues to choose and sing their own songs. *Karaoke* bars are regular bars that have a small stage in each and *karaoke* equipment; guests go up on the stage to sing. Some smaller *karaoke* bars often have no stages at all; customers simply pass the microphone around the room and sing from their seats. *Karaoke* boxes are generally more popular, because the prices are reasonable and people are not bothered by poor singers from other groups!

If Japanese colleagues or friends invite you to join them for *karaoke*, try your best to participate even if you cannot sing well. This will make others treat you as 'part of the group'. Many *karaoke* boxes and *karaoke* bars in Tokyo feature Western as well as Japanese songs.

LEARNING THE LANGUAGE

CHAPTER 8

'Lost in Translation'
—The title of an award-winning
movie directed by Sofia Coppola

The language barrier is the challenge most frequently mentioned by foreigners living in Tokyo. It is highly recommended that you study the Japanese language while you are in Tokyo, or ideally, before you go. Your daily life will be made much easier if you are able to say even a few phrases in Japanese, and the more you learn, the more you will improve the quality of your experience. Even if you are not fluent in Japanese, people will appreciate your effort and are more likely to open up to you.

OVERVIEW OF THE JAPANESE LANGUAGE

The exact origin of the Japanese language is not known. Some scholars claim it is similar to other languages in the Altaic language family (which includes Turkish, Mongolian and Korean); other scholars observe similarities with Polynesian languages. Japanese people developed a writing system based on the Chinese written language, but the two languages are completely different in terms of grammar and pronunciation, and are not mutually intelligible.

The Japanese language used in the media and taught in schools (including language schools) is called *hyojungo* (standard language). In addition, a large number of dialects are spoken throughout the country. In these dialects, some words are pronounced in unique ways and/or some vocabulary is different. The dialect spoken in Tokyo is very similar to the standard language. People from other parts of

Japan think that people in Tokyo speak very fast and some people feel that the Tokyo dialect sounds cold.

Pronunciation

All Japanese syllables end either in vowels or a nasal **n**. There are five vowels:

- **a**   as in *father*
- **i**   as in *machine*
- **u**   as in *dude*
- **e**   as in *end*
- **o**   as in *over*

If two vowels appear together, they should be pronounced separately (such as the **a-i** in 'naïve'). Because vowel sounds are prominent in the Japanese language, Japanese people tend to add vowels to the ends of syllables and words when they speak in other languages. For instance, they tend to pronounce the English word *house* as **how-su** and the word *stop* as **su-top-pu**.

There are 14 consonants, most of which are pronounced approximately as they are in English. However, the Japanese language does not distinguish between **r** and **l** and there is no **th** or **v**; thus, it is difficult for Japanese people to pronounce these sounds when speaking in English or other languages containing these sounds.

Writing Systems

The Japanese writing system consists of four different sets of symbols: *kanji, hiragana, romaji* and *katakana*. Japanese people use a mixture of these symbols when writing.

Kanji is the set of Chinese characters imported into Japan about 1,500 years ago. Chinese characters originated as pictographs and each character has a meaning. In the Japanese language, the same character can be pronounced differently depending on its usage (for example, whether the character is used independently or in combination with other characters). The Japanese government has identified about 2,000 *kanji* that are used in daily communication. Even Japanese people have difficulty memorising their meaning, writing and pronunciation. The widespread use of computers and word processors now allows people to choose the character they want from a list of homonyms, so less time and energy is spent memorising how to write the characters.

Hiragana is a simplified symbol system created from Chinese characters about 1,000 years ago. There are 51 *hiragana* symbols—they represent sounds, but do not have any meaning. *Hiragana* is often used after *kanji* to form verb endings and is also used for particles. ('Particles' are used to indicate the function of words in sentences.) While entire sentences can be written in *hiragana*, Japanese people find them cumbersome to read, sometimes ambiguous in meaning and too simplistic.

Basic Japanese Writings
Hiragana

a	i	u	e	o
あ	い	う	え	お
ka	ki	ku	ke	ko
か	き	く	け	こ
sa	shi	su	se	so
さ	し	す	せ	そ
ta	chi	tsu	te	to
た	ち	っ	て	と
na	ni	nu	ne	no
な	に	ぬ	ね	の
ha	hi	fu	he	ho
は	ひ	ふ	へ	ほ
ma	mi	mu	me	mo
ま	み	む	め	も
ya	(i)	yu	(e)	yo
や	(い)	ゆ	(え)	よ
la	li	lu	le	lo
ら	り	る	れ	ろ
wa	(i)	(u)	(e)	wo
わ	(い)	(う)	(え)	を
n				
ん				

Katakana is the third writing system. It contains 51 symbols just as *hiragana* does and represents the same sounds, but the symbols look different. *Katakana* is used to express words or concepts imported from other languages. For example, when computers were introduced into Japan, there was no Japanese word for 'computer', so *katakana* symbols were used to simulate the English pronunciation of 'computer'.

Katakana				
a	i	u	e	o
ア	イ	ウ	エ	オ
ka	ki	ku	ke	ko
カ	キ	ク	ケ	コ
sa	shi	su	se	so
サ	シ	ス	セ	ソ
ta	chi	tsu	te	to
タ	チ	ツ	テ	ト
na	ni	nu	ne	no
ナ	ニ	ヌ	ネ	ノ
ha	hi	fu	he	ho
ハ	ヒ	フ	ヘ	ホ
ma	mi	mu	me	mo
マ	ミ	ム	メ	モ
ya	(i)	yu	(e)	yo
ヤ	(イ)	ユ	(エ)	ヨ
la	li	lu	le	lo
ラ	リ	ル	レ	ロ
wa	(i)	(u)	(e)	wo
ワ	(イ)	(ウ)	(エ)	ヲ
n				
ン				

Romaji, the fourth writing system, uses Roman letters to spell Japanese words. In Tokyo, most train stations' names are displayed in *romaji* in addition to Japanese symbols. Many Japanese language textbooks are written in *romaji* so that foreigners can study the spoken language without having to learn the writing system.

In the past, Japanese script was usually written vertically and from right to left, but because of increased exposure to Western languages (especially English), more people today write Japanese horizontally and from left to right. Most Japanese books are still written vertically, however, and open from the right.

Grammar

In the Japanese language, verbs normally come at the end of a sentence, and the indication of positive or negative also comes at the end. In other words, people must listen carefully until the end of the sentence for what is sometimes the most important part of the message. Verbs are not conjugated based on the gender or the number of subjects.

The subject of a sentence is often omitted in Japanese. People guess what the subject is based on the context, such as the subject of the previous sentence, the nature of the topic or the choice of words. In particular, they will often omit 'I' or 'me', so one must infer from the context that the subject refers to themselves—this frequently becomes a source of confusion to many foreigners.

Japanese people change the way they speak depending on whom they are speaking with. First, there are several levels of formality and informality that can be expressed by the choice of verbs and their conjugations. For example, *arigato gozaimasu* (thank you) is more formal than *arigato* (which also means 'thank you'). Japanese people use more formal forms when speaking to people they are not well-acquainted with, when they do business or when they talk to older people. As individuals get to know each other better, they often change to more informal forms, although they will continue using formal forms when speaking with older people.

To reduce confusion for foreigners learning the Japanese language, Japanese language textbooks are usually written in the formal form. As a result, foreigners who studied Japanese abroad may find that the Japanese they speak is too formal for daily life in Japan, especially when dealing with people similar in age to themselves. Not that this should hold you back from studying Japanese prior to your arrival, as you will quickly learn the more informal forms through daily interactions with Japanese people.

In addition to the distinction between formal and informal forms of Japanese language, there is a distinction between honorific forms and humble forms. In conversation, people use the honorific form to refer to others and the humble form to refer to themselves when they want to show respect to their counterparts. The honorific form is used to 'elevate' the other person and the humble form is used to 'lower' the speaker. People generally use these forms when speaking with clients, with someone senior to them in either age or rank, or with people they do not know well. Both forms are expressed by different patterns. For example, the word 'to come' can be expressed in three different ways: *kuru* (neutral formal form); *irrassharu* (honorific form); and *mairu* (humble form).

Finally, there is a distinction between some word choices made by males and females. For example, when people refer to themselves (that is, when they say 'I'), both males and females use either *watashi* or *watakushi,* but only males may say *boku* or *ore* in casual conversations. In addition, males and females often use different word endings, especially in informal settings. For example, to say "This is good, isn't it?", a man might say "*Kore ii daro?*" and a woman may say "*Kore ii desho?*". In general, females tend to use more polite language than males do, although gender differences in language are less obvious among younger people.

Learning Difficulty for Foreigners

One of the greatest challenges foreigners experience when they study Japanese is that the vocabulary and grammatical forms vary according to the level of politeness required in each situation. Foreigners are usually taught one polite form that can be used in many situations, but they may find that the forms used by their Japanese friends, their Japanese boss, and Japanese service people (bank tellers, for example) are different. Japanese choose the appropriate form based on personal relationships and relative status. Even Japanese people these days have problems mastering the appropriate usage of different forms.

Another challenge is learning how to write the language in *Hiragana, Katakana*, and *Kanji*. Learning *Hiragana* and *Katakana* is not very difficult because they each consist of 51 symbols. Studying *Kanji* (Chinese characters) can be very time-consuming, however, and requires a lot of effort; there is no systematic way to remember these characters. As the Japanese language is written using all three systems, you will not be able to read even simple document unless you understand some *Kanji* characters.

The good news is that the long-term reward of being able to communicate in and read some Japanese is significant. You do not have to be fluent, but even just making the effort to study the language counts in making a good impression and in building relationships with Japanese people.

Japanese English

Japanese people have adopted and sometimes modified the pronunciation of many English words, using them in daily conversations when speaking in Japanese. They also try to use these words when they speak in English, but these words can sometimes cause misunderstandings when pronounced differently or used with a slightly different meaning. Here are some examples:

- ***terebi—television***
  (The original word has been shortened; the sound **b** replaces **v**, which does not exist in Japanese.)
- ***G-pan—jeans***
  ('Jeans pants' is abbreviated, with '**G**' standing for 'jeans'.)
- ***OL—female support staff***
  ('OL' stands for 'Office Lady', which is not widely used among native English speakers.)
- ***kura—air conditioner***
  (cooler)
- **manshon—apartment or condominium**
  (mansion)

UNDERSTANDING NON-VERBAL CUES

Non-verbal cues can provide much information about the meaning of messages, but as these cues and their meanings vary from culture to culture, they can be easily misinterpreted. Here are some gestures that may be observed in Japan and which may be different from those used in other cultures:

- The Japanese rarely maintain direct eye contact. As a matter of fact, looking into another person's eyes can be perceived as being challenging or threatening; instead, Japanese people may look in the direction of the other person's forehead or throat. People try especially not to sustain eye contact with those senior to them (either in age or rank).

- A smile can have several different meanings in Japan. In addition to express happiness, people may smile when they do not understand what is said, when they are embarrassed, and/or when they do not agree with you.

- When beckoning someone to approach, Japanese people will usually extend their hands with the palm down and move the fingers back and forth toward the palm, while the same gesture performed with the palm up is used when beckoning to somebody very junior to them, or a dog.

- A hand waved in front of the face indicates 'No'. For example, if you ask a Japanese woman something in English and she does not understand you, she may wave her hand to signal that she does not understand English.

- During conversations, Japanese people nod frequently to indicate that they are listening. Note that a nod does not necessarily mean that the listener agrees with the speaker.

- Japanese women generally cover their mouths with one hand when they laugh.

DOING BUSINESS IN JAPAN

CHAPTER 9

'In every culture in the world such phenomena
as authority, bureaucracy, creativity, good fellowship,
verification and accountability are
experienced in different ways.'
—Fons Trompenaars and Charles Hampden-Turner,
international business consultants

FOREIGNERS WORKING IN TOKYO will be in a business environment that has, in some respects, seen dramatic changes over the past few decades. In the 1980s, the country experienced a 'bubble' in its economy; in the 1990s, it suffered a significant downturn. Many companies were forced to restructure to cut costs, drastically altering their business strategies. Many were also forced to modify certain traditional business practices that were impeding their ability to keep up with their competitors in global business. While these factors have changed some aspects of how business is done in Japan, much remains the same.

To assist you in navigating the Japanese workplace, this chapter discusses issues that will affect foreigners working in Tokyo, including etiquette, business style and challenges.

BUSINESS ETIQUETTE

While working in Tokyo, you might encounter several features of protocol and business practices unique to Japan. In Tokyo, business etiquette is generally formal, especially in government circles and conservative industries such as banking and manufacturing.

What to Wear

In most workplaces in Tokyo, business people normally wear business suits. Men working in government agencies and in the financial and manufacturing industries tend to wear conservative suits in navy blue, grey or dark brown, with white, beige or light blue shirts. Those working in fashion-related or mass communication industries may wear more trendy and colourful shirts and suits. In some high-tech companies or subsidiaries of foreign companies, casual wear is gradually being introduced. Many companies have also introduced 'casual Friday', a day when employees are allowed to dress less formally; the definition of 'casual' varies, but most companies do not allow male employees to wear shorts or sandals.

Similar customs apply to the business attire worn by women, although a greater variety of colours is acceptable. Career women usually wear suits or jackets with skirts (pantsuits are acceptable but less common.) They usually avoid large jewellery, excessive make-up and strong or flashy colours such as bright yellow or hot pink. In many Japanese companies, female workers who are not on a career track wear uniforms provided by the employer. On casual days, women may wear T-shirts, pants or dresses; shorts and tank tops are usually not allowed. In general, Japanese women dress rather formally.

Greetings

Japanese people customarily bow when they meet. (Some Japanese businesspeople may also offer to shake hands with Westerners, knowing that this is their custom.) As the depth of the bow indicates the level of respect one desires to show, people try to bow more deeply than their counterparts if those counterparts are customers, senior in rank to them or are otherwise important people. A formal bow is made by putting the hands at the sides of the thighs with the fingers straight, and bowing deeply with the eyes facing the floor.

When two people meet for the first time, they generally bow and then exchange business cards (*meishi*). This is an essential part of greeting others in Japanese business settings. It is recommended that you have your business cards printed in both Japanese and your native language, as this will help your Japanese counterparts pronounce your name and your company's name (if it is a foreign firm), and also indicates your strong willingness to do business in Japan.

Business cards are considered to be representations of their owners, should be handled properly and with respect. When offering your card, hold it with both hands, the lettering on the card facing the recipient so that they can easily read your name, and introduce yourself by saying your name clearly.

When someone offers you a business card, receive it with both hands and glance at it for a moment to read the information. You can even say your counterpart's name aloud to make sure you are pronouncing it correctly. (It is not impolite to ask for the pronunciation if you are uncertain.) Put the cards you receive into a business card holder; do not put them into your pocket. (In particular, do not put them into the back pocket of your trousers, as it would be disrespectful to sit on the cards.) If you receive cards prior to a meeting, you can lay them on the table before you in the order in which their owners are sitting. Do note that it is generally considered rude to write on another person's name card.

Japanese businesspeople generally use their family (last) name in business settings, and when addressing others they usually add the suffix '-san'. Follow this custom unless Japanese counterparts invite you to call them by their given (first) names; even then, address them by family name plus '-san' when in groups and formal settings. Knowing that many Westerners use given names in business, Japanese people often address Western counterparts by their given names plus '-san'. Sometimes people add the title of a person instead of '-san'; for example, a person with the family name Sasaki who is the president (*shacho*) of a company would be addressed as Sasaki-*shacho*, or President Sasaki.

Gift-giving
Gift-giving was once a popular way of building interpersonal relationships with colleagues and customers, but because of budget constraints in recent years, lesser people opt for this practice.

One interesting gift-giving custom unique to the Japanese workplace is that women workers give male colleagues chocolates on Valentine's Day (14 February), which traditionally in Japan, is the day when a woman confesses her love through gifts of chocolates. This custom has been so vigorously promoted by chocolate companies and the media that women feel pressured to follow the custom, even if they do not actually 'love' any of their male co-workers.

Usually all the women in a work group will pitch in and buy *giri-choko* (obligatory chocolates) for their male colleagues. This custom has become so popular that a significant portion of annual chocolate sales takes place around Valentine's Day! More recently, a new marketing opportunity, what's come to be known as 'White Day' (March 14), has been vigorously promoted. 'White Day' sees men giving 'return' gifts (there's that reciprocity again!) to the women who gave them *giri-choko*, and of course, to their sweetheart(s) as well. (*See* 'Gift-giving' *in Chapter 4.*)

Seating Arrangements

Japanese people pay careful attention to seating arrangements. People are usually seated according to their rank in the hierarchy. In general, seats of honour—which are those furthest from the door—go to senior persons and guests. A business person visiting a client's office for a meeting, for example, might be led to a conference room and invited to sit farthest from the door. At a round table or when seating arrangements are unclear, guests wait for senior members of the hosting group to show them where to sit.

When business counterparts are invited out for meals, the host will formally invite the principal guest to sit in the seat of honour (middle of the table, farthest from the door). To show modesty and respect for the host, the guest may then decline at least once, claiming to be undeserving of the honour. The host will persist however, and eventually the guest will acquiesce. Senior members of each group usually sit across from each other.

Entertainment

Entertaining for business purposes has long been popular in Japan. With success in business based largely on interpersonal relationships, companies have spent large amounts of money on entertainment to maintain such relationships.

Nowadays, many companies have taken cost-cutting measures, significantly reducing their entertainment budgets. As a result, businesspeople do not entertain clients as extravagantly, and as often, as they once did; They treat them to lunch instead of dinner, or forego after-dinner drinks.

Business dinners are still a common venue for relationship building, however, and if you work in Japan, you will surely be expected to participate. (*For hosting business dinners, refer to* 'Business Entertainment' *in Chapter 6.*)

Nightclubs are popular venues for after-dinner entertainment. In these nightclubs, hostesses sit next to customers to serve drinks and to chat with them. Although most nightclub customers are men, hostesses usually welcome the opportunity to serve women customers. Foreigners who realise that their business counterparts are planning to take them to a hostess club but who feel uncomfortable going, can turn down the offer by saying they are tired; an indirect communication style that is more tactful than saying you do not want to join in. (*See* 'Japanese Communication Styles' *in Chapter 4.*)

Golfing is the most popular sport among Japanese businesspeople, and knowing how to golf has long been an essential component of conducting business. Because many golf courses are far from Tokyo, when people invite business associates for a day of golfing, they often arrange transportation in advance or personally drive their associates to the course.

THE JAPANESE WORK FORCE
Hiring Practices, Job Security and Promotion

In general, Japanese companies prefer to hire inexperienced staff (typically fresh university graduates) with good potential and then train them, rather than to hire people with work experience. The assumption is that people who have established their careers elsewhere would not blend well into a new corporate culture.

The hiring of university graduates takes place once a year and all new staff start work on the same date, 1 April. Recruitment of candidates takes place more than a year before the actual date of hire. Students find information about job openings through university bulletin boards, job fairs and alumni networks. Qualifications looked for are: a degree from a good university (students from the top public universities are the first choice of most employers) good grades and suitable personal characteristics (for example, team-orientated, diligent and sincere).

These days many companies cannot afford the time and expense of developing a young workforce, so some experienced and skilled staff are employed in addition to university graduates. Some companies have also realised the benefits of recruiting executives who can compete effectively in the global business arena, and who can drastically change the way the companies operate; thus they are turning increasingly to foreign executive search firms for assistance in locating such talent.

Foreign companies in Japan have traditionally hired more mid-career workers than have Japanese companies because training inexperienced workers was not cost-effective, and because Japanese companies offered more stability. Younger Japanese are now attracted to foreign companies because salaries and advancement opportunities are generally better there.

Many Japanese companies used to guarantee lifetime employment, so workers were reluctant to change jobs. Those who did so were regarded as lacking in patience or as troublemakers. Now, few companies offer job security, so some people choose to change companies to advance their careers, while others have been forced to do so as a result of restructuring and downsizing. As a result, employers are becoming less prejudiced toward those who change jobs. Nevertheless, the percentage of people who change jobs in mid-career is still lower than in the United States and some European nations, and Japanese people still try to stay as long as possible in the company they joined immediately after university.

In the past, a strong sense of loyalty to their employers and colleagues meant workers were hesitant to take vacations or leave on time at the end of the official workday. Given the decline in job security and greater emphasis on life outside of work, younger employees are less hesitant about enjoying time for themselves.

To cut costs, many companies are hiring part-time employees for administrative, data entry or simple manufacturing jobs. Most part-timers are women; many of whom are married and are trying to earn additional income for their families or themselves. The number of men applying for part-time jobs is increasing, however. While some men choose this route because they cannot find full-time work, many young men do so because they prefer the flexible lifestyle that part-time jobs offer.

In an attempt to boost productivity, the practice of promotion based on performance has been introduced in a number of Japanese companies, but some observers think that it will not be effective in Japan—the strong emphasis on teamwork makes evaluating individual performance difficult. Young talent may be promoted to managerial levels if they are exceptionally competent, but in most cases, age and seniority still take precedence.

The Employment of Women

Many Japanese organisations are still male-dominated. The percentage of women at managerial level in Japan is less than 10 per cent. After the economic downturn, finding a job has become especially difficult for women—companies have reduced the number of new staff, and when they do hire, they prefer males.

Large Japanese companies usually offer college-graduate female applicants two different tracks: career track (*sogo-shoku*) and administrative track (*ippan-shoku*). Those who choose the former can potentially be promoted to management level in exchange for working long hours and accepting transfers to other locations. Those who choose the administrative track will be engaged in support jobs and are rarely offered transfers. There is the unspoken expectation that women in administrative jobs will get married and leave the company after four or five years of work.

Some talented women find that certain foreign firms offer more opportunities for meaningful work and advancement than Japanese companies, because these companies, modelling the cultures of their home countries, encourage equal treatment of women and men.

Many women who do not actively pursue careers or who prefer to have flexible schedules work as independent contractors. They register with human resource agencies that have contracts with mid- and large-sized companies, and are then sent to work at these companies when there is a demand. The agencies take a certain percentage out of the contract fees as commission.

The Business Environment for Women

The business environment is especially difficult for women with children, regardless of their work status. In general, employees are expected to spend long hours at the office and socialise with co-workers afterwards. It is difficult for working mothers to do so, as their working husbands face the same pressures, and because the number of child-care facilities, though growing, is still inadequate. As a result, women lose precious opportunities to gather inside information and build rapport with co-workers, both of which are keys to success in Japanese organisations.

JAPANESE BUSINESS STYLES

One outcome of Japan's economic success in the 1980s was intense international interest in Japanese business style and practices. Now that the Japanese economic bubble has burst, it is Japan's turn to analyse its business practices to determine its shortcomings. This has resulted in a gradual modification of the country's business culture, although many traditional practices, especially those that reflect wider cultural values and beliefs, remain in place.

Following are corporate characteristics found mostly in large, older Japanese firms. Young companies and subsidiaries of foreign firms are more similar to those found in the West, but with a Japanese flavour.

Hierarchy

Within most Japanese organisations, hierarchy is highly respected. Employees are expected to defer to the authority of people who are senior to themselves (in title or age). When a decision is needed, for example, a proposal has to be brought up through the chain of command, even if the work of some people in the chain is not directly related to the proposal.

Rank and File

During a meeting, senior members of the company are sometimes invited just as a sign of respect for their rank, even if they do not have expertise in the areas of discussion. Also, subordinates will never confront their manager in front of customers or in internal meetings; they are unlikely to correct their superior's mistakes in front of others.

A typical Japanese company has several tiers of hierarchy, with only subtle differences between each level. Because most people have stayed with the same company for a long time, they know to which positions they will be promoted and at what age. Generally, most employees in an organisation with similar qualifications advance to the same level at the same pace, with a few rising more rapidly and higher than others. Young employees, however, are generally not promoted beyond the level of older employees, because seniority is highly valued.

The layers in the hierarchy are so thin that there are no major differences between them in terms of responsibility or salary. It is interesting to note that although hierarchy is respected in Japan, the actual salary difference between a junior rank employee and a top manager tends to be far smaller than in other countries.

Manager-Subordinate Relationships

A good manager in a Japanese organisation is someone who takes care of subordinates and who acts as a professional and personal mentor to them. A manager is also, of course, expected to have technical expertise, but that is not always a priority—they are, more often than not, expected to be generalists than specialists. The manager's job is to use effectively their subordinates' talent and knowledge and to increase the group's morale so that performance increases.

Employees in Japan are rotated among several departments for the first couple of years to learn how the entire company operates. An engineer may spend a few years in Human Resources, and a salesperson may learn accounting before finally being assigned to Sales and Marketing—even then employees may still be transferred to another department

Workplace Do's and Don'ts

Do's

- Study the Japanese language so you can begin to bridge the language barrier.
- Speak slowly and clearly when you speak to someone in English.
- Socialise with your Japanese colleagues and clients outside of the office to get to know them personally.
- Do your homework before meeting clients. (Learn about their backgrounds and their past relationships with your company.)
- Be aware of the hierarchy that exists among Japanese colleagues and clients.
- Bring a group gift to the office when you return from trips. (*Refer to* 'Gift-giving' *in Chapter 4.*)

Don'ts

- Assume that all the Japanese staff working for the Tokyo subsidiaries of foreign firms are fluent in English.

if there is an opening. Employees in the management track are rotated among key positions more frequently than those in the engineering track. As a result, employees who have worked in the same group for a long time may have gained more technical expertise than their manager.

Good manager-subordinate relationships often resemble family relationships in that the manager's role is similar to that of a parent or older sibling. In addition to assigning tasks, a manager ensures that the emotional and psychological needs of subordinates are met. When a subordinate appears to have a problem, it is the manager's responsibility to recognise and take care of it, even if it is personal in nature (such as a family matter or a conflict with a loved one). Thus, a manager must develop interpersonal relationships with subordinates, taking them out for drinks or dinner; that

- Assume that if Japanese colleagues do not say anything, there is no problem. Be aware of their indirect communication style. (*Refer to* 'Japanese Communication Style' *in Chapter 4.*)
- Forget to take your business cards when you plan to visit someone outside of your company.
- Take just any seat in meeting rooms or restaurants. Recognise and respect seating arrangements. (*Refer to* 'Seating Arrangements' *in this chapter.*)
- Mention at the office any topics that are discussed during out-of-office socialisation; out-of-office discussions are usually expected to be off-the-record.
- Expect to be invited to the homes of your Japanese colleagues and clients as it is not customary for Japanese to invite business counterparts to their homes.

is, spend time with them outside the office. Business may or may not be discussed on such occasions. The goal is to create trusting relationships so that when problems arise, subordinates feel comfortable approaching their manager.

Good subordinates support their managers by making them 'look good' and by keeping them informed about every aspect of work. In private, the communication between a manager and a subordinate with a close relationship can be very direct and open. However, when they are in public, such as in front of a client, a good subordinate is expected to show the manager respect.

Customer Relations

'Customers are gods' is a phrase that describes aptly the expectation of how customers should be treated in Japan. Customer satisfaction is not just a priority; rather, it is the premise on which most businesses are based. Product and service consumers may express their opinions directly and exhibit a superior attitude when interacting with merchants and suppliers, who are expected to meet the buyers' needs, even when those seem unreasonable (for example, changing product specifications on short notice, or lowering the price after a contract is signed). Salespeople must develop good relationships with clients by regularly taking them out for entertainment such as golf or dinner. When transferred, salespeople usually introduce their replacements to their customers personally in order to foster the continuance of smooth relations.

Because of this personal emphasis in business, personal referrals are critical when pursuing new customers. Even when products are of high quality and good value, many Japanese buyers hesitate to work with unfamiliar suppliers. Introductions from other organisations, such as banks, or from influential people with existing bonds to the potential customer, can help establish these relationships. Some foreign companies have difficulty entering the Japanese market because they do not have strong networks in place. Many successful foreign firms in Japan partner with local companies to gain access to customers via existing networks.

Many foreigners are impressed by the quality of Japanese goods and services, and the goal of Japanese salespeople is to meet their customers' needs. Rather than using 'hard selling', they work hard to learn the customer's preferences so that they can offer exactly (or sometimes more than) what the customer wants. Although retail customers seldom bargain in shops, salespeople sometimes offer discounts and other *sabisu* ('service', or related items and services included free of charge) to frequent customers or those who buy in bulk. For example, *afuta sabisu* (after-sales service) in the form of free maintenance check-ups or repairs are common. Salespeople use very formal language with customers and apologise profusely if they have made even a minor mistake.

Decision-making

One prominent characteristic of the Japanese internal corporate business style is the decision-making process. Japanese organisations are very consensus oriented. Decision-makers must seek input and acceptance from all those who will be affected by the decision to ensure implementation. It is rare for a single person to have decision-making authority, except in a one-person company.

Many Japanese companies employ a document system called *ringi-seido* to make a decision. When people at the operational level come up with a new idea, they prepare a *ringi-sho* (written proposal requiring a decision). To compose the document, they hold a series of informal meetings or conversations to gain input and endorsement from colleagues of the same level. The proposal is then sent to people one level higher to request their input and endorsement. Those who agree, stamp their seals on the proposal so that others can see who has already agreed to it. If any modifications are suggested, the proposal is sent back to the lower level. Once the modified proposal is endorsed by all members on the first two levels, it is sent to the next highest level for review. The same process takes place and continues until the seals of all people, including top management, have been added.

As mentioned previously, in order to garner the approval of others, the composers of a proposal often conduct a series of informal meetings with key people. This process of influencing opinions is called *nemawashi,* which literally means 'to dig around the roots' (of a tree before transplanting); that is, for a transplanted tree to grow, thorough preparation is necessary. In the decision-making process, this means that for proposals to be endorsed, key people must be adequately informed and persuaded. Originators of proposals use socialising, 'confidential' private conversations and small, informal meetings as forums for encouraging colleagues to exchange information, express ideas and air disagreements. By the time a proposal gets to the top level of an organisation, everybody has been informed about it and has agreed to go along with it, so last-minute conflict or changes are unlikely to occur.

A large formal meeting is usually held at the end of the decision-making process to announce the proposal, ensure comprehension and confirm endorsement. Again, by this time, everyone who is affected by the proposal has been fully informed and consensus has been reached, so no surprises or disagreement will be expressed during the meeting.

The benefits of going through this elaborate process are that potential mistakes are avoided and implementation of the decision will be smooth. On the other hand, this formal process is time-consuming and with so many people involved, it is unlikely any one person will take responsibility for identifying and remedying any problems that may arise down the line.

Working Hours

The official working hours for most offices in Tokyo are from 9:00 am to 5:00 pm, but many people stay at work until 10:00 pm or 11:00 pm. There are several explanations to why people work such long hours.

Firstly, as 'customers are gods', employees are expected to deliver products or services of exemplary quality to ensure customer satisfaction; these expectations create extra work for the detail-oriented Japanese worker.

Secondly, the typical Japanese decision-making process involves a lot of people and much information, time and data are required to build consensus. People stay late to handle all the groundwork and paperwork before and after decisions are made.

Thirdly, in Japanese organisations, performance evaluations are based on teamwork and attitudes toward work as well as on results produced, so working late is one way for employees to show their commitment. Thus even those who accomplish their tasks in fewer hours may be evaluated negatively if they leave while others are still toiling. In addition, people are expected to help others, so if they leave the office after meeting their individual responsibilities when others are still working, they can be perceived as not being team players. In addition, because of adherence to hierarchy, younger people feel they should not leave the office until their manager and other senior people have left.

Given these long working hours, *karoshi* (death from overwork) has become a serious problem in Japanese society. If it is determined that an employee died from the stress and fatigue of working too hard, a company can be held responsible for the employee's death, and be made to provide his or her family monetary compensation; compensation, however, is rarely paid as it is usually difficult to determine *karoshi* with legal certainty.

Japanese people often arrive home late because they spend a lot of time socialising with colleagues after work, in order to develop essential personal relationships with colleagues and managers. Socialising provides employees with the opportunity to complain openly to their managers about work and to share inside information about certain issues. As neither of these things is likely to occur at the office, socialising plays an important role in building good working relationships and in allowing employees to air potentially explosive or sensitive issues.

CHALLENGES FOR FOREIGNERS

Expatriates working in Tokyo report challenges due to cultural differences in language, communication styles, working hours, decision-making styles and gender issues.

The Language Gap

The most frequently-mentioned challenge for expatriates working in Japan is language.

Expatriates who work for the Tokyo subsidiaries of foreign firms may assume that English is commonly used for written and verbal communication, and that they will have few problems communicating with Japanese colleagues. However, this is an erroneous assumption. In most subsidiaries, a mixture of Japanese and English is used, and while a few employees can speak English fluently, especially those who have lived or have obtained degrees abroad, most will not feel comfortable speaking English, and some have very weak command of the language.

Furthermore, English-speaking expatriates who interact with employees of Japanese companies will find that the number of Japanese staff fluent in English to be very limited. If you have a chance to visit Tokyo before beginning your assignment, talk to some of your potential colleagues so that you will start work with realistic expectations regarding this issue.

Studying Japanese prior to your move and continuing to do so in Tokyo will help bridge the language barrier. Your knowledge of the Japanese language, as well as the effort made to communicate, will be much appreciated by Japanese colleagues and can create a good impression. Speaking a second language often requires a lot of effort and is stressful for some people; but by doing so, you can sympathise with your Japanese colleagues who are struggling to improve their command of English.

Differences in Communication Style

Misunderstandings are not solely caused by differences in language, but also by differences in communication style. Expatriates who have worked with Japanese people often feel that they do not receive enough information from Japanese colleagues about a variety of work-related topics such as personnel issues, decision-making, and ongoing projects.

As Japan is a group-oriented culture, its people place priority on maintaining harmony within groups and therefore often employ an indirect communication style. (*Refer to* 'Japanese Communication Styles' *in Chapter 4.*)

For example, Japanese people think twice before voicing their opinions (especially negative ones), and sometimes convey messages through a third person. Other approaches employed to maintain group harmony are using hints and suggestions, and avoiding direct confrontation.

As Japanese people usually convey negative feedback or suggestions subtly, foreign workers sometimes do not take their Japanese counterparts' comments seriously, and sometimes do not even notice that a message has been communicated. On the other hand, Japanese workers are not used to being confronted directly and may feel offended or threatened by such encounters.

Expatriate managers sometimes fail to recognise the capabilities of Japanese employees because, in general, Japanese workers tend to downplay their abilities and performance in front of others, in order not to stand out from the group. They expect managers to recognise their abilities and effort, and to promote them accordingly. In addition, Japanese workers who do not feel comfortable speaking in English may not mention their achievements at all. It is thus likely for an expatriate manager to overlook an employee's contributions or neglect to use the employee's talents.

Even positive feedback is communicated indirectly in order to maintain harmony among group members. Praising an individual worker openly may make that person stand out from the group, and make both the individual and group members feel uncomfortable. Thus, in Japan, managers generally reward and praise the entire group instead of just the individual, or give positive feedback to an individual employee only in a private setting or through a third person. One of the greatest frustrations of foreigners who work with Japanese people is the lack of feedback on their achievements; thus, it is hard to know whether Japanese people think they are performing well. On the other hand, Japanese people often feel that they are being coddled when they receive constant praise from a foreign manager.

What can you do to reduce misinterpretation and maximise your working experience with Japanese colleagues? First, try to cultivate multiple sources of information and feedback. Differences among Japanese employees, in terms of communication styles and proficiency in English, may mislead you if you rely only on feedback from a small group of people. Learn what is really going on by listening to people from different areas and positions in the company. At the same time, be sensitive to the company hierarchy—junior staff members sometimes may not feel comfortable talking to you unless their bosses have been informed. There is a delicate balance between respecting the hierarchy and getting to know enough people to be effective in your work.

By building personal relationships with Japanese workers, you will be able to receive more candid and direct feedback from them. After-work socialising is a prime opportunity to develop relationships with your colleagues and to get to know them better; they may behave very differently when they are away from the office. People who are usually business-like in the office might be open and casual at dinner or at a bar, offering valuable feedback that you would have never had the chance to hear in the office. It may only be through such informal interactions that you discover important information, such as who's the most influential person in a particular work group, as an individual's level of influence may not be reflected in the organisational chart!

Of course, because of the language barrier and differences in communication style, both you and your Japanese colleagues may initially feel uncomfortable socialising after work. But what matters to Japanese workers is that you are willing to spend some time with them; it is not important what is actually discussed on such occasions. Issues raised during after-work gatherings are considered off-the-record and people generally do not bring them up at the office the next day.

However, if you are successful in building rapport with Japanese colleagues through such gatherings, they are likely to provide you with more work-related information in the future. Try to speak with colleagues regularly outside the office, even if the occasion is only lunch or a coffee break. Some may be more open when you meet with them individually than in the presence of others.

Another way to develop and nurture relationships with Japanese colleagues is to brief them thoroughly about the background of a particular project. When people from different backgrounds work together, shared goals or common interests tie them together. As Japanese people value group goals and achievements, their motivation will increase when they understand the aims of the group and how their roles fit with that of the group. Regular group meetings should be held to keep track of progress, remind the group of the goals and redefine direction. This will help to establish common ground among group members—an essential ingredient of teamwork and productivity, as Japanese people can be very open and direct with people with whom they share similar interests. In addition, share with Japanese colleagues what is going on at headquarters or in other international offices of your company. This will increase their sense of being part of the company and your credibility will rise because you are able to provide such information.

Long Working Hours

Many expatriates find that they spend a lot more time at work in Tokyo than in their home countries, primarily because their Japanese colleagues and clients work long hours. Because a large part of this work ethic can be attributed to cultural values and societal norms, expatriates find that it is not easy to change either the working style of their Japanese colleagues or of themselves. Many expatriates are not willing to stay at the office longer than necessary

Riding the subway after a long day's work.

and may even be among the first to leave the office at the end of the day. One risk associated with this approach is that as Japanese people often get more creative after hours and may discuss new ideas or make important decisions late at night, the person who leaves early may remain uninformed.

Again, building good personal relationships with Japanese colleagues can be a good strategy for bridging these differences. If you have developed good communication channels, you will be informed properly about decisions made in your absence, so you would not feel the pressure to be present at all times.

Through the informal communication channels that you cultivate, you should also be able to learn the main factors behind your Japanese colleagues working late. If the reason is due to a heavy workload and you are a manager, you may be able to reduce it, for example, by reducing the number of reports workers must generate for the headquarters.

Due to the time difference between Japan and your home country, you may frequently have to work from home. Usually people in the home country are not particularly sensitive to the time constraints of expatriates; thus, expatriates feel that they work around the clock. It is important to let Japanese colleagues know that you work from home so that your leaving early or arriving late will not become an issue. It is also important to be clear to people in your home country about your working hours, so that they will not call you regularly in the middle of the night.

You may get tired of frequent after-work gatherings, so be sure to pace yourself and do not feel pressured to attend every gathering you are invited to. Try to go out more often in the early stages of your Tokyo assignment, as declining initial offers might make people hesitant to invite you again. Ideally, after a couple of months, you will be able to find a way to balance your time between work and personal life.

Lengthy Decision-making Process

When conducting business with Japanese people, many foreigners feel very frustrated with the long decision-making process. You might not experience this as much in your Tokyo office if you work for the subsidiary of a foreign company, but you might find that it affects your work with Japanese customers. Consequently, you might have to factor in more lead time when you do business with Japanese companies. If people at your company's headquarters will be affected as well, let them know that the decision-making process is somewhat different in Japan and encourage them to modify their expectations.

Patience is the key in dealing with this lengthy process. To find out what is going on with a customer, use several different channels. Your formal contact person within the customer organisation might be able to tell you at what stage of the decision-making process the company is or how long it might take to reach a decision. If your contact seems hesitant to explain the situation, it might be that he or she simply does not know.

It might also be a good idea to take the contact person out for a get-together (for example, lunch, dinner or drinks) to get sensitive information off-the-record. If your contact is not willing to divulge the information, you might ask your Japanese colleagues to find out the information through their personal contacts. Your contact person might not be able to tell you because of hierarchy or obligations to others, but people in other areas in the customer organisation may feel free to disclose the details. Also, if you know other expatriates who have dealt with this organisation before, you could ask for their insights.

Gender Inequality

Female expatriates frequently mention that they observe gender inequality in the Japanese workplace. They often see that Japanese women, equally as competent as their fellow male workers, are promoted less frequently than men, even in the Tokyo subsidiaries of foreign firms. Foreign women, however, generally do not feel that they are affected by gender inequality; that they are treated almost equally (but less so than in their home countries) because they are foreigners. However, due to their gender, many initially do encounter difficulty in establishing their credibility.

For foreign women to establish credibility, either in Japanese organisations or in the subsidiaries of foreign firms, it is essential that they receive support from an immediate supervisor. Women should work to create good personal relationships with their managers through individual meetings, informal get-togethers and after-work socialising. Once they have gained credibility in the eyes of their managers, these managers will generally speak highly of them to others, making it easier for them to establish relationships with other key people at work.

Foreign women in managerial positions sometimes want to promote female Japanese colleagues in an attempt to resolve gender inequality in the organisation. This approach can backfire if there is a lack of consensus in the organisation regarding the issue. Before promoting a particular woman, it is essential to check on her reputation with different people and to be aware of possible reactions to the promotion. If a Japanese woman is promoted without the full agreement of others, she could experience harsh treatment. Try to gain compliance from other workers before making the promotion so that it seems legitimate to most people.

JOB SEARCHES IN TOKYO

Foreigners who arrive in Tokyo looking to work here generally face many challenges in finding a job. First, to be eligible to work in Tokyo, foreigners must obtain a valid employment visa, and to obtain this visa, they must receive sponsorship from a prospective employer. Many employers are reluctant to hire foreigners, however, because of the mountain of paperwork involved. Secondly, to be effective in most jobs, foreigners must have a certain command of the Japanese language, thus employers prefer a Japanese candidate, unless the foreigner has experience or skills (such as computer skills) that significantly outweigh the need for fluency in the language.

In spite of these challenges, some foreigners do find work, the most common of which is teaching their native languages. In particular, numerous English-language schools in Tokyo are constantly looking for native speakers. Some schools require candidates to possess certain credentials for teaching English, while others are more flexible. Foreigners also sometimes find jobs related to writing and editing materials in English. Modelling, particularly for advertisements, is popular with Westerners.

To begin a job search, check employment listings on the Internet, or in English-language magazines and newspapers. The Tokyo Employment Service Centre for Foreigners (http://www.tfemploy.go.jp) is a public organisation offering foreigners in Tokyo placement services. You will also find advertisements for job placement agencies in the media. On Mondays, **The Japan Times** classifieds features a large 'Help Wanted' section; and a list of agencies can be found in the book **Tokyo Finder** (*listed in the* 'Further Reading' *section*).

TOKYO
AT A GLANCE

CHAPTER 10

'Everyday life is like a theatre in the city of Tokyo.'
—Kazusuke Ogawa,
author on Japanese culture and literature

Official Name
Tokyo

Japanese flag
White with large red disk (representing the sun without rays) in the centre

National Anthem
Kimigayo

Time
GMT (Greenwich Mean Time) + 9 hours

Telephone country code
81

Location
Positioned approximately in the centre of Japan's main island (Honshu). Neighbouring prefectures are Chiba, Kanagawa and Saitama prefectures.

Area
2,000 sq km (769 sq miles)

Highest point
Kumotori Mountain 2,000 m (6,600 ft)

Population

Population of Japan: 127 million
Population of Tokyo: 12 million

Ethnic Groups

Japanese 99 per cent, others 1 per cent (Korean, Chinese, Brazilian, Filipino)

Religion

Shinto, Buddhist

Languages and Dialects

Japanese

Government

For administrative purposes, Japan is divided into 47 prefectures, each with its own local government (a single-house legislature) and a governor who is elected by public vote. Local governments manage their own budgets and fund part of their revenues through local taxes paid by corporations and residents. Each of the prefectures elects representatives to the national government.

In accordance with the constitution implemented after World War II, the Japanese national government consists of a two-house legislature called the Diet (*Kokkai*). The upper house, or House of Councillors, currently has 252 members who are elected every six years. The lower house, or House of Representatives, has 500 members elected every four years. Political power resides primarily with the House of Representatives. The Prime Minister is chosen by the Diet and generally is the leader of the majority party or of the coalition of parties that make up a majority. The Diet building, as well as other government buildings, are concentrated in the Kasumigaseki area.

For several decades after the war, the Liberal Democratic Party (LDP) dominated Japanese politics. That dominance diminished after 1993 when a series of political scandals involving the party occurred—for the first time since 1955, a coalition of other parties gained the majority. Although the

LDP is still the largest and most influential party, it is less powerful now as compared to the 1990s. Public interest in politics has declined in recent years, however. This may be due to a relative absence of charismatic leadership in the government and a slowness in implementing strategies to stimulate the economy.

Currency
Japanese yen (¥)

Gross Domestic Product
Japan's GDP—US $4.218 trillion (2006 est). (Tokyo accounts for about 20 per cent of the national economy.)

Industries
Concentrated in the service sector including financial, retail, communication, entertainment and corporate services.

Port and Harbours
Port of Tokyo

Airports
The closest international airport is Narita Airport in Chiba prefecture (about 60 km / 37 miles away from Tokyo). Haneda Airport in Tokyo mainly services domestic flights.

Average Monthly Temperatures in Tokyo

	Jan	Feb	Mar	Apr	May	Jun	Jul	Aug	Sep	Oct	Nov	Dec
°C	5	6	9	14	19	22	25	27	24	18	13	8
°F	41	43	48	57	66	72	77	81	75	64	55	46

Electricity
100 volts and 50 cycles (hertz)

Weights and Measures

Japan uses the metric system.

Acronyms

ANA	All Nippon Airways
BOJ	Bank of Japan
JAF	Japan Automobile Federation
JAL	Japan Air Lines
JAS	Japanese Agriculture Standards Association
JETRO	Japan External Trade Organization
JICA	Japanese International Corporation Agency
JIS	Japanese Institution of Standards
JR	Japan Railway Company
JTB	Japan Travel Bureau
LDP	Liberal Democratic Party
METI	Ministry of Economy, Trade and Industry
MOF	Ministry of Finance
MoFA	Ministry of Foreign Affairs
NASDA	National Space Development Agency
NHK	Nippon Hoso Kyokai (Japan Broadcasting Corporation)
NTT	Nippon Telegraph and Telephone Company
TEPCO	Tokyo Electric Power Company

Famous People

Yasunari Kawabata

Won the Nobel Prize in Literature in 1968. Famous novels include *The Izu Dancer*, *The Snow Country*, and *Thousand Cranes*.

Haruki Murakami

Famous contemporary novelist. His novels include *A Wild Sheep Chase*, *Norwegian Wood* and *Dance Dance Dance*.

Kenzaburo Oe

Won the Nobel Prize in Literature in 1994. His novels include *A Personal Matter*, *The Silent City* and *Awake, New Man*.

Sports
Ichiro Suzuki
Baseball player now playing in the US Major League.

Ryoko Tani
Judo player who won many world titles, including the Olympics.

Movies
Akira Kurosawa
World famous movie director. Famous films include *Rashomon*, *Seven Samurai* and *The Shadow Warrior*.

Hayao Miyazaki
Best-known maker of animated films. Famous films include *Neighbor Totoro*, *Princess Mononoke* and *Spirited Away*.

Business and Politics
Carlos Ghosn
Appointed as the first foreign CEO in Japan in 1999, saved the Nissan (automobile maker) from bankruptcy and revived the company.

Junichiro Koizumi
Prime Minister of Japan from 2001–2006 who worked on economic reform, focusing on improving the government's debt.

Akio Morita
Known in international business market as a co-founder of Sony.

Places of Interest
Asakusa
Considered as 'downtown' Tokyo, this is a great place to experience the ambience of old Tokyo.

Tsukiji Fish Market

The largest wholesale fish market in Japan where visitors can observe the auction of fish from all over the world and enjoy fresh *sushi* after that.

Imperial Palace

The residence of the imperial family. Tourists are not allowed to enter the palace except on New Year's Day and the Emperor's birthday, but they can enjoy the view of the castle and beautiful gardens.

Ginza

The most high-class shopping area in Tokyo where world-famous brand shops are located.

Akihabara electronic district

In this district, there are more than 600 shops selling a variety of electronic products at reduced prices.

CULTURE QUIZ

SITUATION 1

You recently moved to Tokyo. At your new apartment, one of your Japanese neighbours greets you. He does not speak fluent English, but he seems interested to know you. He says, "My name is Miki". What is the appropriate way to address him?

Ⓐ Just call him Miki; it must be his given name if he mentions only one name.

Ⓑ Call him Miki-*san*.

Ⓒ Ask him whether Miki is his given name or family name, and ask how he wants to be addressed.

Ⓓ Call him Mr. Miki.

Comments

Japanese people usually address each other by their family (last) name plus '-*san*'. They use the given (first) name only among family members and very close friends. Thus, when only one name is provided during introductions, it is likely to be the family name. However, Japanese people who are knowledgeable about Western customs might introduce themselves by their given name. Using the name plus '-*san*' is the safest course of action, as it can be used for both the given and the family name, and for both men and women. At some point, you should clarify whether 'Miki' is his first or last name. Even if he asks you to call him 'Miki', it is polite to address him as 'Miki-*san*'; he will probably also appreciate your knowledge of this Japanese custom.

Answer(s): **Ⓑ**, **Ⓒ** and **Ⓓ** are all acceptable but **Ⓑ** is the best.

SITUATION 2

You and your spouse are renting a house from a Japanese landlord. Since moving in, a couple of appliances have broken down, and the dishwasher is now on the blink. You like the house but you are frustrated that so many things need fixing. Each time a problem arises, you call the landlord who then hires contractors to fix the appliances. As the landlord does not speak English well, you have tried communicating with her in what little Japanese you know. This time she has not returned your calls even though you left two messages. What should you do?

A Stay calm, explain the situation one more time and politely ask for help.

B Raise your voice to show her you are frustrated and that you want the appliance fixed immediately.

C Tell the landlord that you will hire a contractor yourself and charge it to her later.

D Ask a Japanese person to speak to her on your behalf; there might be a language problem.

Comments

In Japan, dealing with problems calmly and politely, even if you are very frustrated with the person, is the most effective way of solving the problem. Japanese people are put off by a show of anger as such behaviour is considered immature and will harm the relationship. Getting a third person, such as a Japanese friend or colleague, to help is better than risking a direct conflict. That person might be able to interpret the situation from a Japanese cultural perspective, or clear the air over possible misunderstanding. There is also the possibility the landlord has been away and did not receive your messages.

Answer(s): **A** is the best response; **D** is an alternative.

SITUATION 3

You have come to know one of your Japanese neighbours quite well. She seems very open and friendly, and you are happy to have a Japanese friend. Your neighbour speaks English fluently and helps you with your Japanese. One day, on the way to the train station, you see your neighbour with a Japanese person you have never met before. You stop to make small talk with your neighbour, but she does not introduce you to her friend. During the conversation, the other person stands a little behind your neighbour and never looks at you. You feel uncomfortable and wonder why your neighbour did not make any introductions.

Ⓐ Your neighbour does not consider you as a friend.

Ⓑ Your neighbour does not think that you and her friend would meet again, and so does not bother to make any introduction.

Ⓒ Your neighbour's friend cannot speak English, so your neighbour does not want to make her friend uncomfortable or awkward.

Ⓓ Your neighbour thought that you and her friend would not get along well.

Comments

There are several possible explanations. Japanese people usually do not make introductions if they assume that the people involved will have no reason or chance to build a relationship—your neighbour probably assumed that you and her friend would never meet again. In addition, Japanese people tend to separate friends into groups based on factors such as age, background and common interests; thus your neighbour may see her friendship with you as different from that with her friend. Another possible reason is that Japanese people who are not used to interacting with foreigners can be shy and hesitant to communicate, even if the foreigners speak some Japanese. Your neighbour's friend avoided looking at you probably because in Japan, direct eye contact between people who have just met is considered rude (although you may experience people staring at you out of curiosity when you travel outside Tokyo).

Answer(s): Either **Ⓑ**, **Ⓒ** or both are possible explanations.

SITUATION 4

You and your spouse have invited your Japanese colleagues to your home for drinks and dessert. Not knowing the guests' preferences, you have prepared a variety of both. When you ask your Japanese guests what they would like to drink, they look at each other and do not respond. Then, you tell them what kinds of drinks you have, and ask one of them what he wants. He says, "Anything is fine". When you ask the others, all give a similar answer. Not knowing what is best, you serve everyone a glass of wine but realise that some are not drinking it. Next you list the desserts available. After a pause, a senior person mentions a preference, and then everyone else asks for the same thing. You wonder why this is happening.

Ⓐ They all have the same tastes.

Ⓑ They do not know what to ask for.

Ⓒ The senior person has pressured everyone to request the same thing.

Ⓓ They feel that it is not polite to assert their preferences.

Comments

Japanese people generally feel that it is not polite to assert to a host their preferences and simply accept whatever is offered. If they must choose, they often select what others have requested because they do not want to trouble the host to serve different kinds of drink or food. Also, the person who chooses first is often the most senior, because Japanese people tend to observe the hierarchy even when away from the office. Hosts who genuinely want guests to state individual preferences should be persistent. In addition, they should offer food or drinks a few times, because Japanese guests tend to decline the first offer out of politeness.

Answer(s): The most likely explanation is **Ⓓ**.

SITUATION 5

Some time ago, you heard from a colleague that he and his wife were looking for an English-language teacher for their daughter, so you introduced the family to one of your friends. A couple of weeks later, you received a gift from the colleague who said, "It is just a little thing". However, when you opened the box you found a gorgeous Japanese doll. You feel uncomfortable about accepting such an expensive gift for such a small favour and are wondering what to do now.

Ⓐ Thank your colleague, but return the gift, telling him that you cannot accept such an expensive gift.

Ⓑ Thank your colleague, but refuse to do him anymore favours from then on.

Ⓒ Thank your colleague, telling him how much you liked the gift.

Ⓓ Thank your colleague, and give him something in return on a different occasion.

Comments

It is very common for Japanese people to offer gifts in return for favours. If the gift is an expensive one, it may indicate that the person really appreciated your favour. The best option is to accept it, because returning it would seriously hurt the feelings of that person and could damage the relationship. When Japanese people feel that a gift is very expensive, they sometimes give a present in return on a different occasion (for example, a souvenir from holiday).

Answer(s): **Ⓒ** is the best, although **Ⓓ** is also a possibility.

SITUATION 6

You are the manager of an engineering group at your company's Tokyo subsidiary. One of the Japanese engineers came up with a great idea that has significantly increased the productivity of the group. You want to acknowledge the performance of this young member and wonder what is the best way to do it.

Ⓐ Reward the group by taking them out to dinner and commending their increase in productivity.

Ⓑ Convey to the engineer, through other Japanese members of the group, the message that you are happy with the performance.

❻ Call the engineer into your office, and personally acknowledge the exemplary performance.

❼ Praise this engineer in front of other group members.

Comments

Because Japanese people are group-oriented, rewards are usually given to the entire group. Although to you it was the young engineer's idea, some form of teamwork could have taken place giving rise to the engineer's idea. Thus, giving him the reward might not be accepted well by group members. As your employees work for a foreign subsidiary, they might not expect the traditional Japanese management style, and might be willing to accept individual rewards. Even so, praising the engineer in front of the other members of the group would probably make him feel uncomfortable. It would be more culturally appropriate to use an indirect approach such as conveying praise through a third person (probably the senior group member, to show respect for the hierarchy within the group) or praising the engineer in an individual setting.

Answer(s): **❶** is the best; **❷** and **❻** are possibilities.

DO'S AND DON'TS

DO'S

- Bow when you greet someone.
- Take off your shoes when you enter a room with *tatami* mat at restaurants and/or when you enter a Japanese home.
- Bring a gift if you are invited to someone's house.
- Say *Itadakimasu* before a meal.
- Always carry at least ¥10,000 as some shops, restaurants and taxis do not accept credit cards.
- Watch carefully for cars before you cross the street (look right then left).
- Be prepared to walk a lot and climb a lot of stairs as public transportation will be the main transportation in Tokyo and escalators are not installed at all stations.
- Write things down if your spoken English is not understood. Japanese people comprehend better reading English rather than listening or speaking it.
- Make an effort to study the Japanese language. Many people are not fluent in English.
- Be punctual. People generally try to arrive a few minutes before the appointment.

DON'TS

- Don't call Japanese people by their first name unless you are invited to do so.
- Don't forget business cards when you visit someone outside of your company.
- Don't speak in a loud voice in a public place.
- Don't point your fingers at people.
- Don't force people to open a gift in front of others.
- Don't use a handkerchief when you blow your nose. Use a tissue paper.
- Don't eat food while you are walking.
- Don't pour soy sauce over rice.
- Don't pour your own beer. Wait until someone next to you pours it for you.
- Don't wash your body inside a bathtub. There is a washing place outside of the tub.

GLOSSARY

NUMBERS

ichi	one
ni	two
san	three
shi or *yon*	four
go	five
roku	six
shichi or *nana*	seven
hachi	eight
aagon	nine
ju	ten

GREETINGS AND BASIC PHRASES

Ohayo gozaimasu.	Good morning.
Konnichiwa.	Good afternoon/Hello.
Konbanwa.	Good evening.
Sayonara.	Goodbye.
Dewa mata.	See you later.
Ogenki desuka?	How are you?
Okagesamade genki desu. (Literally it means 'Owing to you, I am fine'.)	Fine, thank you.
Hajimemashite.	How do you do?
Dozo yoroshiku onegai shimasu. (Literally it means 'Please take care of me'.)	Pleased to meet you.
(Anatano) o-namae wa nan desu ka?	What is your name?
Watashi (no namae) wa _____ desu.	My name is _____.
Arigato gozaimasu.	Thank you.

Dohitashimashite.	You are welcome.
Sumimasen.	Excuse me./Sorry.
Eigo wa hanashimasu ka?	Do you speak English?
Hai.	Yes.
Iie.	No.
Nihongo wa wakarimasen.	I do not understand Japanese.
Dozo. (as in 'Go ahead.' or 'Have some.')	Please.
Onegai shimasu. (when asking for something)	Please.
_____ *o kudasai.*	Please give me _____.

GETTING AROUND

densha	train
chikatetsu	subway
eki	station
kippu	ticket
basu	bus
basu noriba	bus stop
takushi	taxi
migi	right
hidari	left
massugu	straight
ushiro	behind
_____ *made onegai shimasu.* (said to a taxi driver)	To _____, please.
_____ *wa doko desu ka?*	Where is _____?
_____ *e wa doh ikeba ii desu ka?*	How can I get to _____?

_____ *made ikura desu ka?*	How much is it to _____?
Jikan wa donokurai kakari masu ka?	How long does it take?

SHOPPING

yaoya	vegetable shop
kudamonoya	fruit shop
nikuya	meat shop (butcher)
sakanaya	fishmonger
panya	bakery
honya	bookstore
suhpah	supermarket
depahto	department store
konbini	convenience store
genkin	cash
otsuri	change
kurejitto kahdo	credit card
Sore (kore) wa ikura desu ka?	How much is that (this)?
Sore (kore) o kudasai. ____	Please give me that (this) one.
____ *wa arimasu ka?*	Do you have _____?
Motto chiisana (ohkina) saizu wa arimasu ka?	Do you have a smaller (larger) size?

EATING OUT

resutoran	restaurant
menyuh	menu
Eigo no menyuh wa arimasu ka?	Do you have a menu in English?
_____ *o kudasai.*	_____, please.
Are wa nan desu ka?	What is that?
_____ *wa arimasu ka?*	Do you have _____?

_____ *wa taberaremasen.*	I cannot eat _____.
Kore wa oishii desu.	It is delicious.
Kanpai! (before drinking)	Cheers!
Itadakimasu. (before eating)	I humbly receive the meal.
Gochiso sama deshita (after eating)	Thank you very much for the meal.
O-kanjoh-o onegai shimasu.	The bill, please.

HEALTH PROBLEMS AND EMERGENCIES

isha (Use *sensei*, when addressing the doctor.)	doctor
byohin	hospital
kyukyusha	ambulance
yakkyoku	pharmacy
kusuri	medicine
itamidome no kusuri	pain killer
Kega o shimashita.	I have been injured.
Shukketsu shiteimasu.	I am bleeding.
Kibun ga warui desu.	I am feeling sick.
Netsu ga arimasu.	I have a fever.
Itai desu.	It hurts.
Atama ga itai desu.	I have a headache.
Onaka ga itai desu.	I have a stomachache.
Ha ga itai desu.	I have a toothache.
Yakedo o shimashita.	I have got a burn.
Ishiki ga arimasen.	She/he is unconscious.
Tasukete!	Emergency! Help!
keisatsu	police
Keisatsu o yonde kudasai!	Please call the police!
kaji	fire

shohbohsha	fire truck
doroboh	thief
_____ *o nusumaremashita.*	_____ was stolen.
kohtsuh jiko	traffic accident
jishin	earthquake

RESOURCE GUIDE

IMPORTANT NUMBERS

Police: 110
Fire: 119
Ambulance: 119

To report a burglary or any incidents that require the help of police officers, call 110. An English-speaking operator is on duty around the clock.

To report a fire, ask for rescue, or request an ambulance, call 119. An English-speaking operator is on duty 24-hours a day. If you place a call to 119, state the type of emergency, your address, and your name.

Calling an Ambulance

Many public phones allow callers to connect directly to 119 without inserting a coin, simply by pushing a button. On telephones that do not have this type of button, just dial 119; the call will go through directly without the insertion of a coin. Pink and red phones (which are very rare now) require a 10-yen coin to dial 119.

Dialing 119 connects you to the central calling centre of the Tokyo Fire Department. You must tell the operator that you need an ambulance (*kyukyu-sha*), because this number is also used to call fire engines. Give the following information to the operator:

- The address where an ambulance is needed.
  Jusho wa _____desu. (Address is _____.)
- The name, age and the gender of the patient.
  Namae wa _____ desu. (Name is _____.)
  _____ *sai desu.* (Age is _____.)
  Josei desu. (It is a woman.)
  Dansei desu. (It is a man.)

If you do not speak Japanese, ask to speak to an English-speaking operator. They are on duty 24 hours a day. Do not hang up if you are not transferred immediately to an

English-speaking operator, or if you think the operator did not understand what you said. Emergency operators will try to trace the origin of any telephone call, determine the location, and send an ambulance.

While waiting for the ambulance, it is important to prepare the patient's passport, Foreign Registration Card and insurance card (if the patient is enrolled in public health insurance plan). Also, gather some cash—at least ¥ 30,000—to cover any initial medical costs at the hospital (the ambulance ride is free). Patients who do not have their insurance cards available or who are not enrolled in a public health insurance plan will probably have to pay the full amount of any expenses in advance and receive reimbursement afterwards.

If you have insufficient cash, try borrowing from family and friends, or withdraw money from ATMs (which are abundant in Tokyo). If that is not possible, hospitals or clinics are likely to accept whatever money the patient has as a deposit, and/or you should keep a form of the patient's identification until full payment is made.

The Tokyo Fire Department has paramedics available who sometimes perform emergency medical procedures under the guidance of doctors working at a command and control centre. The ambulance usually transports the patient to the nearest hospital capable of handling the patient's condition. A patient can request to be sent to the hospital to which his or her personal doctor is affiliated. The ambulance personnel may comply if the doctor agrees to see the patient and if the hospital accepts ambulances.

MAKING CALLS AND INTERNET SERVICES
Choosing Telephone Carriers

A new system called MYLINE lets customers use different telephone carriers for different distances without dialling each telephone carrier's access code. Before the system was implemented, all local calls and long-distance calls (except international calls) automatically went through NTT, and people who wanted to use different carriers had to dial prefixes such as '0055' before dialling the individual telephone numbers. Now, by pre-selecting and registering your preferences with various telephone carriers, calls can be connected through those designated carriers each time you make calls. You can select a telephone carrier for each of the following four categories of calls: 1) local; 2) in-prefecture long distance; 3) out-of-prefecture long distance; and 4) international.

Each carrier offers a unique pricing structure. Application forms are available directly from each carrier or at the MYLINE Center. For further information, contact MYLINE Center Phone-in customer service (tel: 0120-000-406 in English, Chinese, Spanish and Portuguese, or log onto http://www.myline.org).

You can also make telephone calls without registering with MYLINE. Simply dial the area code (for a call outside your own area) followed by the number, and the call will automatically go through NTT. To use different telephone carriers, simply dial the prefix numbers designated for those carriers before dialling the area codes.

Making Local Calls

Telephone numbers in Tokyo consist of an area code followed by an exchange number and the subscriber's number. Telephone numbers within the 23 wards are indicated by the area code '03', followed by eight-digit numbers: (03) 1111-1111. In several areas (including Koganei-shi and Kokubunji-shi), the area code is '042' followed by seven-digit numbers: (042) 111-1111. In other areas (such as Chofu-shi, Hachioji-shi, and Ome-shi), telephone numbers are prefixed with a variety of area codes including '0424', '0426' and '0428', followed by six-digit numbers, for example, (0424) 11-1111. Area codes are not necessary when placing a call within the same area code. Area codes are also unnecessary when calling emergency numbers (such as '110' for police or '119' for fire-fighting and ambulance services). Telephone numbers starting with '0120' are toll-free numbers.

Making International Calls

- If you have registered with the MYLINE system and have pre-selected an international carrier, dial:
  010 + country code + your counterpart's number.
- If you have not registered with MYLINE, dial:
  the prefix of the carrier of your choice + 010 + country code + your counterpart's number.

Internet Services

The broadband access such as ADSL and Cable connection has become the popular method for the Internet connection. Popular Internet providers include Nifty, So-net, Yahoo and Biglobe.

It is also common to use cell phones for Internet access. In addition to exchanging e-mail through cell phones, people can receive information such as weather forecasts, stock quotes and train schedules and can also complete transactions such as making reservations, purchasing tickets, and transferring money from their bank accounts. The most popular Internet service on cellular phones is 'i-mode' provided by NTT DoCoMo.

COMPARISON OF SIZES
Women's Clothing

Japanese	7	9	11	13
American	4	6	8	10
English	6	8	10	12
Continental	36	38	40	42

Men's Clothing

Japanese	S	M	L	LL
American	34	36	38	40
English	34	36	38	40
Continental	44	36	48	50

Women's Shoes

Japanese	22.5	23	23.5	24
American	5.5	6	6.5	7
English	4	4.5	5	5.5
Continental	35	36	37	38

Men's Shoes

Japanese	25.5	26	26.5	27
American	8	8.5	9	9.5
English	6	7	8	9
Continental	40	41	42	42.5

HEALTH CARE PROVIDERS
International Clinics

The following clinics serve the foreign community. The doctors and staff of these clinics speak English.

International Clinic
1-5-9 Azabudai, Minato-ku, Tokyo
Tel: (03) 3583-7831

National Medical Clinic
#202, 5-16-11, Minami-Azabu, Minato-ku, Tokyo
Tel: (03) 3473-2057; http://www.nmclinic.net

The King Clinic
6-31-21 Jingumae, Shibuya-ku, Tokyo
Tel: (03) 3409-0764;
http://www.thekingclinic.com

Tokyo British Clinic
Daikanyama Y Building. 2 Floor. 2-13-7, Ebisu-Nishi,
Shibuya-ku, Tokyo
Tel: (03) 5458-6099;
http://www.tokyobritishclinic.com

Tokyo Medical and Surgical Clinic
32 Mori Building, 2 floor. 3-4-30 Shiba-Koen, Minato-ku, Tokyo
Tel: (03) 3436-3028; http://www.tmsc.jp

Tokyo Midtown Medical Center
Midtown Tower 6F, Akasaka 9-7-1, Minato-ku, Tokyo
Tel: (03) 5413-0080; http://www.tokyomidtown-mc.jp

Pharmacies
The following pharmacies cater to the foreign community
and may carry some imported products.

American Pharmacy
Marunouchi Building. 2-4-1 Marunouchi,
Chiyoda-ku, Tokyo
Tel: (03) 5220-7716

Medical Dispensary
32 Mori Building. 3-4-30 Shiba-Koen, Minato-ku, Tokyo
Tel: (03) 3434-5817

National Azabu Pharmacy
4-5-2 Minami Azabu, Minato-ku, Tokyo
Tel: (03) 3442-3181

Roppongi Pharmacy
6-8-8 Roppongi, Minato-ku, Tokyo
Tel: (03) 3403-8879

RESOURCES AND SUPPORT GROUPS FOR NEW PARENTS

In Tokyo, there are a number of resources and support groups for expatriates who are expecting or caring for newborns, such as those listed below.

La Leche League Japan

http://www.lalecheleague.org

La Leche League is an international non-profit organisation that provides education, information and support for mothers and pregnant women who wish to breast-feed their babies. They arrange monthly meetings and offer telephone counselling.

Tokyo Pregnancy Group

http://www.geocities.com/tokyopregnancygroup

This group holds regular meetings featuring keynote speakers and provides a forum for attendees to exchange information and share experiences with others.

Tokyo with Kids

http://www.tokyowithkids.com

This website hosts discussion forums on several topics including giving birth in Tokyo and child education.

ORGANISATIONS OFFERING COUNSELLING IN FOREIGN LANGUAGES

Ikebukuro Counselling Centre

Tel: (03) 3989-4953; http://www.hozumiclinic.com

Professional counsellors provide services in English and other languages. If necessary, they can refer patients to medical doctors and psychiatrists at the Hozumi Clinic.

TELL Community Counselling Service

Tel: (03) 3498-0231; http://www.telljp.com

Professional counselling available for adults, teenagers and children in English, Japanese and other languages.

EDUCATIONAL FACILITIES
Preschools

Plenty of international preschools are available in Tokyo. Most international schools have affiliated preschools, while independent preschools are also available, such as:

Child's Play
18-8 Motoyoyogi, Shibuya-ku, Tokyo
Tel: (03) 3460-8841;
http://childs-play.org

Gregg International School
1-14-16 Jiyugaoka, Meguro-ku, Tokyo
Tel: (03) 3725-8000;
http://www.gis-j.com

Kids World
Has more than 10 sites in central Tokyo and surrounding areas.
Tel: (03) 3234-8322;
http://www.pigeonhearts.co.jp/kidsworld

Komazawa Park International Preschool
2-12-16 Fukasawa, Setagaya-ku, Tokyo
Tel: (03) 5707-0979;
http://kpipk.com

Maria's Babies' Society
Tomy's House #101, 3-36-20 Jingumae, Shibuya-ku, Tokyo
Tel: (03) 3404-3468;
http://mariasbabies.co.jp

International Schools
Schools with English-Language Curricula

The American School in Japan

1-1-1, Nomizu, Chofu-shi, Tokyo
Tel: (0422) 34-5300;
http://www.asij.ac.jp
Founded in 1902, this is the largest and oldest international school in Tokyo. It offers co-educational classes from Kindergarten through Grade 12 and is attended by 1,500 students from 40 countries. The curriculum follows the American system but is modified to fit the Japanese environment. Nursery School and some Kindergarten classes are held at the school's second campus in Meguro.

Aoba-Japan International School

2-10-7 Miyamae, Suginami-ku, Tokyo
Tel: (03) 3335-6620;
http://www.a-jis.com
Founded in 1980, this is a co-educational school offering classes from Kindergarten through Grade 9. The school accepts students who are fluent in English as well as those with limited English proficiency. Japanese language study is an integral part of the curriculum. Currently enrolment is at 600. Its Nursery School is located in Meguro.

The British School in Tokyo

1-21-18, Shibuya, Shibuya-ku, Tokyo
Tel: (03) 5467-4321;
http://www.bst.ac.jp
Founded in 1989, this school provides a British-style primary education. Co-educational classes are offered from Kindergarten through Year 8 (age 13). Majority of the nearly 400 students are British.

The Christian Academy in Japan
1-2-14 Shinkawa-cho, Higashi Kurume-shi, Tokyo
Tel: (0424) 71-0022;
http://caj.or.jp
Founded in 1950, this school offers a co-educational environment based on the American system, from Kindergarten through Grade 12. Of the more than 400 students enrolled, 54 per cent are the children of missionaries; just over half are Americans, with nearly 30 per cent Japanese, about 10 per cent Korean, and the rest from other countries.

International School of the Sacred Heart
4-3-1 Hiroo, Shibuya-ku, Tokyo
Tel (03) 3400-3951;
http://www.issh.ac.jp
Founded in 1908 by the Society of the Sacred Heart, this school offers a co-educational Kindergarten and all-girls' classes through Grade 12. It has approximately 650 students, and the curriculum is based on both the American and British systems.

Nishimachi International School
2-14-7 Moto Azabu, Minato-ku, Tokyo
Tel: (03) 3451-5520;
http://www.nishimachi.ac.jp
Founded in 1949, this co-educational school offers classes from Kindergarten through Grade 9. Among the 400 students enrolled, approximately 40 per cent are American, 33 per cent are Japanese, 14 per cent are Australian or British, and 13 per cent are from other countries. The curriculum is based on the American model. All students study Japanese as their first or second language.

Saint Mary's International School
1-6-19 Seta, Setagaya-ku, Tokyo
Tel: (03) 3709-3411;
http://www.smis.ac.jp

Founded in 1954 by the Roman Catholic Brothers of Christian Instruction, this is a boys-only school and offers classes from Kindergarten through Grade 12. It has more than 900 students representing 75 different countries. The school uses a curriculum that follows the American model and provides an International Baccalaureate course of study.

Seisen International School
1-12-15 Yoga, Setagaya-ku, Tokyo
Tel: (03) 3704-2661;
http://www.seisen.com
Founded in 1962, this school is run by the Handmaids of the Sacred Heart of Jesus. It offers a co-educational kindergarten and all-girls' classes from Grade 1 through Grade 12. With a student body of nearly 700 representing over 60 countries, the school serves the international community as well as Japanese children who have lived abroad. Like Saint Mary's it offers an International Baccalaureate course of studies.

Tokyo International School
3-4-22, Mita, Minato-ku, Tokyo
Tel: (03) 5484-1160;
http://www.tokyois.com
Founded in 1994, this co-educational pre- and primary school is attended by more than 200 students from over 35 nations and boasts the best student/teacher ratio (15:1) of any primary school in Tokyo. The primary school moved to its current location in 2001, while the preschool is still located at the old Meguro campus.

Schools with Curricula in Other Foreign Languages
Several international schools in Tokyo offer curricula in languages other than English. They include the following:

Lycée Franco-Japonais de Tokyo
1-2-43 Fujimi, Chiyoda-ku, Tokyo
Tel: (03) 3261-0137;
http://www.lfjt.or.jp

Tokyo Chinese School
14 Gobancho, Chiyoda-ku, Tokyo
Tel: (03) 3261-5894;
http://www.tcs.or.jp

Tokyo Indonesian School
4-6-6 Meguro, Meguro-ku, Tokyo
Tel: (03) 3661-2956

Tokyo Korean School
2-1 Wakamatsucho, Shinjuku-ku, Tokyo
Tel: (03) 3357-2233

Adult Education

Foreigners who want to study Japanese intensively or other subjects can take classes offered in English at several universities.

**International Christian University
(ICU/Kokusai Kirisutokyo Daigaku)**
3-10-2 Osawa, Mitaka-shi, Tokyo
Tel: (0422) 33-3038–40;
http://www.icu.ac.jp
ICU offers a liberal arts education in both Japanese and English, including summer courses on Japanese language and culture. Foreigners are required to take intensive Japanese language classes.

Sophia University (Jochi Daigaku)
7-1 Kioi-cho, Chiyoda-ku, Tokyo
Tel: (03) 3238-4018;
http://www.sophia.ac.jp
All classes, except Japanese language classes, in Sophia's Faculty of Comparative Culture are taught in English. Its Japanese Language Institute offers a two-year programme for foreigners wishing to master the Japanese language.

**National Graduate Institute for Policy Studies
(GRIPS/ Seisaku Kenkyu Daigakuin Daigaku)**
7-22-1 Roppongi, Minato-ku, Tokyo
Tel: (03) 6439-6000;
http://www.grips.ac.jp
Courses on areas such as public policy, economics, public finance and leadership are offered in English.

Japanese Language Schools

Academy of Language Arts
2-16 Agebacho, Shinjuku-ku, Tokyo
Tel: (03) 3235-0071;
http://www.ala-japan.com

ARC Academy Japanese Language School
(There are several campuses in Tokyo.)
Tel: (03) 3409-0391;
http://www.arc-academy.net

Association for Japanese-Language Training (AJALT)
3-25-2 Toranomon, Minato-ku, Tokyo
Tel: (03) 3459-9620;
http://www.ajalt.org

**Japan Language Institute (JLI)
(Nichibei Kaiwa Gakuin)**
1-21 Yotsuya, Shinjuku-ku, Tokyo
Tel: (03) 3359-9621;
http://www.iec-nichibei.or.jp

Kai Japanese Language School
1-15-18 Okubo, Shinjuku-ku, Tokyo
Tel: (03) 3205-1356;
http://www.kaij.co.jp

Sendagaya Japanese Institute
(Sendagaya Nihongo Kyoiku Kenkyujo)
1-31-18 Takadanobaba, Shinjuku-ku, Tokyo
Tel: (03) 3232-6181;
http://www.jp-sji.org

ENTERTAINMENT FACILITIES
Amusement Parks

National Children's Castle (Kodomo no Shiro)
5-53-1 Jingumae, Shibuya-ku, Tokyo
Tel: (03) 3797-5666;
http://kodomono-shiro.or.jp
This ten-storey building offers facilities designed to help children develop their artistic, athletic and imaginative talents. Facilities include play halls, music studios, a video library, a swimming pool and a computer room.

Sanrio Puroland
1-31 Ochiai, Tama-shi, Tokyo
Tel: (042) 339-1111;
http://www.puroland.co.jp
Shows are performed here starring Sanrio's famous cartoon characters (such as Hello Kitty). The theme of the park is 'love and dreams' and attractions highlight that theme.

Tokyo Disneyland
1-1 Maihama, Urayasu-shi, Chiba
Tel: (045) 683-3333; http://tokyodisneyresort.co.jp
Modelled after the original Disneyland in California, many features such as landscaping, attractions and services were imported from the US. This is definitely the most popular amusement park in the Tokyo area. Be prepared to spend a long day here because the wait for popular rides such as Space Mountain can easily be more than an hour. DisneySea, an amusement park next to Tokyo Disneyland, features water attractions.

Tokyo Dome City Attractions
1-3-61 Koraku, Bunkyo-ku, Tokyo
Tel: (03) 5800-9999;
http://www.tokyo-dome.co.jp
This park is part of Tokyo Dome City, which contains a baseball field, a bowling alley and a skating stadium. It also has thrilling roller coaster rides and a carousel, and offers shows and events geared toward children.

Tokyo Summer Land
600 Kamiyotsugi, Akiruno-shi, Tokyo
Tel: (042) 558-6511;
http://www.summerland.co.jp
Located just next to Tokyo Sesame Place, this is a place of everlasting summer. Man-made waves dash against the shores of a huge indoor pool and tropical rains create a summer atmosphere all year round. An outdoor pool is also open during the summer. In addition to swimming, children can enjoy several rides, a picnic area, a golf range, tennis courts and a bowling alley.

Toshimaen Amusement Park
3-25-1 Mukoyama, Nerima-ku, Tokyo
Tel: (03) 3990-8800
The park offers a variety of rides for children of all ages. Other popular attractions are water slides and seven different swimming pools.

Yomiuri-land Amusement Park
4015-1 Yanokuchi, Inagi-shi, Tokyo
Tel: (044) 966-1111
In addition to taking thrilling rides such as the roller coaster and the free fall, children can watch sea otters and enjoy performances by seals. The park also features a swimming pool in summer and an ice-skating rink in winter.

Aquariums

Enoshima Aquarium
2-19-1 Katase Kaigan, Fujisawa-shi, Kanagawa
Tel: (0466) 29-9960;
http://www.enosui.com
The first modern aquarium in Japan, it consist of three sites:
1) an aquarium; 2) a marine land featuring dolphin and whale
shows; and 3) a marine zoo where seals, penguins, sea lions
and sea otters live.

Tokyo Sea Life Park
6-2-3 Rinkai-cho, Edogawa-ku, Tokyo
Tel: (03) 3869-5152;
http://www.tokyo-zoo.net/zoo/kasai
Located in Kasai Rinkai Park, the aquarium has a large
doughnut-shaped tank where huge tunas swim in groups. A
guided tour (in Japanese) is offered, taking visitors behind
the fish tanks that contain a total of 62,000 fish belonging
to 540 species.

Shinagawa Aquarium
3-2-1 Katsushima, Shinagawa-ku, Tokyo
Tel: (03) 3762-3433;
http://www.aquarium.gr.jp
The theme of this aquarium is 'communicating with the river
and the sea'. It offers the only dolphin show in Tokyo and
displays more than 10,000 different fish. A big tunnel-shaped
glass tank offers visitors a 180-degree view of the fish.

Sunshine International Aquarium
(Sunshine Kokusai Suizokukan)
Sunshine City 10 Floor, 3-1-3 Higashi Ikebukuro,
Toshima-ku, Tokyo
Tel: (03) 3989-3331
This large aquarium showcases fish from all over the world.
One of the most popular events is an underwater feeding

show during which a diver enters the tank to feed the fish and also answers questions from the audience.

Yokohama-Hakkeijima Sea Paradise Aqua Museum
Hakkeijima, Yokohama-shi, Kanagawa
Tel: (045) 788-8888;
http://www.seaparadise.co.jp
This is a sea paradise built on a little island called Hakkeijima. The aquarium is one of the largest in Japan and displays 100,000 fish representing 500 species. There is also a playground for small children, and a place to feed the penguins.

Zoos

Inokashira Park Zoo
1-17-6 Gotenyama, Musashino-shi, Tokyo
Tel: (0422) 46-1100;
http://www.tokyo-zoo.net/zoo/ino
Both the main zoo and the annex are located in Inokashira Park. More than 200 species of wildlife live here, including elephants, monkeys and raccoons. Inokashira Park also has a pond where visitors can ride boats, and is a good place for family picnics. The cherry blossoms are beautiful in spring.

Tama Zoological Park
7-1-1 Hodokubo, Hino-shi, Tokyo
Tel: (042) 591-1611;
http://www.tokyo-zoo.net/zoo/tama
This huge zoo tries to recreate the animals' natural environment. It features a savannah with herbivorous animals and a bus tour that allows visitors an close-up view of the resident lions.

Ueno Zoological Gardens
9-83 Ueno Koen, Taito-ku, Tokyo
Tel: (03) 3828-5171;

http://www.tokyo-zoo.net/zoo/ueno
The oldest zoo in Japan, it is famous for the giant panda
donated by the Chinese government. During the weekends
and holidays, visitors would need to wait very long to view
the panda.

Zoorasia

1175-1 Kamishirane-cho, Asahi-ku,
Yokohama-shi, Kanagawa
Tel: (045) 959-1000;
http://www.city.yokohama.jp/me/ygf/zoorasia
Built in 1999, this zoo's goal is to replicate six different climate
zones so that animals can live in their natural environments.
It also exhibits rare animals in order to protect the species.

Art Museums

Bridgestone Museum of Art (Burijisuton Bijutsukan)

1-10-1 Kyobashi, Chuo-ku, Tokyo
Tel: (03) 3563-0241;
http://www.bridgestone-museum.gr.jp
This small, private museum displays a wonderful collection of
Impressionist (Corot, Monet, Degas, Manet, Renoir, Cézanne,
etc.) and post-Impressionist (Gauguin, Van Gogh, Matisse,
Picasso, etc.) paintings, as well as Western-style paintings by
Japanese artists (Saeki Yuzo, Fujita Tsuguharu, etc.)

Museum of Contemporary Art Tokyo
(Tokyo-to Gendai Bijutsukan)

4-1-1 Miyoshi, Koto-ku, Tokyo
Tel: (03) 5245-4111;
http://www.mot-art-museum.jp
This museum specialises in contemporary art works, mainly
post-World War II, by both Western and Japanese artists.

National Museum of Modern Art (Kokuritsu Kindai Bijutsukan)

3-1 Kitanomaru Koen, Chiyoda-ku, Tokyo

Tel: (03) 3214-2561;

http://www.momat.go.jp

Reopened in January 2002 after more than two years of renovation, Japan's first national art museum showcases a large collection of modern Japanese art, and also hosts temporary exhibitions of works byWestern artists.

National Museum of Western Art (Kokuritsu Seiyo Bijutsukan)

7-7 Ueno Koen, Taito-ku, Tokyo

Tel: (03) 3828-5131;

http://www.nmwa.go.jp

The only museum in Japan to exclusively display Western art, its permanent collection includes the works of French painters (such as Delacroix, Courbet, Renoir and Monet) and sculptures by Auguste Rodin. It also holds temporary exhibitions by Western artists from different periods.

Museums

Fukagawa Edo Museum (Fukagawa Edo Shiryokan)

1-3-28 Shirakawa, Koto-ku, Tokyo

Tel: (03) 3630-8625

Here visitors can experience downtown Tokyo in the mid-19th century (Tokugawa Period). Inside the four-storey building, shops, restaurants, residences and traffic from the Fukagawa district (in the eastern part of Tokyo) are reproduced. Visitors can touch certain exhibits to gain a 'feel' for life at that time and also listen to sounds simulating daily life then.

Ghibli Museum
1-1-83 Shimo-renjaku, Mitaka-shi, Tokyo
Tel: (03) 5800-1978
Hayao Miyazaki, a famous animation producer known overseas for his works, 'Princess Mononoke' and 'The Neighbor Totoro', is the director of this museum. It is designed to be a fantasy world for children and features famous characters from movies as well as the museum's original animated films. Advance tickets specifying time and date are required for entrance; tickets are sold at Lawson convenience stores throughout Tokyo.

National Science Museum
(Kokuritsu Kagaku Hakubutsukan)
7-20 Ueno Koen, Taito-ku, Tokyo
Tel: (03) 3822-0111 Monday through Friday;
Tel: (03) 3822-0114 Saturday, Sunday, and national holidays;
http://www.kahaku.go.jp
This museum covers all the wonders of nature and science, including evolution, meteorites, the solar system and the analysis of sound waves. Children can participate in many hands-on exhibits.

National Museum of Emerging Science and Innovation
(Nihon Kagaku Miraikan)
2-41 Aomi, Koto-ku, Tokyo
Tel: (03) 3570-9151;
http://www.miraikan.jst.go.jp
Opened in 2001, this museum features numerous exhibits and activities to help visitors understand the latest science and technology developments. The director of the museum is the Japanese astronaut Mamoru Mori.

Sunshine City Starlight Dome
Sunshine City 10F, 3-1-3 Higashi Ikebukuro,
Toshima-ku, Tokyo
Tel: (03) 3989-3331
Here children as well as adults can enjoy the spectacular panorama of stars through the use of advanced telescopes.

SHOPPING PLACES
Department Stores

Isetan
Popular for its women's clothing. Foreigners can become members of the I-Club (at no charge) and receive shopping guidance and information about events (such as sales on tall- and large-sized clothing). There are four Isetan stores in Tokyo: Shinjuku, Kichijoji, Tachikawa and Fuchu.

Marui
This chain of department stores targets young customers in their teens and twenties.

Mitsukoshi
Considered the most prestigious department store in Tokyo, Mitsukoshi carries traditional, conservative items. Its four main stores are in Ginza, Shinjuku, Nihonbashi and Ikebukuro.

Odakyu
The Odakyu flagship store is conveniently located at Shinjuku Station. Two other stores are located in Machida and Fujisawa.

Seibu
Targeted at younger clients, Seibu holds a big sale each time the company's baseball team (the Seibu Lions) wins the league championship. The three main stores in Tokyo are in Shibuya, Yurakucho, and Ikebukuro.

Takashimaya
This is another old establishment that targets both adults and younger customers. The four Tokyo branches are in Shinjuku, Nihonbashi, Futako Tamagawa, and Tachikawa.

Tobu
Located in Ikebukuro, Tobu is the largest department store in Tokyo.

Tokyu
The headquarters in Shibuya provides a luxurious shopping experience.

International Supermarkets

Costco
A few stores are located in and near Tokyo.
Tel: (043) 213-4111;
http://www.costco.co.jp

Kinokuniya International
There are several stores in Tokyo.
Tel: (03) 3409-1231;
http://www.e-kinokuniya.com

Meidi-ya
There are several stores in Tokyo.
Tel: (03) 3444-6221;
http://www.meidi-ya-store.com

National Azabu Supermarket
There are two stores in Tokyo.
Tel: (03) 3442-3181;
http://national-azabu.com

Nissin World Delicatessen
2-34-2 Higashi Azabu, Minato-ku, Tokyo
Tel: (03) 3583-4586;
http://www.nissinham.co.jp/nwd

American products can be ordered through the **Foreign Buyer's Club** by telephone: (078) 857-9001 or via the Internet (www.fbcusa.com). This organisation is based in Kobe in western Japan, but offers delivery to Tokyo for a fee. It carries more than 40,000 items including food, home products, and books.

BOOKSHOPS CARRYING FOREIGN READING MATERIALS

Most major bookstores have a section featuring foreign reading materials. One of the largest, **Kinokuniya**, has materials in English and other languages. Listed below are some bookstores that carry foreign language books:

Book 1st
33-5 Udagawa-cho, Shibuya-ku, Tokyo
Tel: (03) 3770-1023
There are several other stores in Tokyo.

Bookstore Fiona
5-41-5 Okusawa, Setagaya-ku, Tokyo
Tel: (03) 3721-8186

Foreign Books BIBLOS
1-26-5 Takadanobaba, Shinjuku-ku, Tokyo
Tel: (03) 3200-4531

Kinokuniya
3-17-7 Shinjuku, Shinjuku-ku, Tokyo
Tel: (03) 3354-0131;
http://www.kinokuniya.co.jp
There is another large branch in Southern Shinjuku, and many smaller stores around Tokyo.

Maruzen (Headquarters)
1-6-4 Marunouchi, Chiyoda-ku, Tokyo
Tel: (03) 5288-8881

Yaesu Book Center
2-5-1 Yaesu, Chuo-ku, Tokyo
Tel: (03) 3281-1811

American books can also be ordered through the **Foreign Buyer's Club** (tel: (078) 857-9001).

ANTIQUE FLEA MARKETS

Togo Shrine (Togo Jinja)
1-5-3 Jingumae, Shibuya-ku, Tokyo
Tel: (03) 3403-3591

Nogi Shrine (Nogi Jinja)
8-11-27 Akasaka, Minato-ku, Tokyo
Tel: (03) 3478-3001

Hanazono Shrine (Hanazono Jinja)
5-17-3 Shinjuku, Shinjuku-ku, Tokyo
Tel: (03) 3209-5265

REAL ESTATE AGENCIES FOR FOREIGNERS

KEN Corporation
1-2-7 Nishi Azabu, Minato-ku, Tokyo
Tel: (03) 5413-5666
http://www.kencorp.com

Kimi Information Center
2-42-3 Ikebukuro, Toshima-ku, Tokyo
Tel: (03) 3986-1604
http://www.kimiwillbe.com

Nord House
Masuya Building. 6F, 3-21-24 Nishi Azabu, Minato-ku,
Tokyo
Tel: (03) 5474-7412
http://www.nord.co.jp

Plaza Homes
1-9-12 Azabudai, Minato-ku, Tokyo
Tel: (03) 3583-6941
http://www.plazahomes.co.jp

INTERNATIONAL ORGANISATIONS IN TOKYO
Culture-Specific Organisations

Indian Community Activities Tokyo
Fax: (03) 3727-4419
http://www.manicat.org

Japan British Society
Tel: (03) 3211-8027
http://www.japanbritishsociety.or.jp

Jewish Community of Japan
Tel: (03) 3400-2559
http://www.jccjapan.or.jp

Singapore Association in Japan (SAIJ)
http://www.saij.org

Tokyo American Club
Tel: (03) 3224-3670
http://www.tokyoamericanclub.org

Tokyo Canadian Club
http://www.tokyocanadianclub.com

Tokyo Japan Australia/New Zealand Society
Tel: (03) 3590-8581
http://www.janz.jp

Professional Organisations
Foreign Correspondents' Club of Japan
Tel: (03) 3211-3161
http://www.fccj.or.jp

Foreign Executive Women
Tel: (090) 7216-5171
http://www.fewjapan.com

Foreign Nurses Association in Japan
Tel: (03) 5469-0966

RELIGIOUS INSTITUTIONS
Buddhist Temples

Sengakuji Temple
2-11-1 Takanawa, Minato-ku, Tokyo
Tel: (03) 3441-5560

Sensoji Temple
2-3-1 Asakusa, Taito-ku, Tokyo
Tel: (03) 3842-0181

Tsukiji Hongwanji Temple
3-15-1 Tsukiji, Chuo-ku, Tokyo
Tel: (03) 3541-1131
http://www.tsukijihongwanji.jp

Shrines

Meiji Jingu Shrine
1-1 Kamizono-cho, Yoyogi, Shibuya-ku, Tokyo
Tel: (03) 3379-5511

Nezu Shrine
1-28-9 Nezu, Bunkyo-ku, Tokyo
Tel: (03) 3821-4817

Yasukuni Shrine
3-1-1 Kudan-shita, Chiyoda-ku, Tokyo
Tel: (03) 3261-8326

Churches

Catholic Shimoigusa Church
2-31-25 Igusa, Suginami-ku, Tokyo
Tel: (03) 3396-0305

Christian Science Church
5-6-3 Jingu-mae, Shibuya-ku, Tokyo
Tel: (03) 3499-3951

International Christian University Church
3-10-2 Osawa, Mitaka-shi, Tokyo
Tel: (0422) 33-3323

St. Ignatius Church
6-5-1 Kojimachi, Chiyoda-ku, Tokyo
Tel: (03) 3263-4584

Tokyo Union Church
5-7-7 Jungumae, Shibuya-ku, Tokyo
Tel: (03) 3400-0047

Others
Islamic Center, Japan
1-16-11 Ohara, Setagaya-ku, Tokyo
Tel: (03) 3460-6169
http://www.islamcenter.or.jp

Jewish Community of Japan
3-8-8 Hiroo, Shibuya-ku, Tokyo
Tel: (03) 3400-2559
http://www.jccjapan.or.jp

ENGLISH LANGUAGE RESOURCES
Newspapers
The following English-language newspapers are published in Tokyo and sold in bookstores that have foreign book sections, as well as at the kiosks in most major train and subway stations. Their websites also contain snapshots of current news and events. Newcomers can arrange for home delivery (refer to the following websites for more information):

International Herald Tribune/Asahi Shinbun
http://asahi.com
This paper contains news and articles from both the International Herald Tribune and the Asahi Shinbun, while the website offers news titbits from Asahi Shinbun.

Mainichi Daily News
http://mdn.mainichi.co.jp

The Daily Yomiuri
http://www.yomiuri.co.jp

The Japan Times
http://www.japantimes.co.jp

The Nikkei Weekly
http://www.nni.nikkei.co.jp
This is primarily a business newspaper.

Major international newspapers such as the *Financial Times*, the *Asian Wall Street Journal*, and *USA Today* can be purchased at major bookstores and large kiosks around Tokyo. Subscriptions are also available.

Magazines
The following are examples of magazines in English published in Tokyo; they are sold at major bookstores that offer foreign book sections. Contents of these magazines include information about Japanese society, current events, interviews with people, restaurant recommendations and classified ads. The magazine websites also contain information on a wide variety of topics about life in Tokyo and Japan in general.

EL Magazine (http://www.elmagazine.com)

Hiragana Times (http://www.hiraganatimes.com)

Japan Select Magazine (http://www.jselect.net)

Metropolis (http://www.metropolis.co.jp)

Tokyo Journal (http://www.tokyo.to)

Tokyo Weekender (free of charge)
(http://www.weekender.co.jp)

Directories

NTT TOWNPAGE
This telephone directory in English is available for free at any NTT office. The directory service is also available on the Internet at http://english.itp.ne.jp.

"Tell me about Tokyo" TELL Directory
Published by Tokyo English Life Line, this directory contains many useful contact numbers. To order copies, visit their website (www.telljp.com) or call them at (03) 3498-0261.

Websites

Homepage of **Tokyo Metropolitan Government**:
http://www.metro.tokyo.jp
Comprehensive advice for general living matters in Tokyo is offered on this official website.

Japan Information Network:
http://jin.jcic.or.jp
This website offers various useful resources such as maps, Japanese arts, statistics and contact information, as well as a bulletin board.

Asia Xpat:
http://Tokyo.asiaxpat.com
Information on a variety of topics for expatriates living in Tokyo is provided.

Tokyo with Kids:
http://www.tokyowithkids.com
Offers various types of information regarding childcare and types of children's education in Tokyo, along with a discussion forum.

TELEPHONE COUNSELLING

Tokyo English Life Line (TELL): (03) 5774-0992;
http://www.telljp.com
Provides information and counselling on a variety of topics that foreigners might encounter while living in Tokyo. Services are free of charge.

Japan Helpline: (0570) 000-911;
http://www.jhelp.com
Provides 24-hour counselling and advice over the telephone on topics ranging from simple questions to emergency situations. Its website also contains useful information and links to other websites.

Japan Hotline: (03) 3586-0110
Provides English-language counselling over the telephone concerning various aspects of life in Japan.

FURTHER READING

DAILY LIFE

A Look Into Tokyo. (JTB's Illustrated Book Series Vol. 7). Tokyo: Japan Travel Bureau, 2001.

Being A Broad: Everything a Western Woman Needs to Survive and Thrive. Pover, Caroline. Tokyo: Alexandar Press, 2001.

Eating in Japan. (JTB's Illustrated Book Series Vol. 3). Tokyo: Japan Travel Bureau, 1987.

Japan for Kids: The Ultimate Guide for Parents and Their Children. Wiltshire, Diana and Huey, Jeanne. Tokyo: Kodansha International, 2000.

Japan Health Handbook. Maruyama, Meredith E.; Shimizu, Louise P., and Tsurumaki, Nancy S. Tokyo: Kodansha International, 1998.

Kid's Trips in Tokyo: A Family Guide to One-Day Outings. Maeda, Ivy; Kobe, Kitty; Ozeki, Cynthia; and Sato, Lyn. Tokyo: Kodansha International, 1998.

Little Adventures in Tokyo: 39 Thrills for the Urban Explorer. Kennedy, Rick. Berkeley, California, USA: Stone Bridge Press, 1998.

Living in Japan: Getting Closer to Japan. Para, Andy D. Tokyo: ASK, 2001.

Living in Japan. Tokyo: The American Chamber of Commerce in Japan, 2002.

Living Japanese Style. (JTB's Illustrated Book Series Vol. 2). Tokyo: Japan Travel Bureau, 1991.

Tokyo Finder: How to Live, Work and Play in the 21st Century. Sasaki, Rie; Ng, Tzyh; and Tsuchiya, Takemi, eds. New York: Y's Publishing, 2001.

Tokyo for Free. Pompian, Susan. Tokyo: Kodansha International, 1998.

Tokyo Living Guide. SOA Communications, ed. Tokyo: Yohan Publications, 1996.

JAPANESE CULTURE

A Look Into Japan. (JTB's Illustrated Book Series Vol. 1).Tokyo: Japan Travel Bureau, 1998.

Behind the Japanese Bow: An In-Depth Guide to Understanding and Predicting Japanese Behavior. De Mente, Boye L. Lincolnwood, Illinois, USA: Passport Books, 1995.

Discovering Cultural Japan: A Guide to Appreciating and Experiencing the Real Japan. De Mente, Boye L. Lincolnwood, Illinois, USA: Passport Books, 1995.

Festivals of Japan. (JTB's Illustrated Book Series Vol. 4). Tokyo: Japan Travel Bureau, 1987.

Japan As It Is. Tokyo: Gakken, 2001.

NTC's Dictionary of Japan's Cultural Code Words. De Mente, Boye L. Lincolnwood, Illinois, USA: NTC Publishing, 1997.

The New Japan: Debunking Seven Cultural Stereotypes. Matsumoto, David. Yarmouth, Maine, USA: Intercultural Press, 2002.

Who's Who of Japan. (JTB's Illustrated Book Series Vol. 9). Tokyo: Japan Travel Bureau, 1987.

BUSINESS

Doing Business with Japanese Men: A Women's Handbook. Brannen, Christalyn and Wilen, Tracy. Berkeley, California, USA: Stone Bridge Press, 1993.

Doing Business with the Japanese. Goldman, Alan. New York: State University of New York Press, 1994.

Doing Business with the New Japan. Hoggins, James D; Sano, Yoshihiro; Graham, John L.; Hodgson, James. Lanham, Maryland, USA: Rowman & Littlefield, 2000.

Going to Japan on Business: Protocol, Strategies, and Language for Corporate Traveler. Brannen, Christalyn. Berkeley, California, USA: Stone Bridge Press, 1997.

Hidden Differences: Doing Business with the Japanese. Hall, Edward T. and Hall, Mildred R. Garden City, New York, USA: Anchor Press/Doubleday, 1987.

How to Do Business with the Japanese: A Complete Guide to Japanese Customs and Business Practices. De Mente, Boye L. Lincolnwood, Illinois, USA: NTC Business Books, 1994.

On Track with the Japanese: A Case-by-Case Approach to Building Successful Relationships. Gercik, Patricia. New York: Kodansha America, 1996.

"Salaryman" in Japan. (JTB's Illustrated Book Series Vol. 8). Tokyo: Japan Travel Bureau, 1987.

The Japanese Negotiator: Subtlety and Strategy Beyond Western Logic. March, Robert M. Tokyo: Kodansha International, 1990.

Working For a Japanese Company: Insights into the Multicultural Workplace. March, Robert M. Tokyo: Kodansha International, 1996.

HISTORY

Japan: A Modern History. McClain, James L. New York: W.W. Horton & Company, 2001.

Japan: The Story of a Nation. Reischauer, Edwin O. Boston: WCB/McGraw-Hill, 1989.

The Japanese Experience: A Short History of Japan. Beasley, W.G. Berkeley, California, USA: University of California Press, 1999.

The Japanese Today: Change and Continuity. Reischauer, Edwin O. and Jansen, Marius B. Cambridge, Massachusetts, USA: Harvard University Press, 1995.

The Rise of Modern Japan. Beasley, W.G. New York: St. Martin's Press, 2000.

ABOUT THE AUTHOR

Yuko Morimoto-Yoshida is an inter-cultural business consultant and trainer. Born and raised in Tokyo, as a child she lived in Europe and Mexico with her family for a couple of years. Currently she resides in California and frequently goes back to Tokyo for work and to visit her family and friends.

While living in Tokyo, Ms Morimoto-Yoshida worked in an international bank for more than ten years and interacted frequently with expatriates. This experience exposed her to the issues of cultural differences between foreigners and Japanese people and led her to pursue a career as an inter-cultural business consultant. Based in the US, she enjoys the opportunity of observing the cultural differences from yet another perspective.

Ms Morimoto-Yoshida holds a Masters' Degree in Speech and Communication from San Francisco State University. In addition to her native Japanese, she is fluent in English and conversational in Spanish. She loves to travel and try cuisines from different parts of the world.

Her e-mail address is yukomor@earthlink.net.

INDEX

Titles in the CultureShock! series:

For more information about any of these titles, please contact any of our Marshall Cavendish offices around the world (listed on page ii) or visit our website at:

www.marshallcavendish.com/genref